THE CATSKILLS

Painters, Writers, and Tourists in the Mountains
1820–1895

Plate 1. Thomas Addison Richards, *Meditations in the Catskills*, 1851. Courtesy J. B. Speed Art Museum.

Kenneth Myers

with contributions by
Margaret Favretti

Introduction by Jules D. Prown

The Hudson River Museum of Westchester

Yonkers, New York
1987

Distributed by University Press of New England
Hanover and London

The Hudson River Museum of Westchester
Trevor Park-on-Hudson
511 Warburton Avenue
Yonkers, New York 10701
914-963-4550

Designed by Kenneth H. Townsend
Typeset in Plantin by Rochester Mono/Headliners, Rochester, New York
Printed by Salina Press, Inc., Syracuse, New York

Exhibitions and programs at The Hudson River Museum are made possible
with assistance provided by the County of Westchester, the New York State
Council on the Arts, the National Endowments for the Arts and Humanities,
corporations and businesses, foundations and individuals. Use of Museum
buildings is contributed by the City of Yonkers.

Library of Congress Cataloging-in-Publication Data

Myers, Kenneth, 1955-
    The Catskills: painters, writers, and tourists in the mountains, 1820-1895.

    Catalog of an exhibition held at the Hudson River Museum, Yonkers, N.Y.,
Feb. 28–June 19, 1988, et al.
    Bibliography: p.
    1. Arts, American—New York (State)—Exhibitions. 2. Arts, Modern—19th
century—New York (State)—Exhibitions. 3. Catskill Mountains (N.Y.) in
art—Exhibitions. 4. Catskill Mountains (N.Y.) in literature—Exhibitions.
I. Hudson River Museum. II. Title.
NX510.N46M94 1988 758'.9974738'0740147277 87-32371
ISBN 0-943651-05-0

The publication of *The Catskills: Painters, Writers, and Tourists in the Mountains, 1820-1895* is made possible by a generous grant from the Luce Fund
for Scholarship in American Art, a program of the Henry Luce Foundation, Inc. The exhibition is supported in part by public funds from the
New York State Council on the Arts and the National Endowment for the
Arts, a federal agency.

Exhibition Tour:

The Hudson River Museum, Yonkers, New York
28 February–19 June 1988

The Margaret Woodbury Strong Museum, Rochester, New York
15 July–16 October 1988

Albany Institute of History and Art, Albany, New York
20 November 1988–12 February 1989

Everson Museum of Art, Syracuse, New York
26 February–23 April 1989

Cover: Detail, Frederic Edwin
Church, *Morning, Looking East
over the Hudson Valley from the
Catskill Mountains*, 1848 (plate 31).

CONTENTS

Foreword

From a spectacular location along the Hudson River and its collections—the works of American nineteenth-century first- and second-generation landscape artists—The Hudson River Museum of Westchester derived its name. Long associated with pioneering projects in the area of nineteenth-century American art, The Hudson River Museum of Westchester has engaged over the past three years in a labor of love—a journey to the Catskills. The product of these efforts is *The Catskills: Painters, Writers, and Tourists in the Mountains, 1820-1895.* The opportunity to embark on a visual journey to this great mountain wilderness, within the four walls of a museum and within the confines of this publication, proved to be exhilarating. This travelogue not only offers an important scholarly contribution, but it also offers the visitor and the reader a greater appreciation and understanding of America's interest in its landscape and its landscape painting. *The Catskills,* as an exhibition, seeks to celebrate the artistic and public love of natural beauty in New York State. This region, captured on canvas by artists and in prose by writers, fortunately is still preserved. This exhibition and catalogue follow in a tradition of outstanding exhibitions that seek to introduce America's nineteenth-century artistic heritage to a twentieth-century audience. The Hudson River Museum of Westchester has become a catalyst in exploring many American art topics during the past decade, exemplified most recently by *Domestic Bliss: Family Life in American Painting, 1840–1910.* In addition, six drawing exhibitions, one every two years during the past decade, explored the careers of Jasper Cropsey, Thomas Cole, Asher B. Durand, Frederic Edwin Church, William Trost Richards, and, currently, David Johnson. The Museum finds its rewards for its pioneering efforts in the fact that these artists, who worked in the Hudson River Valley, have today become household names all across America.

Lenders, sponsors, and supporters, along with past and present staff and trustees of The Hudson River Museum of Westchester, have all played a major role in making *The Catskills: Painters, Writers, and Tourists in the Mountains* possible. Through the combined efforts of Kenneth Myers, guest curator, and The Hudson River Museum staff—Rick Beard, Jan Seidler Ramirez, Sharon Emanuelli, Virginia Rojack, Janet Hawkins, Laura Vookles, John Matherly, Mark Ouderkirk, Alison Paul, Bonnie Levinson Rosenblum, Kim Litsey, Kate Zaenglein, Lucia Persichilli, Margaret Ann Tockarschewsky, and others—the most ambitious project in the Museum's history was realized. Other friends of this project, who lent their expertise and talents, include William H. Gerdts, Donald Keyes, Kathryn Grover as editor, and Kenneth Townsend as designer. Scholarly advice and mentoring was provided by Jules D. Prown, who also wrote the introduction, and J. Francis Murphy, both of whom reviewed the text and gave invaluable advice. Special thanks are offered to the Albany Institute of History and Art and the American Wing of The Metropolitan Museum of Art.

The realization of such an important and spectacular exhibition depends greatly on the generosity of funding sources, whose financial contributions bring such a project to fruition. The significance of *The Catskills* project can be measured in the generous support it has been offered. We are indeed fortunate for and appreciative of the funds provided by The Henry Luce Foundation, Inc., under the category of Scholarship in American Art, The National Endowment for the Arts, a federal agency, and The New York State Council on the Arts, under the category of special exhibition projects.

Lastly, this exhibition could not have been undertaken without the cooperation and generosity of so many lenders, both institutional and individual. Countless collectors and numerous institutions, including historical societies, art museums, art associations, libraries, as well as corporations, foundations, colleges, and universities generously assisted in making material, art work, and expertise available to The Hudson River Museum of Westchester. Some have generously lent works for the entire tour, while others have substituted similar works, especially in the drawing and watercolor media, so that each artist or particular scene would be fully represented in the exhibition.

An important aspect of *The Catskills: Painters, Writers, and Tourists in the Mountains* lies in the research of Kenneth Myers, who not only explored the influence these artists and writers had in the development of American painting but also demonstrated their influence on Americans' understandings of mountains as picturesque settings. The exhibition has relevance in our lives still, because the Catskills are just as inspiring today as they were one hundred years ago.

I am pleased that this exhibition, indirectly, advocates the long-term preservation of this area, which has provided such inspiration to so many. The world of the Hudson River School of painting has recently been described as American Paradise. Paradise is the place where life springs eternal. Inspiration, bliss, and the sublime were terms that Americans associated with the landscape during this seventy-five-year period. The most important American Paradise was, and still is, the Catskills.

Beyond the scholarship and opportunity to view the many spectacular works of art in one place, there awaits the discovery or rediscovery of the beauty and significance of the Catskill Mountains themselves. We encourage present-day Americans to seek out this important region. In doing so, we hope that both art and landscape will continue to be enjoyed and preserved for generations to come. I believe that The Hudson River Museum of Westchester has indeed celebrated and helped to preserve America's artistic heritage. Just as the paintings of the Catskills are a benchmark in American art, so *The Catskills* exhibition is a milestone in the history of The Hudson River Museum of Westchester.

Thomas S. Holman
Director
The Hudson River Museum of Westchester

Introduction

Aesthetic interest in the American landscape has had, like the landscape itself, its ups and downs. As the opening words of Kenneth Myers's catalogue essay indicate, early Americans had only a limited interest in the landscape as landscape (as opposed to the land as a place to build on, grow in, extract from, or travel over). The artist John Smibert in the middle of the eighteenth century did speak of diverting himself "in a landskip way," and topographical drawings and watercolors of utilitarian value became increasingly common around the time of the War of Independence. The important recent exhibition, *Views and Visions: American Landscape before 1830* (The Corcoran Gallery of Art, 1986), has finally given us a clear understanding of the initial growth of interest in landscape painting in America during the late eighteenth and early nineteenth centuries. But widespread enthusiasm for and artistic attention to the American landscape did not really occur until after 1825 in New York, coinciding (not coincidentally) with the opening of the Erie Canal and the arrival of the young artist Thomas Cole in New York in that year, and the founding of the National Academy of Design in the next.

Vigorous interest in the landscape and in landscape painting flourished about a hundred and fifty years ago, involving Cole and the other Hudson River School artists featured in this exhibition and supported by both patrons such as Luman Reed, Jonathan Sturges, and Robert Gilmor (of Baltimore) and institutions such as the National Academy of Design and, later, the American Art Union. The landscape boom lasted for about fifty years, culminating in the colossal paintings of Frederic Church and Albert Bierstadt that lifted the eyes of viewers from scenes of New York and New England to panoramic views of the West, South America, the Arctic, and the Near East. Then landscape interest seemed to turn in upon itself toward more intimate, gentle, crepuscular meditations, often unspecific as to locale, and, slightly later, toward equally gentle but coloristically higher-keyed Impressionist landscapes. The latter remained popular in the twentieth century long after more adventurous artists began to render the landscape in abstract and expressionistic modes (John Marin, Marsden Hartley, Georgia O'Keeffe).

Fifty years ago, there was little art historical interest in American landscape painting. Scholarship was motivated more by interest in genealogy and important historical persons, and the study of American art focused on portraiture. Prior to 1950, Clara Endicott Sears's popular *Highlights among the Hudson River Artists* (Boston, 1947) and Wolfgang Born's rudimentary survey *American Landscape Painting: An Interpretation* (New Haven, 1948) were the primary general works on landscape. No scholarly studies of such nineteenth-century landscape masters as Cole or Church or Bierstadt existed; Martin Johnson Heade, Jasper F. Cropsey, John F. Kensett, Asher B. Durand, Sanford Gifford, and Worthington Whittredge were little known; the American pre-Raphaelites had slipped into oblivion. The subsequent revival of interest in American landscape painting was anticipated by a collector, the energetic Maxim Karolik, whose collection now ornaments the Boston Museum of Fine Arts. It took European immigrants such as Born and Karolik to call the attention of Americans to the importance of American landscape painting. Subsequently, young scholars in the field of American art history, led by Barbara Novak working at Harvard and David Huntington at Yale, *did* turn their attention to landscape. Huntington's *The Landscapes of Frederic Edwin Church: Vision of an American Era* (New York, 1966) was an early

publication in what became a wave of monographs on American landscape
painters. Among early academic studies were dissertations on Bierstadt
(Richard S. Trump, Ohio State University, 1963), George Inness (Nicolai
Cikovsky, Jr., Harvard, 1965), Durand (David B. Lawall, Princeton, 1966),
Gifford (Ila Weiss, Columbia, 1968), and Jasper F. Cropsey (William S. Talbot,
New York University, 1972), most of which were published in 1977 by Garland
in the series "Outstanding Dissertations in the Fine Arts." Important work
was soon published by such younger scholars as Theodore E. Stebbins, Jr.
(Martin Johnson Heade, 1975) and the prolific John Wilmerding, whose
studies of Fitz Hugh Lane, Robert Salmon, and other artists eventually culmi-
nated in the exhibition *American Light: The Luminist Movement 1850–1875*
(National Gallery of Art, 1980). Major surveys of the nineteenth century
emphasizing landscape painting were produced, notably by Novak, whose
*American Painting of the Nineteenth Century: Realism, Idealism, and the Amer-
ican Experience* (New York, 1969) led to the evocative, seminal *Nature and
Culture* (New York, 1980), a book that has given direction to the next generation of scholars.

The study of American landscape art has recently taken a fascinating,
unexpected, and important turn, a turn signaled by the title of Novak's book,
Nature and Culture. The turn has been away from the study of landscape and
landscape painting in and for itself toward their study as a manifestation and
reflection of culture, of the beliefs of Americans who shaped and enjoyed as
well as painted the landscape. This interest in nature as it relates to culture
coincided, again not coincidentally, with the rise of scholarly interest in
cultural geography (see the impressive work of J.B. Jackson, John Stilgoe,
Yi-Fu Tuan, D.W. Meinig, Peirce Lewis, Wilbur Zelinsky and John Fraser
Hart). There has been a union of the concerns of humanists and social
scientists, and much of this has taken place under the scholarly umbrella of
American Studies. In the wake of the art historians who recovered the lives
and work of the great landscape painters and defined the major movements,
younger scholars arrived, many of whom came to American Studies with backgrounds other than art history but absorbed art historical orientation and
methodologies in the course of their studies. Among recent publications in this
vein are Lee Clark Mitchell, *Witness to a Vanishing America* (Princeton, 1981),
Bryan Jay Wolf, *Romantic Revision: Culture and Consciousness in Nineteenth-
Century American Painting and Literature* (Chicago, 1982), and Elizabeth
McKinsey, *Niagara Falls: Icon of the American Sublime* (Cambridge, 1985),
which are the forerunners of work beginning to surface in dissertations
recently completed or in progress.

A more visible manifestation of the new scholarship has been a series of
museum exhibitions accompanied by catalogues, catalogues that not infre-
quently have represented the forward edge of scholarship in our field. In
addition to the *American Light* and *Views and Visions* exhibitions already
mentioned, smaller innovative exhibitions with valuable catalogues include
J. Gray Sweeney, *Themes in American Painting* (Grand Rapids Art Museum,
1977); Donald D. Keyes, *The White Mountains: Place and Perceptions* (University of New Hampshire, 1980); Roger B. Stein, *Susquehanna: Images of the
Settled Landscape* (Roberson Center for the Arts and Sciences, Binghamton,
1981); Martha J. Hoppin, *Arcadian Vales: Views of the Connecticut River Valley*
(George Walter Vincent Smith Art Museum, Springfield, Massachusetts, and
Center for the Arts, Wesleyan University, 1981–82); Kenneth W. Maddox,
In Search of the Picturesque: Nineteenth Century Images of Industry along the

Hudson River Valley (Bard College, 1983); and Patricia Anderson, *The Course of Empire: The Erie Canal and the New York Landscape, 1825–1875* (Memorial Art Gallery of the University of Rochester, 1984). These are but a sampling of the new rush of investigations, frequently thematic, into American art as expressive of American culture that have refocused our interest on the landscapes of 1825–1875. We seem to be as fascinated aesthetically by landscapes as Americans in that period were, perhaps because our culture's new environmental awareness enables us to share their attitudes, values, and concerns. The pervasive influence of the social sciences in our times has attuned us to social, psychological, and cultural issues, and our environmental worries have alerted us to the historical context of which these earlier landscapes stand as material evidence.

Kenneth Myers, an American Studies scholar with a background in literature and environmental studies, has perceived the importance of the Catskills as a physical constant by which shifting cultural attitudes, changes in the relationship between man and nature, and evolving ideas of what has been and what has not been aesthetically appealing during our distant and not-so-distant past can be calibrated. He speaks of artists and paintings, but also of rivers, waterfalls, and mountains; of tourists, artists, and entrepreneurs; of railroads and steamboats; of tanneries and hotels. *The Catskills* is a story, visual and intellectual, that informs us about our past, but it also alerts us to environmental issues of the present and future.

Jules D. Prown
Yale University

Acknowledgments

Many people have helped in the organization of this exhibition and the creation of this catalogue. First and foremost I would like to thank Professor Jules Prown, who encouraged me to pursue my interest in the Catskills and who suggested I take my idea for an exhibition to The Hudson River Museum of Westchester. Former director Rick Beard—now at the Museum of the City of New York—saw merit in my ideas, hired me to organize the exhibition, and shepherded the project through its beginning phases. Chief curator Jan Seidler Ramirez nurtured the project with her encouragement and advice. I cannot thank either of them enough. I have also been advised and encouraged by Thomas S. Holman, the new director of The Hudson River Museum of Westchester. The entire staff of The Hudson River Museum has been a constant help, but I want to single out Virginia Rojack, John Matherly, and Laura Vookles for special thanks. Only they and I know how much of their time and life went into the exhibition. The staff of the Albany Institute of History and Art have been involved in the project almost from its inception. Tom Nelson, Christine Robinson, Daryl McCarthy, Tammis Groft, and Christine Miles have all been generous with their time and expertise. I want to thank Professor Frank Murphy for the care—and speed—with which he read drafts of the catalogue, Richard Arthur for his patience and understanding, Pamela Myers for her help in thinking out the size and shape of the exhibition, Erik Borg for his photographs and good cheer, and Kathryn Grover for editing the catalogue and seeing it through the press. My understanding of the social history of landscape taste has been honed by conversations with Richard Brodhead and Bryan Jay Wolf of Yale University, David Van Lear of the University of California at Davis, William H. Gerdts of the City University of New York, Susan Casteras of the Yale Center for British Art, and my colleagues in American Literature and Civilization at Middlebury College. My family has lived with the project as long as I have; I hope they know how much I have relied on their love and encouragement. Words cannot express my debts to Margaret Favretti.

In organizing this exhibition and writing the catalogue, I have visited many museums and libraries and have been helped by many people. Among the New Yorkers who have shared their time and expertise are Wendy Shadwell of The New-York Historical Society, Roberta Waddell of The New York Public Library, Linda Ferber and Barbara Gallati of The Brooklyn Museum, Clark Marlor of Brooklyn, Kevin Avery and Doreen Bolger Burke of The Metropolitan Museum of Art, Hollee Haswell of Columbia University Libraries, Alexander Acevedo of Alexander Gallery, Fred Bernaski of Kennedy Galleries, Bruce Chambers of Berry-Hill Galleries, Stuart Feld of Hirschl & Adler Galleries, and Alexander Raydon, Ira Spanierman, Joan Washburn, and Deedee Wigmore. Elsewhere in New York State, I have been helped by Joseph Butler of Historic Hudson Valley, Mrs. John Newington and Florence Levins of the Newington-Cropsey Foundation, Raymond Beecher and Mrs. Shelby Kriel of the Greene County Historical Society, Kenneth Van Vechten Parks of Catskill, Justine Hommel of the Haines Falls Free Library, James Ryan of Olana State Historic Site, Sally Bottiggi of the Columbia County Historical Society, and David Wooters of George Eastman House. I would also like to thank Ron Birch and John Shearer at the New York State Museum in Albany. Out of state, I want to express my thanks to Professor Ellwood C. Parry III of the University of Arizona, Alden Gordon of Trinity College, Patrick Noon of the Yale Center for British Art, Helen Cooper and Paula Freedman of the Yale

University Art Gallery, Barbara McCorkle, Ellen Cohen, and Helen Chillman of Yale University Libraries, Thomas Colville of New Haven, Betsy Kornhauser and Elizabeth McClintock of the Wadsworth Atheneum, Edward Nygren of The Corcoran Gallery of Art, William Truettner of the National Museum of American Art, Christine Hennessey of the Inventory of American Paintings, Heidi Gealt of the Indiana University Art Museum, William Johnston of the Walters Art Gallery, Sona Johnston of the Baltimore Museum of Art, Steven Majors of the Washington County (Maryland) Museum of Fine Arts, Judith Barter of the Mead Art Museum of Amherst College, Valerie McWilliams of the George Walter Vincent Smith Art Museum in Springfield, Massachusetts, Louise Leplant of Smith College Museum of Art, Susan Olney and Nicki Thiras of the Addison Gallery of American Art, Carol Troyen of the Museum of Fine Arts, Boston, Nancy Rivard Shaw of The Detroit Institute of Arts, Marge Goldwater of the Walker Art Center, George Keyes of the Minneapolis Institute of Arts, Betsy Rosasco and Barbara Ross of The Art Museum, Princeton University, Don Crosswell of the Philadelphia Print Shop, and Linda Ayres of the Amon Carter Museum. I could not have written the catalogue without the help of the staff of The Egbert Starr Library, Middlebury College. Bob Buckeye, Terry Plumb, Martha Dier, and Fleur Laslocky have been especially helpful. I have not named half the people who helped, but I want to assure those that are unnamed that I remember and am grateful.

The success of the exhibition has been made possible by the generosity and cooperation of the institutions, galleries, and individuals that have lent objects. They are listed elsewhere, but I want to take this opportunity to thank them all.

Kenneth Myers
Middlebury, Vermont

THE CATSKILLS AND
THE CREATION
OF LANDSCAPE TASTE
IN AMERICA

Plate 2. Thomas Cole, *Falls of Kaaterskill,* 1826. Courtesy Gulf States Paper Corporation.

INTRODUCTION: ON THE HISTORY OF LANDSCAPE TASTE

Fig. 1. George Inness, *Leeds in the Catskills*, 1865. Courtesy The Berkshire Museum.

Although we tend to assume that mountains and other wild environments are intrinsically attractive and that all people in all cultures probably think so too, historical and anthropological evidence suggests otherwise. The ability to experience such environments as attractive is learned rather than intuitive or natural, and it is not characteristic of people in all cultures at all periods in their history. Although many twentieth-century Americans will fly or drive hundreds or even thousands of miles in order to spend their vacations in the mountains, few of our seventeenth- or eighteenth-century ancestors had the opportunity, the leisure, or—most importantly—the desire to visit mountains.[1]

Most seventeenth- and eighteenth-century immigrants to North America came from the lowlands of northern Europe and southern England. Like their relatives and ancestors in Europe, they usually settled on low, relatively flat land suitable for intensive agriculture. As European settlers moved west across Massachusetts and Virginia (towards the Berkshires and the Blue Ridge) and north up the Merrimack, Connecticut, and Hudson Rivers (towards the White Mountains, the Green Mountains, and the Catskills), colonial hunters and trappers ventured into the mountains in search of game. But at no time did hunters or trappers represent a very large percentage of the colonial population. Until late in the eighteenth century, the northeastern forests were populated with significant numbers of native Americans. Even after the effective destruction of the native tribes, the northeastern forests and mountains were home to lynx, cougar, and bear. Inexperienced in the ways of the forest and often ill prepared to follow Indian and game trails, most seventeenth- and eighteenth-century Americans were frightened both of getting lost in the wilderness and of being attacked by Indians or wild animals and therefore sought to avoid mountains and wilderness.[2]

Most inhabitants of the Northeast colonies during these centuries were knowledgeable about religion and had learned to think of the wilderness as the haunt not only of wild beasts and wild men, but also of spiritual temptation. In both the Hebrew and the Greek books of the Bible, the word translated into English as "wilderness" is the same as the word translated as "desert" and means a place without human inhabitants. In both the Old and the New Testaments, the wilderness or desert is always identified as a place of spiritual trial. After bringing them up out of Egypt, God tried the Israelites by keeping them on a forty-year trek through the wilderness. Only a new generation of the spiritually clean—those who had never been slaves—were allowed to exit into the promised land of Canaan. Just as he tried the Israelites, God tried Christ in the wilderness. After his baptism by John, Jesus "was led by the Spirit into the wilderness," where he was tempted by the devil for forty days and nights before he proved his spiritual mettle and returned to his Galilean ministry. Protestant ministers throughout North America adapted the biblical imagery of the wilderness and desert to the facts of the local North American environment and warned their congregants that the forest and mountain wildernesses beyond the edges of their cleared fields were places of spiritual as well as physical danger.[3]

Although historians of early modern European and North American culture sometimes point to Petrarch's fourteenth-century ascent of Mont Ventoux as marking the substantive beginning of the taste for wild environments, this taste did not become common among any segment of these populations until the mid seventeenth century. Until the twentieth century, the tastes of Europeans living in North America almost always lagged behind the tastes of the European elites. The appreciation of mountains and wilderness did not begin to become widespread among any segment of the North American population until the early nineteenth century. In the United States, the development and popularization of the new taste for wild environments was an effect both of the expansion of the national economy, which led to development of an increasingly large middle class, and of the importation of new kinds of environmental attitudes, literature, and paintings from Europe.[4]

In Europe, the taste for mountains first developed in Italy. The taste seems to have become popular among some elements of the elites of the Italian city states by the end of the sixteenth century. During the seventeenth and eighteenth centuries, the new taste spread northward from Italy to France, Holland, and England. In each of these states, the development and popularization of the new taste required the existence of an agricultural or mercantile elite that was not tied to the cycles of agricultural production and was able to look on the natural world not simply as a source of sustenance, but also as an object of aesthetic satisfaction.[5]

The key word in the last sentence is *object*. Aesthetic appreciation is a kind of judgment, and the development of this judgment entails a degree of *objectification*. In order to experience an object as attractive or unattractive, an individual needs to be free mentally to step back from an immediate involvement with it so as to be able to apply his or her aesthetic criteria to it. An eighteenth-century New England farmer reaping his hay might see the evening sun glinting off the Berkshires, but, in order to notice the effect and appreciate it as beautiful, he would have to free his mind from his immediate task and make the beauty of the glinting sun the object of his attention. While the mental freedom to step back from the natural world to experience it aesthetically does not necessarily entail the economic freedom to step back from the labor of actually working the land, in both Europe and North America these two kinds of freedoms almost always went together. The taste for wilderness did not develop among agricultural workers who lived near the mountains or the remaining European wildernesses but among the agricultural and mercantile elites who lived in the most developed agricultural areas or in cities. The taste for mountains and other wild environments first developed among members of these elites because the mental skills necessary to success in the increasingly complex market economy of sixteenth- and seventeenth-century Europe required similar kinds of mental skills. Just as an aesthetic judgment necessitates the objectification of a part of the natural world as an attractive or ugly *view* or *landscape*, so a business decision requires the objectification of natural goods as marketable commodities. Members of the agricultural and mercantile elites who were adept at thinking of natural objects as commodities to be bought and sold were well prepared to pick up the less common but no more complex mental skills necessary to the formation of an aesthetic judgment. A view or landscape that is appreciated either directly by a traveler who spends money to see it or indirectly by a mental traveler who reads about it or views an image of it is itself a kind of aesthetic commodity. The rise of landscape tourism, literature, and painting, like the rise of the modern market economy and of modern science, depends on the objectification and commodification of the natural world.[6]

The development of new mental skills often either requires or leads to the creation of new words. The mental skills necessary to the formation of aesthetic judgments concerning the attractiveness of natural environments did not begin to become widespread among the agricultural and mercantile elites of England until the end of the sixteenth century. Something of the process by which these new mental skills were popularized is suggested by the history of the word *landscape*. Although *landscape* sounds as though it would have a good Anglo-Saxon origin, it is actually a very late seventeenth-century borrowing from the Dutch *landschap*. Until the seventeenth century, the Dutch word *landschap*, the French word *pays*, and the English word *countryside* all denoted "a collection of farms or fenced fields, sometimes a small domain or administrative unit."[7] As an English word, *landscape* or its equivalent *landskip* was originally used not as a synonym for countryside but to denote a Dutch painting of the countryside. Whereas *countryside* denoted a place, the English *landscape* denoted a representation of a place. The borrowed word quickly began to be applied to natural environments as well as to Dutch paintings. But throughout the seventeenth and eighteenth centuries, the word always carried pictorial connotations. *Countryside* denoted an inland environment. *Landscape* denoted an inland environment looked at or experienced as if it were a painted picture. Peasants lived in the countryside. Educated aesthetes traveled to the countryside where they sought out the best vantage points from which to appreciate the countryside as a landscape. Atop these vantage points, they mentally organized the geography in front of them—using conveniently located trees, rocks, or structures to frame the view, cropping unattractive elements, locating appropriate "staffage"—in precisely the same way that a landscape painter composed his or her pictures.[8]

Until the middle of the eighteenth century, English connoisseurs preferred landscapes well domesticated. As late as 1791, the well-known theoretician of the "picturesque," William Gilpin, complained that "the idea of a wild country, in a natural state, however picturesque, is to the generality of people but an unpleasing one. . . . There are few, who do not prefer the busy scenes of cultivation to the grandest of nature's rough productions."[9] In England, the popularization of mountains and other wild landscapes dates from the latter half of the eighteenth century and is most often associated with Edmund Burke's *Philosophical Enquiry into the Origin of Our Ideas of the Sublime and Beautiful* (1757), the gardens of Lancelot (Capability) Brown (1716-1783), the midcentury paintings of Welsh and English mountains by Richard Wilson (1713-1782), the development of mountain tourism in Wales and the Lake District, and—especially—the poetry of William Wordsworth (1770-1850). In the United States, the popularization of mountains and other wild landscapes dates from the period of rapid economic expansion that followed the conclusion of the War of 1812 and is most often associated with the Leather-stocking novels of James Fenimore Cooper (1789-1851), the landscape paintings of Thomas Cole (1801-1848), and the development of mountain tourism in the White Mountains of New Hampshire and—especially—the Catskills of New York.

THE CATSKILLS
BEFORE THE TOURISTS

THE LAND

A heavily eroded and moderately glaciated section of the Allegheny Plateau, the Catskill Mountains are located in South Central New York State. Twentieth-century geographers usually define the Catskills as extending from the Hudson River northwest to the Batavia Kill and the Schoharie River, west to the West Branch of the Delaware River, southwest to the main body of the Delaware River, and southeast to the Neversink River and Rondout Creek. Nineteenth-century geographers had much less detailed information to work with, but they too usually defined the Catskills as extending from the Hudson River west to the Delaware. For much of the nineteenth century, however, the southern and western reaches of this area were accessible only by horseback or stagecoach, and the vast majority of nineteenth-century painters, writers, and tourists identified the Catskills with the much smaller and much more easily accessible area of the Allegheny Plateau immediately west of the Hudson River port of Catskill.[10]

THE INDIANS

Twentieth-century historians estimate that when Henry Hudson and his crew sailed up the Hudson River in September 1609, there were less than ten thousand Indians belonging to two main language groups living in the Hudson River-Lake Champlain corridor. From the mouth of the river north towards the site of the village of Catskill, both banks of the Hudson River were inhabited by Indians who spoke one of several Munsee dialects and who later confederated with the Delaware tribes. In 1609, there seem to have been about forty-five hundred Munsee-speaking Indians living in the Hudson River Valley.[11] From just south of the site of the village of Catskill north to Lake Champlain, west to the base of the Catskills and Adirondacks, and east to the base of the Taconic and Green Mountains, the Hudson River-Lake Champlain corridor was home to about forty-five hundred other Indians who called themselves Mahicans. The Mahicans spoke an eastern Algonquian language.[12] Both Munsee and Mahican villages usually contained about two hundred individuals and were located in river or creek valleys where the soil was richer and the game more plentiful than on the valley uplands or in the mountains. Munsees and Mahicans supplemented their diet with fish and game, but both lived mainly on corn and other cultivated crops raised in small garden plots planted just outside the villages and on nuts and berries harvested from the surrounding forests. In both cultures, most of the agricultural work was done by women. Villages were moved every eight to twelve years when the soil of the garden plots had been exhausted. Every November, most Munsees and Mahicans left their villages and traveled to their hunting territories, where they stayed until midwinter. Hunting territories were located on the upper reaches of the rivers and creeks. Munsee and Mahican hunters rarely visited the mountain tops, both because they were poor in game and because they were thought to be inhabited by potentially evil spirits.[13]

By 1670, the Munsee population had been decimated by warfare with the Dutch and by the ravages of smallpox, and most of the survivors had migrated west towards the Delaware River. The Mahicans survived a few years longer, but, by 1680, the combined onslaughts of smallpox, the Dutch, and the Mohawks had driven most of them out of the central Hudson Valley, north towards the site of the modern town of Hoosic or east into the Berkshires. By 1689, there were fewer than nine hundred "River Indians" living in their traditional homeland, and almost all of these were living north of Albany. By the end of the eighteenth century, the Hudson Valley Munsees and Mahicans had been almost completely destroyed. Their destruction is clearly visible in the map of the Six Iroquois Nations that Guy Johnson prepared for the Royal Governor of New York, William Tryon, in 1771 (fig. 3). Johnson did not bother to show the location of Indian villages on the Hudson and eastern Mohawk Rivers for the simple reason that significant numbers of Indians no longer lived near those rivers. In 1774, Tryon estimated that the various Long Island and Hudson Valley tribes could jointly muster no more than three hundred warriors and that these were "in general so scattered and dispersed, and so addicted to wandering that no certain account can be obtained of them."[14]

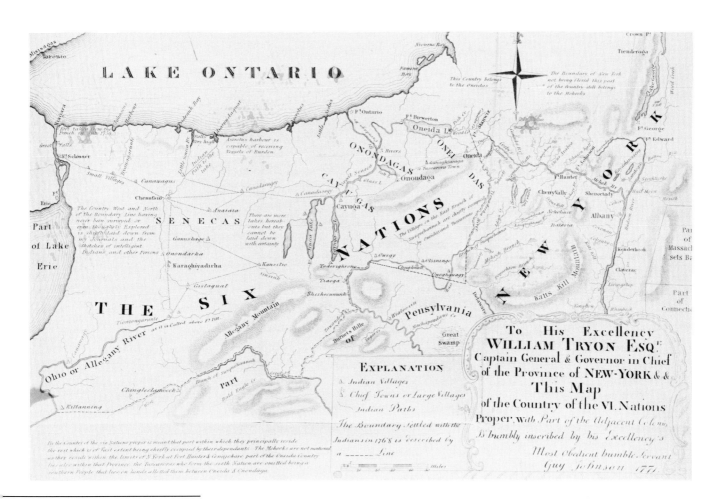

Fig. 3. Guy Johnson, *Map of the Country of the VI Nations*, 1771.

THE DUTCH

Dutch settlement of the Hudson River Valley began between 1624 and 1626 with the establishment of forts on Manhattan and in the area of modern Albany. Unlike the Puritan colonies of Massachusetts and Connecticut, the New Netherlands was primarily a trading colony, and its population grew slowly. When the colony was conquered by the English in 1664, it boasted fewer than nine thousand inhabitants. In the same year, there were more than twenty-five thousand Europeans living in the various New England colonies. Most of the Dutch population was clustered in and around Manhattan with a secondary development near Fort Orange (Albany). In 1664, no more than a few hundred Dutch farmers seem to have been living in the mid Hudson Valley. Most of these settled on the east bank of the river. Like the Munsees and Mahicans before them, the Dutch settlers avoided the mountains and settled on lowland creeks and rivers. Unlike New England farmers, the rural Dutch tended to settle on isolated farms rather than in villages. At the end of Dutch rule, the only European village in the entire Hudson River Valley between Manhattan and Fort Orange was Esopus (renamed Kingston by the English), which contained only sixty or seventy inhabitants.[15]

The number of Europeans living in the middle Hudson Valley increased during the latter half of the seventeenth and the first half of the eighteenth century, but not rapidly. In 1698, there were only about three thousand non-native Americans living in New York north of present-day Westchester County, and most of these lived south of Kingston or around Albany. By 1749, this number had grown to about twenty-three thousand. But much of this growth was concentrated either in the area of Albany or along the border with Massachusetts and Connecticut, where land-starved New Englanders had begun to settle early in the century. Except for a few hundred Palatine Germans who settled on both banks of the Hudson above Kingston and a scattering of Scotch-Irish who settled throughout the valley, there was no significant immigration to the middle Hudson Valley until after the American Revolution.[16]

Population growth along the river was almost entirely due to the fertility of the Dutch, and the valley therefore kept its Dutch character. One of the most observant mid eighteenth-century visitors to the Hudson Valley was the Swedish botanist Peter Kalm. In his 1749 journal, Kalm noted with surprise that although the Hudson Valley had been ruled by the English for more than eighty years and although the Hudson Valley Dutch had begun to dress like Englishmen, their houses, manners, and language were still Dutch. Like later visitors, Kalm also noticed the lack of towns and the wide gaps of uncultivated land between farms on the west bank of the Hudson north of Kingston. Like later historians, Kalm suggested that the Hudson Valley was so under-populated and still so Dutch because most of the land was controlled by a few wealthy landowners who hired tenant farmers to work their vast estates. Because the large landowners were rarely willing to sell land, most mid eighteenth-century European immigrants to the middle Atlantic colonies avoided the Hudson River Valley and settled in New Jersey or Pennsylvania, where good land was both plentiful and for sale.[17]

Something of the prosperity, the isolation, and the Dutch character of the middle Hudson Valley in the middle of the eighteenth century is suggested by the painted overmantel from the Marten van Bergen house near Catskill (plate 3). The van Bergen overmantel is the only eighteenth-century representation

Plate 3. Attributed to John Heaten, *The van Bergen Farm* overmantel, c. 1733. Photograph courtesy New York State Historical Association.

of a New York Dutch farm known to exist and is the earliest known American genre scene. The van Bergens were among the first major landholders on the west bank of the Hudson between Kingston and Albany. On 8 July 1678, Silvester Salisbury, commander of the then-English fort at Albany, and Marte Gerretse van Bergen, the commissary general for the fort, bought thirty-five thousand acres of land from the Indians. Their purchase was located on the south side of Catskill Creek, a few miles upstream from the modern village of Catskill. Van Bergen seems to have bought the land as an investment, because within two years he had built a small stone house and a barn which he immediately leased to one of his wife's relatives. Marte Gerretse van Bergen never lived on his Catskill property, but fifty years later his sons Marten and Garret moved south from Albany (or perhaps Coxsackie) and built themselves two fine stone homes on the site. Both houses were built in 1729, and the surviving overmantel may have been painted to commemorate the completion of Marten's. Garret's house is visible in the distance on the far right. The *stoep*, double doors, and hipped red-tile roof with pedimented dormer windows are characteristically Dutch. Family records suggest that the building on the right was a blacksmith shop. Bricks for the gables are supposed to have been imported from Holland. The black slaves serving as milkmaid and servant, the heavy-wheeled sloped-box wagon, the octagonal hay barracks (five poles supporting an adjustable roof), and the raised-floor corn or grain barracks are also characteristically Dutch and typical of prosperous Hudson Valley farms of the time.[18]

The van Bergen overmantel both illustrates what one prosperous eighteenth-century Hudson Valley Dutch farm looked like and suggests something about eighteenth-century Hudson Valley Dutch attitudes towards the physical environment. Where nineteenth-century painters of this view might have used farm buildings or human figures to establish scale or to add a bit of color to the foreground or middleground of their work, they would probably have emphasized the distant prospect. Alternatively, the focus of the overmantel is not on the background prospect, but rather on the enclosed space pictorially defined by the foreground road and the middleground fence. The van Bergen house is situated so that it faces the road that links the family to the larger world outside the picture frame. The cultural importance of the road is emphasized by the fact that all the movement in the painting is located on or just off it. At the same time that the road suggests a connection between the seemingly isolated farm and the larger world, the fence suggests a sharp break between the foreground farm, the unbroken forest in the middleground, and the generalized representation of the Catskills in the background. The fence is a symbolic boundary marking the historical as well as the physical limit of the wilderness. Physically, the wilderness ends at the fence. Historically, the wilderness ended when it was brought under cultivation by the man who built the fence.

The enveloping oval of the road and fence is echoed by the oval formed by the outstretched arms of Marten and his wife. Standing in front of their new house, they have come up to the road in order to greet the figures entering from the right. These three figures probably represent Garret van Bergen and his sons. The outstretched arms and turned hands of Marten and his wife are a conventional image for ownership. They are displaying their property to Garret and to us. Their pose suggests pride not only in what they own, but also in what they have accomplished. In this painting, Marten van Bergen and his wife step forward as creators of their environment. They spread their hands in a gesture that says not only "look what we own," but also—and more fundamentally—"look what we have *made;* look what we have wrested from wilderness." Outside the forest and within the cultivated space defined by the road and the fence is the prosperous world of a successful mid eighteenth-century middle Hudson Valley Dutch farm. Outside this space is the brooding and undifferentiated unknown.[19]

By 1771, the population of New York north of Westchester County had grown to about eighty thousand, but the west bank of the Hudson between Kingston and Albany was still only sparsely settled. Captain Montresor's 1775 *Map of the Province of New York, with Part of Pensilvania, and New England* (plate 4) accurately illustrates both the location and the extent of Dutch settlement. Although there had been a landing on Catskill Creek near where it emptied into the Hudson from about 1650, it had not evolved into a village. The Dutch population was still concentrated in a narrow band in the most fertile part of the valley along Catskill and Kaaterskill Creeks.[20] The almost complete lack of geographical detail in Montresor's representation both of the main ridge of the Catskills and of the land to its west illustrates the limited extent both of Dutch settlement and of Dutch knowledge (detail).

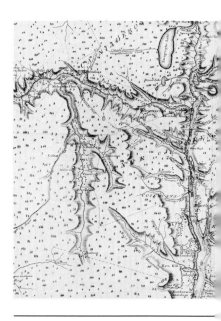

Plate 4 detail. The area of the Catskills, as shown on Montresor's 1775 map.

Plate 4. Captain John Montresor, *A Map of the Province of New York, with Part of Pensilvania, and New England,* 1775. Courtesy Sterling Memorial Library, Yale University.

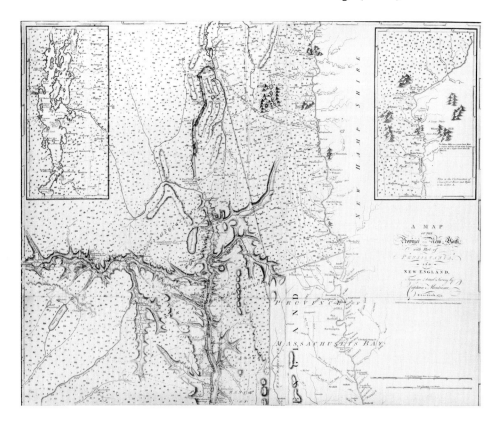

During the American Revolution, the Hudson Valley-Lake Champlain corridor from New York City towards Montreal was the most fought-over area of the colonies. The population of the middle Hudson River Valley stopped growing and may even have declined as the British burned the town of Kingston and their Iroquois allies attacked isolated farms throughout the area.[21]

THE YANKEES

At the end of the Revolution, fewer people lived in New York State than lived in Virginia, Massachusetts, Pennsylvania, North Carolina, Maryland, or Connecticut. Virtually no one of European extraction lived in the vast areas of New York west of the Catskills. The movement of large numbers of people into New York State began with the cessation of hostilities and was the greatest land rush of the post-Revolutionary period. Between 1790 and 1830, the population of the state quadrupled from 340,000 to a little less than 1,400,000. Some of the thousands of immigrants to the New York frontiers came from Europe, but the vast majority came from New England. Emigrants from Vermont settled the upper Hudson Valley and the Adirondacks west of Lake Champlain. Emigrants from central New England traveled to Albany and then followed one of the numerous turnpike roads west. Emigrants from coastal New England usually traveled to New York City and then up the Hudson by boat. Once in the Hudson Valley, they would disembark for the West in Newburgh, Kingston, or Albany. Emigrants from central and western Connecticut traveled overland to the Hudson and entered the New York frontier over the turnpikes starting in Newburgh and Kingston. The pace of emigration was so rapid that by 1820 Timothy Dwight estimated that sixty to sixty-seven percent of all New Yorkers had been born in New England.[22]

Although most of the immigrants settled on the frontiers north of Albany and west of the Catskills, many stopped in the Hudson River Valley south of Albany. The number of persons living on the west bank of the Hudson between Kingston and Albany increased so rapidly that in 1800 a new county named after the Revolutionary War General Nathaniel Greene was created out of parts of Ulster and Albany Counties. It is impossible to determine how many people were living in the area of Greene County in 1783. By 1790, the population had grown to about seven thousand. By the time Greene County was organized in 1800, the population had reached about thirteen thousand. By 1810, it was just less than twenty thousand. Immigration into the county slowed after passage of the 1808 Embargo Act forbidding the importation or exportation of goods, and it remained sluggish through the end of the War of 1812. Immigration into New York State increased rapidly after the end of the war in 1815, but by the mid-1820s most areas of the state had been settled. Immigration therefore declined as potential settlers began to look further west. In 1820, there were about twenty-three thousand people living in Greene County.[23]

The growth of the town and village of Catskill was even more rapid than the growth of Greene County as a whole. In 1783, the area that was later included in the town of Catskill (a political rather than a spatial term) was home to a few hundred Dutch farmers living on a small number of widely dispersed farms. The site of what later became the village of Catskill was merely a landing with a few neighboring farms. The town of Catskill, then part of Albany County, was incorporated in 1786. The 1790 census shows that there were fewer than two thousand people living in the new town. When the town was incorporated, the area it encompassed was almost entirely rural, and almost all the inhabitants lived on their farms. In 1786, the landing on Catskill Creek contained no more than five houses and a single store. By 1792, the landing had grown only slightly: it consisted of about ten buildings. By 1797, however, the landing had become the substantial village pictured in the drawing by Alexander Robertson (plate 5) and the engraving after A.P. (plate 115), and both the town and the village had been annexed to Ulster County. By 1802, the new village at Catskill landing was home to just under two thousand people—as many people as had lived in the entire *town* of Catskill in 1790—and contained more than 180 buildings. In 1810, there were more than four thousand people living in the town of Catskill, most of them in the Hudson River villages of Catskill and Athens. In 1810, the village at Catskill landing contained more than two hundred houses and shops, and the village of Athens contained about 150. In 1815, Athens was incorporated as a separate town; by 1820, the combined population of the towns of Catskill and Athens had risen to more than fifty-five hundred.[24]

Plate 5. Alexander Robertson, *Catskill*, 24 September 1796. Courtesy Albany Institute of History and Art.

Immigration to the open lands of New York was fueled both by the over-population of the New England states and by the steady demand for agricultural products caused by the Napoleonic wars and the attendant disruption of European agriculture. If they did not settle in one of the villages, immigrants to Greene County settled on the hilly land west of the established Dutch farms and east of the mountains. Unlike the Dutch, the New Englanders were commercial farmers who produced for the European market. Far and away the most important local crop was wheat, although pot and pearl ashes made by burning timber felled to clear new fields were also important sources of income. Wheat and ashes for export as well as lesser amounts of other grains and lumber for domestic consumption were carted or (in winter) sledded to Catskill or Athens, from which points they were shipped to New York City. The rapid development of commercial agriculture in the Hudson River Valley was a major reason for the rapid growth of New York City. New York City did not begin to move more goods than Philadelphia until 1797, and it was only after 1815 that it secured its position as the commercial capital of the nation.[25]

The local economies of the village of Catskill and the village of Athens developed in different directions. By 1800, Catskill had gained control of most of the shipping between Greene County and New York City, and the economic base of Athens had begun to shift towards shipbuilding. Athens remained an important center of Hudson Valley shipbuilding through the end of the nineteenth century.[26] The economic ascendancy of Catskill village over Athens village was cemented in 1803 when a group of local entrepreneurs formed the Susquehanna Turnpike Company and built turnpike roads east to Salisbury, Connecticut, and west through the village of Windham to the Susquehanna River. The new turnpike followed the route of older colonial roads and Indian trails, but the improved condition and maintenance of the turnpike attracted the business of immigrants heading west, settlers shipping agricultural products east to the Hudson Valley ports, and Hudson Valley merchants shipping finished goods west to the new settlements. With the completion of the Susquehanna Turnpike, the village of Catskill joined Newburgh, Kingston, and Albany as one of the major gateways to the western frontier.[27] In 1805, another group of local entrepreneurs formed the Little Delaware Turnpike Company in order to build a more southerly turnpike road across the mountains. The Little Delaware Turnpike ran from the village of Catskill to the twin lakes atop the Catskill escarpment by way of the ravine that would later become known as Sleepy Hollow. From the twin lakes, the Little Delaware Turnpike joined the Schoharie River in the area of the present-day village of Hunter. From Hunter, it was supposed to run to the village of Delhi on the west branch of the Delaware River. The Little Delaware was never as popular as the Susquehanna Turnpike, however, and the company failed within a few years of its formation.[28]

The most vivid surviving description of the village of Catskill as it appeared early in the nineteenth century is from a letter written by a journeyman cabinetmaker named Andrew Backus. Born in Plymouth County, Massachusetts, Backus arrived in Catskill in June 1815. On 16 July he wrote his father,

> There is a good deal of business done here. There is considerable building going on this season. There is building in one block one dwelling house and four stores all of brick three story high. The Catskill Mountains are plain in site. From here they are a bought ten miles distant from this place. The soil here is quite clayey so that the streets are very muddy if there is much rain, but they dry very quick again in fair weather and are hard. There is two meeting houses here, one for Presbyterians, one Episcopalian. There is a court house, jail, academy and bank. There is a good many stores here for a place this size. There is mechanicks shops here of a most all kinds. A great many wagons come in here every day from the westward that bring in lumber of a most all kinds, flour, corn, rie, &c.. The inhabitance here are part Dutch but more than half of the people of this village come from Connecticut. Mr. Whittimore that I am at work for moved from Stonington two years ago.[29]

The already diversifying Greene County economy became even more diversified after 1817 when Jonathan Palen opened a large tannery at the foot of Kaaterskill Clove (fig. 4), and Colonel William Edwards (a grandson of the Reverend Jonathan Edwards) opened what was then the largest tannery in the nation at its top.[30]

By the late 1820s, Kaaterskill Clove, the largest of the gaps providing access to the mountain top and to areas west of the mountains, was a center of an international leather trade. Uncured hides were shipped to the Clove from as far away as South America and California, cured with tannin made from local hemlock trees, and shipped to New York or Boston, where they were turned into finished leather goods. The development of this circular trade required the creation of improved roads that could be used by the large wagons that carried the uncured hides to the tanneries and the cured hides to the Hudson River ports. In 1824, the tannery operators therefore formed the Hunter Turnpike Company in order to improve and maintain the existing late eighteenth-century road running through Kaaterskill Clove. In 1825, Zadock Pratt opened another large tannery, this one located near the village of Windham on the Susquehanna Turnpike. By the mid-1830s, Pratt's tannery was the largest in the Catskills and had become one of the largest in the nation. Tanning was the most important industry in the Catskills from the early 1820s until after the Civil War.[31]

But even as the first tanneries were opening, the post-war prosperity was threatened by the construction of the Erie Canal. Completion of the Erie Canal in 1825 made the old turnpike roads economically obsolete and shifted the flow of immigrants and trade north to Albany, Troy, and Schenectady and

Fig. 4. Thomas Hilson, *Tannery in the Catskills*, c. 1825-1830. Courtesy Museum of Fine Arts, Boston.

away from the middle Hudson Valley ports of Newburgh, Kingston, and Catskill. Even more damaging, however, the opening of the canal threatened the economic viability of middle Hudson Valley wheat farming. Middle Hudson Valley wheat farmers could not get the same yields from their long-used fields as farmers working newly opened fields in the Genesee Valley. With the opening of the canal, the Genesee Valley wheat farmers and flour manufacturers gained ready access to the New York City market and quickly drove their Hudson Valley competitors into bankruptcy.[32]

The creation of mountain tourism as a major Greene County industry dates from the mid-1820s. It was created by entrepreneurs who realized that there were increasing numbers of New Yorkers and other potential tourists willing to pay money to see the mountains. But the decision of individual entrepreneurs to enter the tourism industry was also motivated by the declining importance of the wheat and flour trade. Catskill wheat might not be able to compete with Genesee Valley wheat, but Genesee Valley entrepreneurs did not have mountains to sell.

THE BEGINNINGS OF TOURISM

The most spectacular scenery in the entire Catskill range lies in the narrow rectangle of land west of the main Catskill escarpment and between Kaaterskill Clove on the south and the Susquehanna Turnpike on the north and northwest. Limited numbers of visitors began to find their way to this area soon after the Susquehanna Turnpike opened in 1803, but almost all of these early visitors were local residents, scientists, or immigrants on their way west. The number of tourists who traveled to the area simply to see the sights increased with the opening of tannery roads through Kaaterskill Clove, but as late as 1819 Henry Dwight reported that although the scenery between Kaaterskill Clove and the Turnpike was "in the highest degree beautiful and sublime, . . . little or nothing is known of the existence of such scenery, excepting in the immediate vicinity. Few even of those who live within a few hours ride, have curiosity enough to visit it. . . . I have mentioned these mountains to more than fifty persons since I visited them, but I have not met with more than five or six who had ever heard of this sublime display of nature's workmanship."[33]

Mountain tourism did not become a major part of the Greene County economy until after the development of a public that valued landscape experiences and was both willing and able to pay for them; a transportation system able to move significant numbers of these people to and from the mountains with a fair degree of reliability and comfort; satisfactory overnight accommodations in the mountains; and a public awareness of the Catskills as both scenically spectacular and physically accessible. By 1819, two of these four conditions had been met. The development of the national economy and the attendant growth of the Northeast cities, together with the importation of landscape literature and engravings from Europe, had already led to the development of landscape taste among leading elements of the urban elites. The spread of the new taste is evidenced by the popularity of the nature poetry written by William Cullen Bryant (1817 and after) and picturesque engravings such as those published in William Guy Wall's *Hudson River Portfolio* (1821-1825) (plate 6). The taste for mountains and wilderness began to spread at the same time that the development and rapid improvement of steam navigation on the Hudson River made it much easier to travel between New York and the village of Catskill. Robert Fulton and Chancellor Robert Livingston built the first Hudson River steamboat in 1807. The first steamboats were slow and cramped compared to later steamboats, but they were roomier and faster than the Hudson River sloops and packets and quickly became the preferred mode of Hudson Valley transportation (plate 7). The dominance of passenger trade by the steamboats became complete when previously high prices dropped after the 1824 United States Supreme Court decision declaring the Fulton-Livingston monopoly unconstitutional.[34] At the same time that the development of reliable steam navigation made Catskill much more readily accessible to New York City, the opening of new turnpike and tannery roads made the scenic area between Kaaterskill Clove and the Susquehanna Turnpike much easier to reach from the village of Catskill.

From after the development of the steamboat until after the development of the railroad, no other mountain range in the United States was as accessible to a major population center as the Catskills were to New York. But, in 1819, few New Yorkers had heard of the wonders of the Catskills, and there were no comfortable accommodations in the mountains. Except for a single article published in 1794 by the Frenchman Pierre DeLabigarre, early articles on the Catskills were written by scientists, published in limited-circulation scientific journals, and said nothing about the scenery. These articles may have led to a heightened awareness of the Catskills among the scientific community, but they would have had little direct influence on popular taste.[35]

Plate 6. William Guy Wall, *Troy from Mount Ida*, 1821-1822. Courtesy The Hudson River Museum of Westchester.

Plate 7. Pavel Petrovich Svinin, *Deck Life, Probably on the "Paragon," one of Fulton's Steamboats, with Fort Putnam and West Point in the Background,* c. 1811. Courtesy The Metropolitan Museum of Art.

The first widely distributed publication to notice the existence of Catskill Mountains scenery was Horatio Gates Spafford's 1813 *Gazetteer of the State of New-York.* In their description of Windham, the local editors of Spafford's *Gazetteer* noted that the Little Delaware Turnpike crossed the mountains "at a surprising altitude. . . . The view from this [South] mountain is unexpressibly grand and well merits the attention of those who delight to contemplate the stupendous scenery of nature. The high fall of the Kaaterskill is about a half mile from this road, near the summit of the mountain, and 12 miles from Catskill."[36] Except for this short blurb, promotion of the Catskills did not begin until after the conclusion of the War of 1812. The most influential early works to describe the wonders of the region were Washington Irving's story "Rip Van Winkle" (1819), Timothy Dwight's *Travels in New-England and New-York* (1821-1822), the two engravings showing the Catskills in William Guy Wall's *Hudson River Portfolio* (1821-1825) (plate 125), and James Fenimore Cooper's *The Pioneers* (1823). The most widely distributed of these were "Rip Van Winkle" and *The Pioneers.*

Like many other early nineteenth-century Americans, Irving first saw the Catskills from the deck of a Hudson River sloop. Late in his life, Irving recalled the encounter, which took place on a trip up the river to Albany in 1800: "Never shall I forget the effect upon me of the first view of them predominating over a wide extent of country, part wild, woody, and rugged; part softened away into all the graces of cultivation."[37] However often Irving referred to the effect the Catskills had on his youthful imagination, he did not actually disembark in Catskill and visit them until July 1832. He set "Rip Van Winkle" at the foot of the "fairy mountains" he had seen from the river, but at the time he wrote the story he had never visited the mountains and was living in England (plates 8 and 9).[38] It is, therefore, not surprising that the landscape descriptions in "Rip Van Winkle" are generalized and bear no direct relationship with the actual geography of the Catskills. Nonetheless, Irving's fiction both introduced the Catskills to large numbers of European and American readers and gave the mountains a history with which they have been identified ever since. Even today, the Rip Van Winkle Motor Lodge stands beside the New York State Thruway, and the Rip Van Winkle Bridge crosses the Hudson just north of the village of Catskill. Nineteenth-century entrepreneurs made even greater historical claims. From the 1830s until after the Civil War, the main road into the mountains led up a ravine called Sleepy Hollow, and the stagecoaches stopped at the "Rip Van Winkle House," where the horses were watered and the innkeeper would introduce himself as one of Rip's descendants (fig. 5).

Plate 8. Thomas Cole, *Rip Van Winkle*, n.d. Courtesy Albany Institute of History and Art.

Plate 9. Felix O.C. Darley, *Rip's Return*, c. 1848. Courtesy Historic Hudson Valley.

James Fenimore Cooper wrote five novels describing events in the life of the frontiersman Natty Bumppo. *The Pioneers* was the first, and in it Natty, also called Leather-stocking, is already an old man. All the action takes place in a frontier New York town called Templeton, which is located at the source of the Susquehanna River on a lake called the Glimmerglass. Templeton is modeled on the frontier village of Cooperstown, and Glimmerglass is a stand-in for Lake Otsego. The action is set in 1793, seven years after the founding of Templeton. In one of the best-known scenes in the novel, Natty and his companions are fishing on the Glimmerglass. One of his companions praises the beauty of the local scenery, and Natty responds by comparing it with the beauties of the Catskills:

"I have travelled the woods for fifty-three year, and have made them my home for more than forty, and I can say that I have met but one place that was more to my liking; and that was only to eyesight, and not for hunting or fishing."

"And where was that?" asked Edwards.

"Where! Why up on the Cattskills.... next to the river, where one of the ridges juts out a little from the rest, and where the rocks fall for the best part of a thousand feet, so much up and down, that a man standing on their edges is fool enough to think he can jump from top to bottom."

"What see you when you get there?" asked Edwards.

"Creation!" said Natty. ....[39]

Natty does not stop with his description of the view from the escarpment. Like subsequent painters, writers, and tourists, he proceeds to describe the double waterfall at the head of Kaaterskill Clove:

"But there's a place, a short two miles back of that very hill, that in late times I relished better than the mountains; for it was kivered with the trees, and nateral."

"And where was that?" inquired Edwards, whose curiosity was strongly excited by the simple description of the hunter.

"Why, there's a fall in the hills, where water of two little ponds that lie near each other breaks out of their bounds, and runs over the rocks into the valley. The stream is, maybe, such a one as would turn a mill, if so useless a thing was wanted in the wilderness. But the hand that made that 'Leap' never made a mill! There the water comes crooking and winding among the rocks, first so slow that a trout could swim in it, and then starting and running just like a creater that wanted to make a far spring, till it gets to where the mountain divides, like the cleft hoof of a deer, leaving a deep hollow for the brook to tumble into. The first pitch is nigh two hundred feet, and the water looks like flakes of driven snow, afore it touches the bottom; and there the stream gathers together again for a new start, and maybe flutters over fifty feet of flat-rock, before it falls for another hundred, when it jumps about from shelf to shelf, first turning this-away and then turning that-away, striving to get out of the hollow, till it finally comes to the plain."

"I have never heard of this spot before: it is not mentioned in the books."

"I have never read a book in my life," said Leather-stocking.[40]

The immediate popularity of *The Pioneers* meant that Natty's paean to the Catskills received wide dissemination among the English and American reading public.[41] With Dwight's *Travels in New-England and New-York*, it both advertised the wonders of the Catskill scenery and helped to establish the views from the escarpment and Kaaterskill Falls as the two major tourist sites in the area. Moreover, the influence of Natty's description did not fade as Cooper's novel got older. From 1823 until after the Civil War, travel narratives describing a visit to the Catskills regularly quoted Natty's description. One of the reasons that it remained so well known for so long is that in 1846 it was reprinted as the first item in an anthology of Catskill narratives titled *The Scenery of the Catskill Mountains*. Regularly reprinted, *The Scenery of the Catskill Mountains* was the most popular Catskill Mountain guidebook until the 1876 publication of Walton Van Loan's *Catskill Mountain Guide*. The regularity with which subsequent visitors quoted Natty's account suggests that,

Fig. 5. John Rubens Smith, *Rip Van Winkle's House*, 1846. Courtesy Museum of Fine Arts, Boston.

both as a part of *The Pioneers* and as the lead item in *The Scenery of the Catskill Mountains*, his description not only advertised the sites to be seen, but also—and more importantly—offered guidance as to what emotions the sites could or ought to provoke. Along with other early Catskill narratives, Natty's account helped teach early tourists *how to* experience the mountains and waterfalls as aesthetically satisfying. Potential tourists would read Natty's or other accounts before going to the sites in order to learn what he or she could expect to experience. Or they might read the descriptions after visiting the sites. In either case, the written texts provided vocabularies and interpretive frameworks that largely defined the content of individual tourists' "personal" responses to the sites.[42]

The declining value of Greene County wheat, the declining volume of local flour manufacturing, the growth of a well-to-do audience interested in mountain scenery, the rapid improvement of the local transportation network, and the popularization of Catskill Mountain scenery by the various print and graphic media all encouraged the development of mountain tourism in the area between Kaaterskill Clove and the Susquehanna Turnpike. A refreshment stand with a few bunks had been built on the shoulder of South Mountain by about 1819. In 1822, a group of Yankee entrepreneurs—not a Dutchman among them—from the village of Catskill bought the seven most scenic acres on the shoulder of South Mountain and built a simple dormitory to shelter overnight visitors. The dormitory had separate wings for men and women and was situated so as to command a view of the sunrise over the Hudson Valley. James Fenimore Cooper probably stayed in this building during his visit to the area. Business proved good, and the owners bought more land and set about building a hotel. Their new building opened in the spring of 1824 and contained about ten private rooms. By the spring of 1825, the owners had added two wings containing about forty more rooms. The new hotel could accommodate about two hundred guests, was called the Pine Orchard House, and was the first successful mountain tourist hotel in the United States (plate 10).[43]

THE RISE OF CATSKILL MOUNTAIN TOURISM, 1824-1838

Plate 10. John Rubens Smith, *Catskill Mountain-House. A Celebrated Summer Hotel...*, 1830. Courtesy The New York Public Library.

The hotel at Pine Orchard, more popularly known as the Catskill Mountain House, was an immediate success. In the nineteenth century as today, the height of the tourist season ran from the Fourth of July to the end of September. Few tourists traveled after the beginning of September, and the hotel usually closed by the middle of the month. On 13 August 1829, the *Catskill Recorder* reported that more than five hundred persons a week were passing through the village on their way to it (plate 11).[44] Early nineteenth-century travel narratives and guidebooks reveal that the number of visitors was so high because by the end of the 1820s the hotel had joined Niagara Falls and the springs at Saratoga as a regular stop on the American equivalent of the European Grand Tour.[45] But although both the opening and the immediate popularity of the Catskill Mountain House clearly mark an important stage in the history of the taste for wild environments in the United States, it would be a mistake to conclude that the taste for these environments was *already* characteristic either of most Americans or even of most well-to-do Americans. Indeed, the fact that the Pine Orchard House remained the only large mountain tourist hotel in the United States until the 1840s suggests that the taste for undomesticated environments spread slowly.

European and American analysts who found mountains and wilderness attractive often noted the absence of this enthusiasm among the mass of Americans. In the second volume of *Democracy in America* (1840), Alexis de Tocqueville noted that few Americans appreciated the beauties of wild environments and suggested that Americans had not developed a taste for them because they were too busy bringing them under cultivation:

Plate 11. Unknown artist, *Catskill Mountain House,* after 1839. Courtesy Kennedy Galleries, Inc.

I readily admit that the Americans have no poets; I cannot allow that they have no poetic ideas. In Europe people talk a great deal of the wilds of America, but the Americans themselves never think about them; they are insensible to the wonders of inanimate nature and they may be said not to perceive the mighty forests that surround them till they fall beneath the hatchet. Their eyes are fixed upon another sight: the American people views its own march across these wilds, draining swamps, turning the course of rivers, peopling solitudes, and subduing nature. This magnificent image of themselves does not meet the gaze of the Americans at intervals only; it may be said to haunt every one of them in his least as well as in his most important actions and to be always flitting before his mind.[46]

Tocqueville did not condemn the fact that few Americans appreciated wilderness because he understood it as a natural effect of the underdeveloped condition of their material environment and economy. The clear implication of his analysis is that Americans would develop a European-style taste for wilderness as soon as they had finished settling it.

The American landscape painter Thomas Cole shared Tocqueville's views on the seeming unwillingness of Americans to experience the attractions of wilderness. Cole insisted, however, that most Americans failed to see the beauties of wild nature not because they were too busy pursuing the noble work of progress but because they were too preoccupied with making money. In his 1835 "Essay on American Scenery," Cole exclaimed "against the apathy with which the beauties of external nature are regarded by the great mass, even of our refined community" and complained that although it

would seem unnecessary to those who can see and feel, for me to expatiate on the loveliness of verdant fields, the sublimity of lofty mountains, or the varied magnificence of the sky; . . .the number of those who *seek* enjoyment in such sources is comparatively small. From the indifference with which the multitude regard the beauties of nature, it might be inferred that she had been unnecessarily lavish in adorning this world for beings who take no pleasure in its adornment. Who in grovelling pursuits forget their glorious heritage. Why was the earth made so beautiful, or the sun so clad in glory at his rising and setting, when *all* might be unrobed of beauty without affecting the insensate multitude, so they can be "lighted to their purposes?"[47]

Like Tocqueville and almost all nineteenth-century Americans, Cole accepted both the inevitability and desirability of economic progress, but he insisted that such progress was compatible with the development of landscape taste: "If men were not insensible to the beauty of nature the great works necessary for the purposes of commerce might be carried on without destroying it, and at times might even contribute to her charms by rendering her more accessible; but it is not so. They desecrate whatever they touch. They cut down the forests with a wantonness for which there is no excuse, even gain, & leave the herbless rocks to glimmer in the burning sun."[48] In both his public and his private writings, Cole insisted not only that the mass of Americans *could* learn to appreciate wild environments, but that it was spiritually important that they do so. For Cole, the wanton destruction of wilderness was a "desecration" because wild environments were unmarred revelations of the deity. It was important for every American to learn to appreciate mountains and other wild environments because the appreciation of landscape was a way of worshipping God. Cole therefore both began and closed the "Essay on American Scenery" by insisting on "the importance of *cultivating* a taste for scenery."[49] Just as farmers cultivated their land, so Americans should cultivate their taste for natural environments. Americans who had not yet acquired this taste should cultivate it in themselves; Americans who had already acquired it had a social and even spiritual responsibility to cultivate it among those who had not.[50]

Of course, in teaching the mass of Americans how to experience natural environments as beautiful expressions of the deity, painters, writers, and resort operators were also creating an audience for the landscape paintings, landscape writings, and hotel rooms they had to sell. The regularity with which nineteenth-century guides to the Catskills cited Irving and Cooper and mentioned specific painters of the local scenery suggests that businessmen were well aware of the value of landscape paintings and literature as advertisements. But the alliance between painters, writers, and businessmen was informal, not collusive. Painters, writers, and the developers of landscape tourism pursued their own interests, but the growing popularity of the goods offered by each group redounded to the benefit of the others. I do not mean to overemphasize the extent to which painters, writers, and tourists *created* the taste for landscape. It arose among a numerically small group of well-to-do and cosmopolitan Americans *before* the beginning of domestic tourism and *before* the creation of native schools of landscape painting and writing. Indeed, it was the existence of these consumers that made possible the development of landscape painting, writing, and tourism in the 1820s. But even as the existence of this originally small group of consumers made possible these developments in the United States, so the growth of native schools of landscape writing and painting and of domestic tourism helped spread the taste for landscape and thus led to the creation of new consumers. From the 1820s on, the relationship of landscape consumers with the purveyors of landscape was fully reciprocal: the popularization of landscape taste led to the growth of landscape tourism and made possible the production of more landscape art and literature; the growth of landscape tourism and the production of steadily increasing amounts of landscape art and literature led to the creation of steadily increasing numbers of landscape consumers.

THOMAS COLE PAINTS THE CATSKILLS, 1825-1830

Thomas Cole was the first and by far the most influential visual artist to work in the Catskills. He first visited the area in the late summer of 1825 and, like other early visitors, spent most of this first visit in the immediate area of the Mountain House. After a short time on the mountain top, Cole returned to New York City, where he finished five paintings of Hudson River and Catskill Mountain scenery. Probably completed by late October, these paintings were exhibited in the shop of the book and picture dealer William Coleman, and they quickly brought the twenty-four-year-old painter his first public recognition. According to contemporary accounts by the painter and historian William Dunlap (1766-1839), the painter Colonel John Trumbull saw three of Cole's 1825 paintings in the shop window and bought a view (as yet unlocated) of *Caatterskill Upper Fall, Catskill Mountains.* He then reported his "discovery" to Asher B. Durand and Dunlap. Durand and Dunlap hurried to the shop, where Dunlap bought *Lake with Dead Trees* (plate 12) and Durand bought the last of the five paintings—an unlocated *View of Fort Putnam. Lake with Dead Trees* is a view looking southwest towards the outlet of South Lake.[51] Trumbull

continued to help Cole by allowing Dunlap to publish a newspaper story in which he reported Trumbull to have said, "This youth has done at once, and without instruction, what I cannot do after 50 years practice."[52] In December, the paintings bought by Trumbull, Dunlap, and Durand were added to the American Academy of Fine Arts exhibition, where they were widely noticed and favorably reviewed. The *Lake with Dead Trees* and the *Caatterskill Upper Fall, Catskill Mountains* were the first images of the Mountain House area publicly displayed in New York City and no doubt helped spur interest in the new resort.[53] At about this time, Daniel Wadsworth, Trumbull's nephew-in-law, saw *Caatterskill Upper Fall, Catskill Mountains* and commissioned Cole to paint him a view of the same scene (fig. 6).[54]

In a 1 August 1826 letter to Cole in which he praised the "desolate wildness" of *Lake with Dead Trees*, the Baltimore collector Robert Gilmor commissioned a pair of landscapes: "Water should be introduced at least in one, and would be well in both, one being *falling* water, & the other *still*, lake, water, reflecting the tints of sky, foliage, grass & shewing the play of light on a slight motion of part of it, which may be also effected by introducing deer or cattle drinking, or a canoe with Indians paddling on it."[55] Although Gilmor's letter does not suggest that he understood Cole's first two Catskill landscapes as forming this kind of pair, a comparison of *Lake with Dead Trees* with Wadsworth's copy of the unlocated *Caatterskill Upper Fall, Catskill Mountains* suggests that Cole conceived them as pendants.

In both paintings, Cole represented the already settled mountain top as wilderness. The dead trees in *Lake with Dead Trees* may be an indirect reference to the impact of lumbering and tourism on the appearance of the mountain top. While visiting Kaaterskill Falls, Cole would have noticed Silas Scribner's sawmill and dam on Lake Creek between South Lake and the top of the falls. It was Scribner who had sawed the lumber used to build the

Fig. 6. Thomas Cole, *Katerskill Falls*, 1826. Courtesy Wadsworth Atheneum.

Mountain House, and it was his dam that had flooded and killed the trees along the shores of South Lake. Similarly, Cole may have chosen to paint Kaaterskill Falls from within the cavern so as to avoid showing the observation platform that had already been built at its top (plate 13 and fig. 7).[56]

But if both paintings represent the mountain top as wilderness, the still water and subdued sky of *Lake with Dead Trees* represent the beauty of wilderness, while the swirling water and storm clouds of *Kaaterskill Falls* (fig. 6) evoke its sublimity. Both canvases represent the passage of time. In *Lake with*

Fig. 7. Thomas Hilson, *Platform and Hut Overlooking Cauterskill Falls*, c. 1825-1830. Courtesy Museum of Fine Arts, Boston.

Dead Trees, this movement is most obviously figured by the dead trees, but it is also suggested by the movement of the clouds, the autumnal coloring, the late afternoon light slanting out of the southwest, and—especially—the placement of the two deer. The organization of *Lake with Dead Trees* derives from the compositional formulas associated with the French painter Claude Lorrain (1600-1682): the brightly lit trees in the left foreground and the shaded trees in the right middleground frame the central lake and encourage the viewer to look down the lake towards the brightly lit patch of sky, High Peak, and the implied but hidden outlet at the rear. The introduction of the foreground deer diverts the viewer's attention from the middleground and background, however, and encourages him or her to read the canvas as moving horizontally from the brightly lit dead trees in the left foreground, to the stationary deer in the center foreground, to the bounding deer that leaps off the canvas to the right. Silhouetted against the storm clouds, the upper branches of the dead trees at the left resemble the antlers of the two deer and suggest that the organization of the foreground is both from left to right and from death to life.

In *Kaaterskill Falls,* the passage of time is most obviously figured by the rapid flow of Lake Creek, but it is also suggested by the autumnal coloring, the evening sky, and the passing of the storm. As in *Lake with Dead Trees,* the organization of the foreground and middleground is along the central diagonal. But where the diagonal regression in *Lake with Dead Trees* is satisfyingly closed by High Peak and the patch of blue sky, the diagonal regression in *Kaaterskill Falls* is unclosed. The organization of the canvas encourages the viewer to follow the white line of the creek, but the second leap of the creek and the darkness of the Clove conceal the exact relationship of the middleground to the background.

Lake with Dead Trees* and *Kaaterskill Falls* are organized so as to involve the viewer in two fundamentally different kinds of relationship with the represented scene. In *Lake with Dead Trees*, the rotting log in the central foreground and the fixed stare of the central deer distance the viewer from the scene. In *Kaaterskill Falls*, the overhanging arch of the cavern, the absence of any solid foreground, and the viewer's inability to see the full course of the creek pulls the viewer into the scene. The swirling white paint of the creek hurries the viewer along so that he or she joins the central Indian on the last outcropping overlooking the abyss of the Clove. The organization of *Lake with Dead Trees* enables the viewer to distance himself or herself from the scene so as to objectify it in either one of two distinct ways. On the one hand, the viewer can fix his or her attention on the diagonal joining the foreground tree with the distant outlet and *appreciate* the scene as a picturesque landscape. Or the viewer can fix his or her attention on the horizontal joining the foreground tree with the bounding deer and *interpret* the progression from dead tree to bounding deer as morally significant. Thus, although *Lake with Dead Trees* is not didactic in any obvious way, the foreground details suggest a moral truth along the lines of "in nature is no death" or "out of death, life." The important point is that as different as these two ways of experiencing the scene of *Lake with Dead Trees* are, they both depend on the viewer's awareness of separation from a scene that he or she makes the object of aesthetic appreciation or intellectual understanding.

Alternatively, the organization of *Kaaterskill Falls* denies the viewer this kind of physical and interpretive distance in order to draw him or her into a less mediated encounter with the scene. The perilousness of the Indian's position figures the immediacy of his relationship with the surrounding environment. Instead of standing back from the view in order to appreciate or interpret it, he has already stepped into it. Of course, both the Indian's relationship with the abyss of the Clove and the viewer's relationship with the swirling motion of *Kaaterskill Falls* are still shaped by the fact of human consciousness. But the distinguishing characteristic of the kind of aesthetic experience figured by the Indian and—Cole must have hoped—evoked by *Kaaterskill Falls* is that the individual momentarily forgets his or her apartness from the observed scene and experiences it *as if* directly.

Visual analysis suggests that Cole intended *Lake with Dead Trees* and *Kaaterskill Falls* as pendants and that they involve the viewer in two distinct ways of experiencing the represented scene. The actual geography of Lake Creek—which flows from South Lake over Kaaterskill Falls—and the awkwardly leaping deer in the right foreground of *Lake with Dead Trees* suggest that Cole intended *Lake with Dead Trees* to be hung to the left of *Kaaterskill Falls*. With this configuration, both ways of reading *Lake with Dead Trees*—along the diagonal from left front to right rear, and along the horizontal from left front to right front—lead to the Falls. The implication of this placement is that the kind of experience evoked by *Lake with Dead Trees* is—or ought to be—preliminary to the kind of experience evoked by

Plate 14. Thomas Cole, *View from the Top of Kaaterskill Falls*, 1826. Courtesy The Detroit Institute of Arts.

Plate 15. Thomas Cole, *Stony Gap, Kaaterskill Clove*, c. 1826. Courtesy Joslyn Art Museum.

Kaaterskill Falls. It is good to be able to step back from a landscape and either appreciate its picturesque beauty or moralize on its meaning. It is better to be able to step into it and experience it *as if* directly.

Cole spent the winter of 1826 on the estate of George William Featherstonhaugh (pronounced Fanshaw), which was located on the Schoharie River in Duanesburg, New York. While living with Featherstonhaugh, Cole worked up sketches from his fall trip to the Catskills and both sketched and painted scenes of the Schoharie Valley. The most important painting Cole completed while living with Featherstonhaugh was probably *Falls of Kaaterskill*, which had been commissioned by the New York City merchant William Gracie (plate 2). *View from the Top of Kaaterskill Falls* (plate 14) and *Stony Gap, Kaaterskill Clove* (plate 15) may also date from the three months Cole spent with Featherstonhaugh.[57] Cole returned to New York City by May, when he sent seven paintings to the American Academy of Fine Arts exhibition. Among the seven were Trumbull's *Catterskill Upper Fall, Catskill Mountains* and Gracie's *Landscape, Falls of Kaaterskill*. In the same month, he sent three paintings to the first annual exhibition of the National Academy of Design. *Snow Squall, Winter Landscape in the Catskills* (fig. 8) was probably one of these.[58]

By May 1826, Cole had sold enough paintings and had received enough new commissions that he could afford to spend the entire summer and fall in the mountains. He left New York in late May or early June. In the winter of 1826, James Fenimore Cooper had published his second novel featuring Natty Bumppo. Set on Lake George, *The Last of the Mohicans* proved even more successful than *The Pioneers*. Perhaps inspired by Cooper's novel, Cole proceeded to Lake George. How long he stayed at Lake George is unclear, but by the beginning of July he had returned to the Catskills, where he spent the remainder of the summer and early fall.

Cole returned to the Catskills with a commission from Robert Gilmor for a view of the Mountain House from the road. Although it was Cole who had originally recommended the subject to Gilmor, once he returned to the site he decided that there was not enough "distance" between the bend in the road and the Mountain House to give the picture "air" and therefore requested permission to deliver another subject.[59] The evidence of his 1825-1826 paintings of the Catskills suggests that Cole had spent most of his short 1825 visit in the area of the Mountain House. The evidence of his 1826-1827 paintings suggests that he spent most of the summer and fall of 1826 either in the village of Catskill or in the area of Kaaterskill Clove. Although there is no written

Fig. 8. Thomas Cole, *Snow Squall, Winter Landscape in the Catskills*, c. 1825-1826. Courtesy R. W. Norton Art Gallery.

evidence to suggest why Cole stopped working in the area of the Mountain House, one suspects that he was put off by the number of tourists in the areas nearest to the hotel.

That Cole was bothered by the number of tourists in the area of the Mountain House is also suggested by the fact that in both 1827 and 1828 his major sketching trips were to the more remote and less easily visited White Mountains of New Hampshire. If Cole visited the Catskills in 1827 or 1828, there is no evidence of it. He left the United States for Europe on 1 June 1829 and remained there for three and a half years.

Between the fall of 1826 and his 1829 departure for Europe, Cole finished perhaps ten major paintings of the Catskills. All seem to have been based on drawings he did in either 1825 or 1826. Immediately upon his return to New York in the early fall of 1826, Cole finished *Kaaterskill Falls* for Wadsworth. Later that winter he finished a large horizontal view of the falls for a stateroom of the steamboat *Albany* (fig. 9). Unlike the stylized *Falls of Kaaterskill* he had painted for William Gracie, this *Falls of the Kaaterskill* is a topographically persuasive view of the falls as seen from below. Because of its placement in a steamboat stateroom, it was probably the most widely seen of Cole's five known paintings of Kaaterskill Falls.

Except for these two paintings of Kaaterskill Falls, the paintings Cole completed after his fall 1826 return from Catskill and before going to Europe are scenes either of the mountains from near the village of Catskill or of the less traveled areas of the Catskills to the south of Kaaterskill Clove. *Autumn in the Catskills* is one of two paintings commissioned by the New York collector Henry Ward in 1827 (plate 16). The other is the well-known *Sunny Morning on the Hudson River* (Museum of Fine Arts, Boston), a view of Roundtop from the western edge of the ridge dividing Kaaterskill from Plattekill Clove.[60] The subject of *Autumn in the Catskills* has not been identified.

Fig. 9. Thomas Cole, *Falls of the Kaaterskill*, 1827. Private collection; photograph courtesy Vose Galleries.

Plate 16. Thomas Cole, *Autumn in the Catskills*, 1827. Courtesy Arnot Art Museum.

Fig. 10. William Guy Wall, *Cauterskill Falls on the Catskill Mountains, Taken from under the Cavern*, c. 1827. Courtesy Honolulu Academy of Arts.

Plate 17. Gherlando Marsiglia, *Catskill Falls*, c. 1828. Courtesy The New-York Historical Society.

PAINTING THE CATSKILLS, *1826-1838*

The success of Cole's 1825-1829 paintings of the Catskills encouraged other painters to produce oil paintings of the area. The most prominent artist to follow Cole's lead was William Guy Wall, best known as a watercolorist, who painted at least one and probably more oil views of the Catskills in the late 1820s. Wall painted *Cauterskill Falls on the Catskill Mountains, Taken from under the Cavern* (fig. 10) during the winter of 1826-1827 and exhibited it at the National Academy of Design in May 1827. Although Wall deemphasized the abyss beyond the second leap of Kaaterskill Falls and replaced Cole's perilously placed Indian with a group of well-dressed tourists, his decision to paint the falls from the cavern and to use its upper arch as a painted frame shows the influence either of Cole's unlocated *Caatterskill Upper Fall, Catskill Mountains* or of the *Kaaterskill Falls* painted for Daniel Wadsworth. Gherlando Marsiglia, an Italian painter and copyist then living in New York, exhibited four views of the Catskills between 1828 and 1831. None of the four are currently located, but a lithograph of *Catskill Falls* (plate 17) inscribed "Drawn on stone by G. Marsiglia from his own original painting" has survived. Just as Wall borrowed from Cole's *Caatterskill Upper Fall, Catskill Mountains,* so Marsiglia's lithograph suggests that he borrowed from Wall. The similarity of Marsiglia's engraving to Wall's painting together with Marsiglia's reputation as a copyist suggest that all of Marsiglia's oil views of

the Catskills may have been derived from Cole or Wall. Jacob C. Ward's 1833 *Wolf in the Glen* (plate 18) is not as derivative from Cole as the views from the cavern by Wall and Marsiglia, but Ward nonetheless borrowed some ideas. The arrangement of the falls in *Wolf in the Glen* recalls *Falls of the Kaaterskill* (fig. 9), which Ward could easily have seen in the stateroom of the steamboat *Albany.* The wolf in the foreground recalls the equally awkward wolf in Cole's *Snow Squall, Winter Landscape in the Catskills* (fig. 8).[61]

Plate 18. Jacob C. Ward, *Wolf in the Glen,* 1833. Courtesy Wadsworth Atheneum.

Cole returned to the United States in 1832. He traveled to the Catskills in 1833 and painted numerous views of the area until his death in 1848. Except for Cole, few major landscape painters worked in the Catskills during the 1830s and early 1840s.[62] There are at least two reasons why so few other landscape painters were active in the area during this time. The most obvious is that there were few professional painters of landscape working in the United States before the mid-1840s. Moreover, many of the early nineteenth-century landscape painters who were active in the United States lived in Boston, Philadelphia, and Baltimore and concentrated their attention on the environs of those cities.[63]

Less obviously, relatively few landscape painters were active on the mountain top because there were relatively few Americans with the money or—equally importantly—the desire to buy landscape paintings in oil. Although a core group of collectors supported the work of the earliest American landscape painters, significant numbers of new collectors did not begin to buy landscape paintings until the economic boom of the mid-1840s. In the 1820s and through the 1830s, the scarcity of collectors discouraged potential landscape painters from entering the field. Many of the most important landscapists of the middle of the century—including Asher B. Durand, John Casilear, and John Frederick Kensett—spent the early years of their careers working as engravers in large part because they doubted their ability to support themselves as painters. The economic realities that originally deterred Durand, Casilear, and Kensett no doubt discouraged other potential landscape painters. Like the relationship between the development of mountain tourism and the creation of tourists, the relationship between the development of increasing numbers of landscape painters and the creation of new collectors of landscape art was reciprocal. In the 1820s and 1830s, the scarcity of collectors discouraged potential landscape painters from entering the field at the same time that the relative scarcity of landscape paintings discouraged the development of new collectors.[64]

Although the direct effect of Cole's paintings on the spending habits of potential tourists and collectors of painted landscapes is difficult to document, the earliest tourist guidebooks show that at least some nineteenth-century observers recognized connections between the development of landscape taste, the rise of mountain tourism, and the popularization of landscape painting. Until the late 1820s, the best available guides to North American scenery were books such as Spafford's *Gazetteer of the State of New-York,* primarily designed for use by immigrants or business travelers. One of the first guides specifically intended for the use of New York State tourists was James Kirke Paulding's *The New Mirror for Travellers; and Guide to the Springs* (1828). In *The New Mirror,* Paulding encouraged "the picturesque tourist" to visit the new hotel at Pine Orchard and the neighboring waterfall. Once he had directed his readers to Kaaterskill Falls, however, Paulding interrupted his description of the local scenery in order both to inform his readers that they *could* buy landcape paintings of the sites and to insist that they *should* buy such paintings:

> Messrs. Wall and Cole, two fine artists, admirable in their different, we might almost say, opposite styles, have illustrated the scenery of the Kaatskill, by more than one picture of singular excellence. We should like to see such pictures gracing the drawing rooms of the wealthy, instead of the imported trumpery of British naval fights, or coloured engravings, and above all, in the place of that vulgar, tasteless, and inelegant accumulation of gilded finery, which costs more than a dozen fine landscapes. These lovers of cut glass lamps, rose wood sofas, and convex mirrors, have yet to learn that a single bust or picture of a master adorns and enriches the parlour of a gentleman, in the eyes of a well bred person, a thousand times more than the spoils of half a dozen fashionable warehouses.[65]

Where Paulding's guide documents something of the process by which mountain tourism fostered the development of increasing numbers of consumers interested in the purchase of landscape paintings, A. T. Goodrich's *North American Tourist* (1839) documents something of the process by which landscape painting fostered the development of landscape tourism. Although he did not go into great detail, Goodrich suggested that the Catskills had become a popular tourist destination in large measure *because* of Cole's paintings of them. He thus urged all of his readers who were "disposed...to seek out gratification and amusement" to visit Kaaterskill Falls and the "other spots that the magic touches of Cole the artist have brought to the public admiration."[66]

MOUNTAIN TOURISM AND THE MASS MEDIA, 1824-1838

The success of Cole's 1825-1829 paintings of the Catskills promoted awareness both of the availability of landscape art and of the accessibility of the
Catskills among those segments of the American populace that frequented art
exhibitions and read exhibition reviews. Larger numbers of Americans and
Europeans were introduced to the resort by means of the print media. As early
as 1824, the newspaper editor William L. Stone helped the developers of the
new hotel by filling pages of the *New-York Commercial Advertiser* with a series
of articles extolling the wonders of the nearby mountains.[67] Even more importantly, Spafford added a section on the new hotel to the second(1824) edition
of his *Gazetteer of the State of New-York*. Despite the publication of Paulding's
guide in 1828, Spafford's remained the most important guide to New York
State until 1830, when Robert Vandewater published the first edition of his
The Tourist or Pocket Manual for Travellers on the Hudson River. The generous
prose in Spafford's 1824 *Gazetteer* directed thousands of potential visitors to
the new hotel. The year after Spafford published his updated *Gazetteer,* one of
the first visitors to the Mountain House described it in his "Descriptive
Journal of a Jaunt Up the Grand Canal; Being a Letter from a Gentleman in
New York to a lady in Washington, in August, 1825."[68] But the first great
wave of print publicity did not hit until 1828 when articles describing the
Mountain House and its environs appeared in Paulding's guidebook, the
7 June issue of the magazine *Rural Repository*, and both of the most widely
distributed literary annuals published in the United States: *The Atlantic
Souvenir; A Christmas and New Year's Offering* and *The Token; A Christmas
and New Year's Present*. More articles appeared in 1829, including a notice in
the 11 July issue of *The Bower of Taste* and a long account in the most important literary annual published in New York—*The Talisman*.[69] The articles in
the *The Bower of Taste, The Atlantic Souvenir* (plate 27), and the *Rural
Repository* (plate 30) were illustrated with engravings. Throughout the 1830s
and 1840s, accounts of visits to the Catskills and engravings of the Mountain
House and its surroundings regularly appeared in a wide range of American
newspapers, magazines, and literary annuals and figured prominently in book-
length travel narratives published by European and American tourists.

The organization of mountain tourism in the Catskills changed as the
aesthetic skills and interests of painters, writers, and tourists changed. From
1824 until the early 1840s, visitors to the mountain top almost always stayed at
the Catskill Mountain House. Travel narratives, engravings, and the 13 August
1829 notice in the *Catskill Recorder* suggest that during the 1820s and 1830s,
few visitors to the Mountain House stayed longer than two or three nights.[70]
Some of these early visitors complained of the cost, and some may have
limited their stay because of the expense, but the travel narratives show that
even well-to-do visitors rarely stayed more than a few days.[71] Other tourists
may have cut short their stays because the public and the private rooms at the
hotel were small and cramped compared to rooms in the hotels at Saratoga or
other lowland resorts. But written descriptions and drawn representations of
the Catskills from this early period suggest that most visitors left after two or
three nights not so much because the hotel was expensive or uncomfortable,
but because one or two days was all the time needed in order to see what they
had come for. Unlike Cole, few early visitors sought out the wilder environments to the south and west of the Mountain House. Uninterested in the

experience of hiking in the surrounding woods or up the neighboring mountains, early tourists traveled to the mountain top in order *to see* Kaaterskill Falls, the view from the escarpment, and the hotel itself—and departed as soon as they had.

Travel narratives and engravings from the 1820s and 1830s show that early tourists were mainly interested in seeing the three major sites and that many early tourists invested these views with religious significance. Except for Natty's description of Kaaterskill Falls and the view from the escarpment in *The Pioneers*, pre-1824 descriptions of the Catskills rarely invoked God.[72] Obvious references to God are also absent from most travel narratives and engravings published in the later 1820s and 1830s by European visitors to the area.[73] Most travel narratives and engravings of the Catskills were produced by Americans, however, and from 1824 through the end of the 1830s most of these represented mountain tourism as a spiritually significant activity and suggested that landscape appreciation was a kind of religious worship.

THE VIEW FROM THE ROAD

Until the 1880s, almost all visitors to the mountain top arrived by way of the Mountain House road up the eastern escarpment. Although later narratives often ignored the journey from the town of Catskill to the Mountain House, most written before the Civil War devoted a good deal of space to a description of the ascent; many described it as a kind of pilgrimage. Sometimes the comparison was made in passing. In his 1828 "Catskill, A Journal of the Grand and Glorious," for example, Grenville Mellen simply noted that he and his companions cut canes "like good pilgrims."[74] But many writers developed the comparison at greater length. In "Ollapodiana" (1837), the New York writer Willis Gaylord Clark compared the ascent with a pilgrimage, the Mountain House with the heavenly Jerusalem, and the Mountain House registry with the heavenly "book" containing the names of the elect:

> Passing the ravine, where the immortal Rip Van Winkle played his game of nine-pins with the wizards of that neighborhood, and quaffed huge draughts of those bewildering flagons, which made him sleep for years, I flung myself impatiently from the 'quarter-deck' of that postillion whose place I had shared; I grasped that goodly globe of gold and ivory which heads my customary cane...and pushed gaily on, determined to pause not, until my weary feet stood on the Platform....
> There is a wonderful deception in the approach to the Mountain-House, which, when discovered, will strike the traveller with amazement. At one point of the road, where the mansion which is to terminate your pilgrimage heaves its white form in view, (you have seen it from the river for nearly half a day,) it seems not farther than a hundred rods, and hangs apparently on the verge of a stupendous crag over your head; the road turns again, it is out of sight, and the summits, near its *locus in quo*, are nearly three miles off. The effect is wonderful. The mountain is *growing upon you.*
> I continued to ascend, slowly, but with patient steps, and with a flow of spirit which I cannot describe.... Hill after hill, mere ridges of the mountain, was attained—summit after summit surmounted—and yet it seemed to me that the house was as far off as ever. Finally it appeared, and a-nigh; to me the 'earth's one sanctuary.' I reached it; my name was on the book; the queries of the publican, as to 'how many coach-loads were behind,' (symp-

toms of a yearning for the almighty dollar, even in this holy of nature's holies) were answered, and I stood on the Platform.

Good Reader!—expect me not to describe the indescribable. I feel now, while memory is busy in my brain, in the silence of my library, calling up that vision to my mind, much as I did when I leaned upon my staff before that omnipotent picture, and looked abroad upon its God-written magnitude.[75]

Despite the gently humorous tone of Clark's account, he does not seem to doubt the spiritual significance either of the mountain landscape or of mountain tourism. His comparison of the Mountain House registry to the book of the elect is funny. But, like thousands of other Americans, when he reached the Platform, Clark leaned on his pilgrim's "staff" and experienced the view of the Hudson Valley as a revelation of a beneficent deity.[76]

Most of the mass-produced images of the Catskills before the Civil War were of the view of the Mountain House from the road. Like most written accounts of the ascent to the Mountain House, most of these engravings suggest that mountain tourism was a spiritually significant activity and that the ascent of the Catskill escarpment would bring the tourist nearer to God.

The earliest known view of the Mountain House from this perspective is an exception to this generalization. Felix Duponchel's 1826 lithograph *Catskill Mountain House* (plate 19) contains no human figures and does not evoke the identification of mountain tourism as a kind of pilgrimage. Instead, the

Plate 19. Felix Duponchel, *Catskill Mountain House*, 1826. Courtesy New York State Library.

swirling storm clouds above, the threatening bulge at the left of the escarpment, the unevenness of the top of the escarpment in front of the hotel, the unsettling pitch of the trees in the foreground, and the striking emptiness of the road all evoke the melodramatic sublimity commonly associated with Gothic fiction.

Duponchel's lithograph was never bound in a book, and nothing is known about the method or extent of its distribution. The impression in the New York State Library is the only one known to exist. Duponchel's lithograph was the immediate source for the transfer-printed earthenware plate *Catskill House, Hudson* produced by Enoch Wood & Son in Staffordshire[77] and seems to have been a source for John Rubens Smith's 1830 engraving of the *Catskill Mountain-House* (plate 10).

The designer of the Enoch Wood & Son plate was faithful to Duponchel's original design and emphasized the lonely sublimity of the Mountain House site, but Smith reworked the design by increasing the relative size of the Mountain House, moving it back from the escarpment, lowering the escarpment, straightening the road, straightening the middleground trees, and adding a stagecoach in the middleground and seven well-dressed tourists in the foreground. The foreground figures point out the view of the Hudson at the same time that the stagecoach carries other tourists towards the even more expansive views from the Platform. Thus, although the gestures of the foreground tourists and the movement of the stagecoach seem to point in different directions, they both suggest that the object of tourism is the enjoyment of views. While Duponchel's lithograph suggested that mountain tourism was a lonely and potentially dangerous activity, Smith's engraving suggested that it was a genteel and altogether safe one. But like Duponchel's engraving, Smith's does not suggest that the appreciation of landscape is a spiritually significant activity. Smith's travelers are picturesque tourists in search of beautiful views, not pilgrims in search of God.

The first mass-produced image to represent the ascent to the Mountain House as a kind of pilgrimage was the engraving after Thomas Cole's unlocated *View of the Cattskill Mountain House, N.Y.* (plate 20). Engraved by the London firm Fenner, Sears, & Co. in August 1831 and originally published in one of the last numbers of the second volume of John Howard Hinton's 1832 *The History and Topography of the United States*, Cole's design was far and away the most influential representation of the view from the road.[78] Cole's engraving is much simpler than Smith's. Where Smith's engraving is organized by both the diagonal of the road and the horizontal established by the outstretched arms of the foreground figures, Cole's engraving is centered on the vertical axis formed by the alignment of the right edge of the Mountain House with both the well-dressed couple in the right middleground and the solitary horseman in the right foreground. Cole created this vertical axis by cropping herbage and sky from both the left and right edges of the Smith-Duponchel design so as to narrow the focus of the composition and emphasize its vertical structure, by moving the road to the right edge of the composition and lining it up directly beneath the Mountain House, and by moving the figures into the reoriented road.

The shadows to the right of Cole's horseman establish the time of day as early morning. The figure has just passed the spring at the lower right and has lifted his head to view the distant hotel. Both the horseman and the hotel are illuminated by the early morning light. Although the presence of small figures on both the Platform and the Mountain House porch imply that the road leads

Plate 20. Thomas Cole, *View of the Cattskill Mountain House, N.Y.*, 1831. Courtesy Mr. and Mrs. R. M. Decker.

to the Mountain House, the exact connection is obscured by the intervening forest. Although he is still in the light cast by the rising sun, the horseman will have to pass through the shadows and forests ahead of him if he is to reemerge into the sunlight of the Platform and gain the view it offers.

The situation of the figure in *View of the Cattskill Mountain House, N.Y.* is similar to that of the horseman in Cole's later *Notch of the White Mountains* (1839; National Gallery of Art) and *Mountain Ford* (fig. 11). In all three images the dwarfed rider follows his path deeper into the mountains which tower over him. The horseman in the *Mountain Ford* is about to cross the swollen river; the figure in *View of the Cattskill Mountain House, N.Y.* is about to enter the dark wood that lies between him and the Mountain House. The situation of the figure in *Mountain Ford* seems dangerous in a way that the situation of the horseman in *View of the Cattskill Mountain House, N.Y.* does not. But this difference derives less from the nature of the thresholds each of them is about to cross than from the fact that the figure in *Mountain Ford* cannot see the country to which he is traveling while the horseman in *View of the Cattskill Mountain House, N.Y.* keeps his eyes on the pearly columns of the beckoning Mountain House. Because the horseman in *View of the Cattskill Mountain House, N.Y.* sees his destination, he is not threatened by the wood that lies in his way but does not *loom* before him.

Fig. 11. Thomas Cole, *Mountain Ford*, 1845. Courtesy The Metropolitan Museum of Art.

Plate 21. Enoch Wood, *Pine Orchard House, Catskill Mountains*, after 1831. Courtesy Albany Institute of History and Art.

Some of the subsequent view-makers and view-buyers probably read Cole's composition from the top down and found it reassuring because, like Willis Gaylord Clark, they interpreted the columns of the Mountain House as the pearly gates of Heaven and the horseman as a Christian on the road to salvation. But the visual and verbal evidence suggests that most probably read the composition from the bottom up and interpreted the horseman as a traveler-pilgrim who journeyed to the mountain not for merely aesthetic pleasures, but for the good of his soul. Later artists and consumers found Cole's composition appealing not because it reassured them that every persevering Christian would get to Heaven, but because it reassured them that although it might *seem* frivolous, mountain tourism was a morally serious activity.

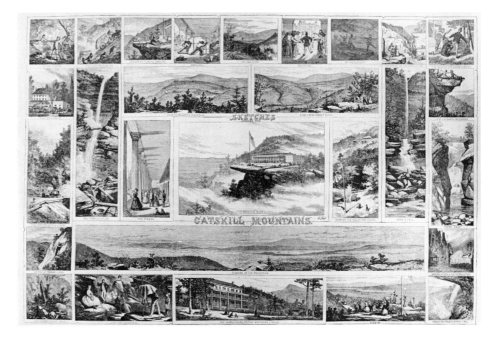

Cole's *View of the Cattskill Mountain House, N.Y.* was the immediate source for the transfer-printed earthenware plate manufactured in 1831 by the English potter J. & J. Jackson; its relationship to most subsequent representations of the view from the road was less direct. Almost every such view produced after the 1831 publication of Cole's design adopted his reworking of the compositional formulas invented by Duponchel and Smith and showed figures making their way up the road to the Mountain House. Among these later images are the transfer-printed earthenware plate *Pine Orchard House, Catskill Mountains*, manufactured by Enoch Wood & Sons after 1831 (plate 21); Alphonse Boilly's 1836 *Cattskill Mountain House* (plate 63); William Endicott's lithograph of C. Parsons's *Catskill Mountain House* (c. 1844); De Witt Clinton Boutelle's oil painting *Catskill Mountain House* (1845; Albany Institute of History and Art); J. H. Bufford's lithograph after B. B. G. Stone's *Catskill Mountain House* (1860); Thomas Nast's satiric *Sketches among the Catskill Mountains* (1866; plate 22); and Gray-Parker's *Climbing the Catskills* (1875; plate 23).[79] The most important exceptions to this generalization are Cole's oil sketch of the *Beach Mountain House* (c. 1846-1847; private collection) and George Harvey's watercolor *The Catskill Mountain House* (c. 1845-1850; plate 24).[80] Harvey's drawing was engraved by James Smillie in 1850. Cole's oil sketch shows the artist seated in the road, while Harvey's watercolor and Smillie's engraving invert Cole's design by showing a stagecoach descending the Mountain House road. Smillie's engraving served as the source for the Currier & Ives lithograph *Scenery of the Catskill. The Mountain House* (after 1857; plate 25).[81]

Plate 24. George Harvey, *The Catskill Mountain House*, c. 1845-1850. Courtesy Mrs. Judith Filenbaum.

Plate 25. Nathaniel Currier and James Merritt Ives, *Scenery of the Cattskill. The Mountain House*, after 1857. Courtesy New York State Museum.

KAATERSKILL FALLS

Through the late 1830s, the only route from the Mountain House to Kaaterskill Falls was a carriage road which followed the south side of North Lake, crossed the stream connecting North and South Lakes, and continued along the west bank of South Lake and Lake Creek to the top of Kaaterskill Falls. The distance from the hotel to the Falls by way of the carriage road was about a mile and a half. The operators of the Mountain House did not own the Falls, but they encouraged their guests to see them and operated carriages for those guests who preferred not to walk. By 1825 or 1826, the owner of the Falls had built an observation platform at their top and a path leading to their base (plate 13).

Many visitors complained that it was difficult to get a feeling for the height or grandeur of the Falls from their summit, and most—like Natty Bumppo and Henry Dwight—emphasized the views from the cavern and from below the second leap. Grenville Mellen's 1828 account is typical:

> We first came to the verge of the precipice, from which the water takes its leap upon a platform that projects with the rock many feet over the chasm. Here we gazed into the dell and the basin into which the stream pours itself from the beetling cliff. But the prospect from this point is far less thrilling than from below; and we accordingly began our descent. Winding round the crags, and following a foot-path between the overhanging trees, we gradually and with some difficulty descended so far as to have a fine view of the station which we had just left. The scene here is magnificent beyond description. . . . Following the guide that had brought us thus far down the chasm, we passed into the amphitheatre, and, moving under the terrific projection, stood in the centre of this sublime and stupendous work;—the black ironbound rocks behind us, and the snowy cataract springing between us and the boiling basin, which still lay under our feet. Here the scene was unparalleled. Here seemed to be the theatre for a people to stand in, and behold the prodigies and fearful wonders of the Almighty; and feel their own insignificance. Here admiration and astonishment come unbidden over the soul, and the most obdurate heart feels that there is something to be grateful for. Indeed the scene from this spot is so sublime and so well calculated to impress the feelings with a sense of the power and grandeur of nature, that, apart from all other considerations, it is worthy of long journeying and extreme toil to behold it. Having taken refreshment, . . . we descended to the extreme depth of the ravine, and, with certain heroic ladies, who somehow dared the perils of the path, we gazed from this place upon the sheet of water, falling from a height of more than two hundred and fifty feet. . . . Mountains ascend and overshadow it [the Falls]; crags and precipices project themselves in menacing assemblage all about, as though frowning over a ruin which they are only waiting some fiat to make yet more appalling. Nature has hewed out a resting place for man, where he may linger, and gaze, and admire! below him she awakens her thunder, and darts her lightning, above him she lifts still loftier summits, and round him she flings her spray and her rainbows![82]

The earliest mass-produced images of the Falls were Marsiglia's lithograph *Catskill Falls* (c. 1828; plate 17) and an 1831 engraving after Cole's *The Falls of Catskill, New York* (plate 26). Like *View of the Cattskill Mountain House, N.Y.*, *The Falls of Catskill, New York* was originally published in the second volume of Hinton's *History and Topography of the United States*. Cole's engraving was the source for Alphonse Boilly's *Chute de Cattskill*, which was published in M. Alcide d'Orbigny's widely distributed *Voyage Pittoresque dans les Deux Amériques* (1836).[83] Except for the print by Boilly, however, *The Falls of Catskill, New York* had little influence on subsequent mass-produced images of the Falls.

Most nineteenth-century mass-produced images of Kaaterskill Falls adopted a vantage point below the second leap. The earliest of these was probably George Ellis's 1828 engraving after Thomas Doughty's *Catskill Falls* (plate 27). Unlike Cole's 1825-1829 paintings of the Falls but like most nineteenth-century written representations of the site, Doughty's design represented them as a

Plate 26. Thomas Cole, *Kaaterskill Falls*, 1831. Courtesy Mr. and Mrs. R. M. Decker.

tourist destination and included both tourists and the observation platform. Doughty's design received an exceptionally wide distribution: it was published both in *The Atlantic Souvenir* for 1828 and as the frontispiece to the third (1828) edition of Theodore Dwight's popular guide *The Northern Traveller*.[84]

Even more widely distributed were two engravings after William Henry Bartlett published in Nathaniel Parker Willis's *American Scenery* (1838-1842). The more topographically accurate of these engravings is *Catterskill Falls from above the Ravine* (plate 28), which rearranges the shape of the Clove in order to suggest its lonely wildness. Despite this emphasis, *Catterskill Falls from above the Ravine* clearly shows the observation platform atop the Falls. *Catterskill Falls from below* (plate 29) both reworks the actual appearance of the Falls and conceals the presence of the building. Bartlett, like every artist who drew the Falls, had to decide whether to represent it as a tourist destination or as wilderness. His innovative solution was to offer his audience two incompatible views of the same site.

The view of the Mountain House from the road and the view of Kaaterskill Falls from below the second leap were far and away the two most popular subjects for early and mid nineteenth-century mass-produced Catskill images. The two subjects were associated with two distinct *kinds* of experiences. Like *Lake with Dead Trees* (plate 12), the engraving after Cole's *View of the Cattskill Mountain House, N.Y.* and subsequent representations of tourists on their way to the Mountain House emphasize the distance separating the observer and the scene he or she observes. Both the viewer of these images and the tourists in them have the physical room and, therefore, the mental freedom to interpret the aesthetic and moral significance of the scene in front of them.

Early and mid nineteenth-century representations of the Falls either lack human figures or contain small figures dwarfed by the vastness of the ravine. In the engraving after Cole's *The Falls of Catskill, New York*, as in the *Kaaterskill Falls* he painted for Daniel Wadsworth, the Indian is placed in the middle of the scene and seems lost in rapt admiration of the abyss before him. The

Plate 27. Thomas Doughty, *Catskill Falls*, 1828. Courtesy Abernethy Library, Middlebury College.

Plate 28. William Henry Bartlett, *Catterskill Falls from above the Ravine*, 1838. Courtesy The Hudson River Museum of Westchester.

Plate 29. William Henry Bartlett, *Catterskill Falls from below*, 1838. Courtesy Albany Institute of History and Art.

figure in the engraving after Doughty's *Catskill Falls* is equally small, but, unlike Cole's Indian, he has turned away from the exaggeratedly large ravine behind him as if stunned by too close an encounter with it.

Eighteenth- and early nineteenth-century aestheticians described experiences of the sublime as containing two distinct phases. At the height of a sublime experience, the individual becomes so involved with the object of appreciation that he or she momentarily forgets his or her independent existence. This is the kind of involvement represented by Cole's Indian. Because it requires self-forgetfulness, an individual cannot be aware of the fact that he or she is having this kind of experience *while* it is still happening. It is only after its conclusion that one realizes that one has had such an experience. The experience of the sublime is thus known only as a memory—only after it is over does the individual remember the self-forgetful involvement with the object of his or her appreciation. The tourist in Doughty's engraving turns from the Falls and remembers both his independent existence and his momentary self-forgetfulness.[85]

Although the engravings after Bartlett work somewhat differently, they too evoke the forgetfulness of self. Unlike the engravings after Cole and Doughty, these contain no human figures. Although the viewer is set at a distance from the waterfall in *Catterskill Falls from above the Ravine*, the lack of foreground leaves him or her hanging in the air. Like the implied viewer of Cole's *Kaaterskill Falls*, the implied viewer of *Catterskill Falls from above the Ravine* is pulled into the midst of the represented scene. In *Catterskill Falls from below*, Bartlett provided a narrow foreground, but he also exaggerated the height of the Falls so as to draw the viewer into the scene. In both engravings, the place of human figures is taken by birds which seem to figure the kind of un-self-reflective experience suggested by the rapt Indian in Cole's painting and engraving.

ABOVE THE CLOUDS

Although most early nineteenth-century paintings and engravings of the Catskills are of either the view from the road or Kaaterskill Falls, the travel narratives suggest that most early nineteenth-century tourists were chiefly interested in the view from the Platform in front of the Mountain House and were especially fascinated by what one early visitor described as "the novel feeling of having the clouds passing beneath me."[86]

Nineteenth-century mountain tourism was largely limited to the months of July, August, and September. During these months, water that evaporates from the Hudson River during the heat of the day often condenses into low-lying clouds during the cool of the night. In summer, the mountain top is also usually considerably cooler than the valley floor. Because of this difference in temperature and because of the height of the Catskills and of the Taconic Mountains on the east side of the Hudson, clouds that form in the Hudson Valley rarely rise above the surrounding mountains and are therefore rarely blown out of the valley. Although these clouds sometimes grow during the day and erupt into short but violent late afternoon thunderstorms, they usually burn off in the heat of the following morning.

Most early nineteenth-century Europeans and Americans lived on lowland farms or in lowland villages or cities, had few occasions or opportunities to ascend great heights, and rarely if ever had the experience of seeing clouds from above. The proprietors of the Mountain House sited their hotel on the edge of the escarpment to give their guests the greatest possible opportunity to enjoy the view and to observe the changing atmospheric conditions. The location of the hotel and its shape were largely determined by the fact that both the proprietors and the guests considered the view from the escarpment the most unusual, the most spectacular, and the most religiously significant of the local sites.

As can be seen in the 1828 engraving of the Mountain House published in the *Rural Repository* (plate 30), the original 1824 hotel was built parallel with the escarpment and was quite narrow. This permitted most of the rooms to face east so that as many guests as possible would be able to see the sunrise

Plate 30. Unknown artist, *Catskill Mountain House*, 1828. Courtesy Mr. and Mrs. R. M. Decker.

from their rooms. The organization of the tourist's day was also determined by the fact that the view of the valley was the most important of the local sites. Tourists usually arrived at the Mountain House in the late afternoon. After arrival, they could examine the view from the escarpment and, if they had time, take a walk to the lake. After supper most visitors retired early, wishing to get up early the following morning in order to watch the sun rise. Lest anyone miss this experience, an employee of the hotel woke all the guests by knocking on their doors and announcing the imminent event. After watching the sunrise, guests would return to their rooms, dress for the day, and have breakfast. Most visitors seem to have spent the morning in the neighborhood of the hotel. If they wished to visit Kaaterskill Falls, they probably did so in the afternoon. After seeing the Falls, guests would return to the hotel where— if they were lucky—they might see an afternoon storm in the valley below them. Retiring early, they would get up the next morning to see another sunrise, eat, and depart. Weather conditions were of course erratic, and a two-night stay did not guarantee that a guest would see a "good" sunrise or an afternoon storm. Guests who did not see spectacular atmospheric effects were often disappointed with the view, and the authors of a number of narratives complain that the Pine Orchard did not live up to its reputation. Guests who stayed more than two nights were often motivated by a desire to see "better" effects.[87]

Early nineteenth-century written descriptions of the view from the escarp-ment usually begin by emphasizing the vastness of the prospect—from the Platform one could see parts of Connecticut, Massachusetts, and Vermont, and the mid Hudson Valley from Poughkeepsie in the south to Albany in the north. After noting the extent of the view, the narratives usually describe the most spectacular atmospheric effect seen by the author. As noted by T. Addison Richards, "Every fashionable 'resort' has its especial points or lions— its great staple 'sights.' The staple, *par excellence*, of the Mountain House is the 'sunrising.' "[88] Nineteenth-century descriptions of the Catskills almost invariably describe the view from the road and Kaaterskill Falls, but they usually pay greatest attention to the effect of the sun rising over the mist-filled Hudson Valley.

As early as 1830, it had already become conventional to compare the morning mist filling the Hudson Valley with the ocean. The first person to make this comparison may have been Henry Dwight who, in 1819, described the morning clouds as an "almost shoreless ocean."[89] In 1823, James Pierce wrote that the cloud-filled valley resembled "a boundless ocean" and noted that the clouds rolled "like the waves of a tempestuous sea."[90] In 1828, the unidentified author of "A Visit to the Cattskills" described how the morning mist "was borne round the mountain, and for a few moments the landscape was as distinct as the light of dawn could show it; but another and another overspread it, until the misty flood was whitened into a sea of foam by the beams of the rising sun; wave followed wave, parting as they rolled, and showing beneath, sunny spots of green fields and sparkling waters."[91] In the same year,Grenville Mellen compared the cloud-filled valley to a "silent and outstretched ocean."[92] In 1829, Robert Sands concluded a description of his first, pre-1823 visit to the Pine Orchard by noting that the morning clouds "presented" to his mind

> a more immediate though cloudy type of that which is without beginning or end, or any confines, than the ocean itself has ever suggested to me. I have been on much more elevated spots, and have powerfully felt the natural

influences of the locality, and the picture before me. But the sense of mighty solitude, of somewhat oppressive and always sublimating abstraction from the peddling concerns of mankind, never overcame me more forcibly than on this occasion. I heard a deep voice, though all was silent, and saw a vast phantom stretching and spreading away forever; and the shadow which this pageant cast over the brain, was constantly that of 'Eternity, Eternity and Power.'[93]

Comparisons of the morning mist with the ocean remained commonplace until the Civil War.[94]

Authors who noted the resemblance between the morning mist and the ocean often completed their descriptions by comparing "the ocean landscape" with either Noah's flood or the primal chaos out of which God created the heavens and the earth.[95] The first writer to do so seems to have been Henry Dwight, who used both comparisons in his 1819 description of the sunrise:

> In the autumn, a dense fog commonly arises during the night, from the streams within the view, covering with its misty waves the whole area, excepting the tops of these lofty mountains. The only land visible, is Saddle Mountain and the Highlands, each sixty miles, and the Taughconnoc Mountain, at nearly the same distance. The fog rises about 1500 feet in height, and is gilded by the beams of the morning sun as it appears above the horizon. For an hour after sunrise, the mist is quiescent, exhibiting an almost shoreless ocean, with the tops of these peaks rising above it, like distant islands in a calm at sea. After the sun has risen a few degrees above the horizon, the fog begins to be agitated, and to move in vast undulations towards the heavens, shooting its needles into the atmosphere, or rolling its lengthening billows into a thousand figures, presenting a glowing picture of the general deluge. It remains agitated about an hour, when, unfolding its misty mantle, the earth below appears here and there illumined by the rays of the sun. When the fog is dispelled by its beams the landscape unfolds all its beauties, as if it had just sprung into existence at the command of the Creator. [96]

Among other writers who developed the comparison of the morning mist with the deluge was the English traveler James Silk Buckingham. In *America, Historical, Statistic, and Descriptive,* he wrote that the scene outside his window

> was most remarkable, and totally different from any thing I had ever before witnessed. The sky above us was a bright clear blue, slightly mottled with white fleecy clouds, as in the finest summer mornings of England. But of the earth beneath us, nothing was to be seen except the rocky platform on which our habitation was built, and a small portion of the brow of the hill on which this stood. All the rest of the great expanse before us, extending to a distance of from 40 to 50 miles, was covered with a thick sea of perfectly white billows, as if there had been a general deluge, and we were occupying the summit of the Ararat which alone rose above the wide waste of the waters around us.[97]

The comparison of the morning mist with the chaos out of which God created nature was even more popular than the comparison with the deluge. Harriet Martineau's use of the comparison is typical. After giving an extended description of the first of the two sunrises she saw while at the Mountain House, Martineau closed her account by noting that she would not give a description of the second because "I would not weary others with what is most sacred to

me. Suffice it that it gave me a vivid idea of the process of creation, from the moment when all was without form and void, to that when light was commanded, and there was light."[98]

Although the written narratives make clear that the view from the escarpment was by far the most important of the views associated with the Mountain House, there are almost no early visual representations of the scene. A rare early image of the sunrise over the Hudson is Thomas Cole's *Sunny Morning on the Hudson River* (1827; Museum of Fine Arts, Boston), which is a view not from the Catskill escarpment but from the south side of Kaaterskill Clove west of the Round Top.[99] The earliest known depictions of the view from the escarpment are Frederic Church's *Morning, Looking East over the Hudson Valley from the Catskill Mountains* (1848; plate 31) and *Above the Clouds at Sunrise* (1849; plate 32).

CONCLUSION: VARIETIES OF CATSKILL EXPERIENCES, 1839-1880

Fig. 12. John William Hill, *Landscape: View on Catskill Creek*, 1867. Courtesy The Metropolitan Museum of Art.

By the late 1830s, significant numbers of well-to-do Americans had developed a taste for mountains. The Catskills had been firmly established as a major tourist resort; the major Catskill sites and the experiences they were supposed to evoke had been defined. Travel narratives and mass-produced images suggest that the view from the road, Kaaterskill Falls, and the view from the escarpment remained the most important Catskill Mountain sites until after the development of tourism in the southern and western Catskills in the 1870s. Indeed, the most popular of the stereoviews manufactured in the 1860s and 1870s reproduced the same subjects from the same points of view as the early engravings after Cole, Doughty, and Bartlett (plates 33 and 34). But although the makers of inexpensive images continued to focus on the familiar views, and although most tourists remained most interested in those views, the structure of Catskill Mountain tourism became more diversified after the late 1830s.

Despite its immediate popularity, the Mountain House never returned much profit to its original owners. Operating expenses were high because of the brevity of the season, and because furnishings and supplies had to be hauled up the escarpment from Catskill. The original owners scraped by until the late 1830s, when the downturn of the national economy and competition from grander hotels drove them into bankruptcy.[100]

Plate 33. E. & H. T. Anthony, *The Bluff by Mountain House,* c. 1860-1870. Courtesy Greene County Historical Society.

Plate 34. E. & H. T. Anthony, *View from the Top of the Kauterskill Fall, Looking down the Glen,* c. 1860-1870. Courtesy Greene County Historical Society.

In 1839, the Catskill businessman Charles L. Beach acquired a controlling interest in the hotel (plate 35). Beach was born and raised in Catskill. During the 1820s, Beach's father had operated the stagecoach line that carried tourists from Catskill landing to the Mountain House. By 1839, the son had built one of the largest stagecoach companies in New York State and was one of the wealthiest men in the mid Hudson Valley. Beach realized that in order to make money the hotel had to attract visitors who would stay longer than two or three nights. Unlike the original proprietors, Beach could afford to make the improvements that would encourage longer stays.

Beach acquired control of the Mountain House in 1839, but he did not gain full ownership until July 1846. Although he did some remodeling shortly after he took over operation of the hotel, the most extensive additions and most of the renovations seem to have been carried out in 1845 and 1846. Before Beach's renovation, the facade of the northern 1825 section of the hotel was set back from the facade of the central 1824 section (plates 10 and 30). In rebuilding the hotel, Beach widened the northern section in order to make its facade flush with that of the original, replaced the original plain pillars with thirteen Corinthian columns, replaced the original side staircases with a single staircase descending from the center of the extended facade, moved the flagpole from the roof to the piazza, and eliminated the gables, balustrades, and catwalk (plate 36). Less visible but as important, Beach enlarged the interior

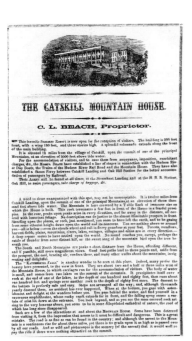

Plate 35. Advertising circular for Catskill Mountain House, c. 1851. Courtesy Greene County Historical Society.

Plate 36. Sarah Cole, *A View of the Catskill Mountain House*, 1848. Courtesy Albany Institute of History and Art.

Fig. 13. S. Root, *Two Views of the Dreer Family at the Entrance to the Catskill Mountain House*, August 1854. Courtesy Greene County Historical Society.

Plate 37. William Henry Bartlett, *The Two Lakes and the Mountain House on the Catskills*, 1838. Courtesy The Hudson River Museum of Westchester.

public spaces by expanding the central section westward away from the front piazza and by shifting the main entrance from the redesigned front to the enlarged rear (fig. 13).[101]

Beach's renovations made the hotel more comfortable, but because of its isolated location the Mountain House could not compete with lowland resorts for the business of patrons solely interested in physical comfort. In order to keep his guests for more than two or three nights, Beach needed to develop new activities so that they would want to stay even after they had seen

Kaaterskill Falls and the sunrise. The engraving after William Henry Bartlett's 1838 watercolor of *The Two Lakes and the Mountain House on the Catskills* (plate 37) is a view from the rocky platform on the shoulder of North Mountain. The fact that Bartlett was able to reach this spot suggests that a trail from the Pine Orchard north along the escarpment to the summit of North Mountain may have been built even before Beach acquired control of the hotel, but no pre-1840 narratives mention the existence of such a trail. Soon after his

acquisition of the hotel, Beach began both to buy as much of the surrounding land as he could and to extend the network of trails and carriage roads crossing the mountain top. By the end of the 1840s, Beach had built trails on North Mountain and a trail from the Mountain House up South Mountain and then along the south edge of Kaaterskill Clove to Kaaterskill Falls. Sanford Gifford's 1862 *Kauterskill Clove* (plate 38) and Jervis McEntee's slightly later *A Cliff in the Kaatskills* (plate 39) are both based on drawings done from new trails on South Mountain.

Beach also arranged for the publication of the first guidebook solely devoted to the Catskills. Edited by a local minister named David Murdoch and first published in 1846, *The Scenery of the Catskill Mountains* is an anthology of poems, short stories, and travel narratives descriptive of the mountain top.[102] Except for essays by Murdoch and well-known American author Elizabeth Fries Ellet, all the pieces are reprints of earlier published works, and therefore emphasize the three most familiar views. Murdoch's essay is a conventional if unusually elaborate description of the view from the escarpment which compares the sunrise both with creation and with the new creation that will mark the advent of the millennium.

In terms of the history of mountain tourism in the Catskills, the most important piece in the anthology is Ellet's essay on "The Fourth at Pine Orchard," in which she announced the existence of the new trails and insisted that there was more to see and do at the hotel than the three best-known sites:

> Visiters at Catskill mountain do not usually give themselves time to see even what they do see to the best advantage. Many of them remain but a single day; paying only a hurried visit to the falls, and neglecting many other scenes almost equal in interest. There are numerous lovely walks in the vicinity, chief among which are those upon the South and North mountain;

Plate 38. Sanford Robinson Gifford, *Kauterskill Clove*, 1862. Courtesy The Metropolitan Museum of Art.

Plate 39. Jervis McEntee, *A Cliff in the Kaatskills*, c. 1866. Courtesy The Brooklyn Museum.

Plate 40. Sanford Robinson Gifford, *Kauterskill Falls*, 1846. Courtesy Alexander Gallery.

Plate 41. Sanford Robinson Gifford, *Tree Trunk, Catskills*, 9 July 1850. Private collection.

and the beautiful lake in the immediate neighborhood of the House is said to abound in fish, affording amusement to those fond of the sport, with boats for rowing or sailing-parties. There is said also to be an ice-glen some miles distant, into the depths of which the sun never penetrates, and where ice may be found deposited by all the winters since creation.[103]

Having announced her theme, Ellet proceeded to give the first extended descriptions of the trails on North and South Mountains. Although the trail system did not replace the major views as the main object of tourism, by 1857 T. Addison Richard's widely distributed *Appleton's Illustrated Hand-Book of American Travel* devoted as much space to the lakes and the trails as to the more famous views.[104]

The diversification of Catskill Mountain tourism in these years is also evidenced by the development of less expensive boarding houses in Kaaterskill Clove and along Lake Creek. Most of the early boarding house operators were local residents who took in a few guests to supplement their income. In many cases, these guests were painters looking for accommodations away from the well-known views and the distractions of the Mountain House.

The first of the mountain top residents to accept boarders was probably the sawmill operator Ira Scribner. Scribner was receiving guests at least as early as July 1844, when Henry David Thoreau and his friend William Ellery Channing boarded with him. Scribner expanded his house in 1845 or 1846, named it the *Glen Mary* in honor of his wife, and began to take in boarders on a regular basis. The artist Sanford Gifford seems to have been a regular guest at Scribner's in the late 1840s and early 1850s. *Kauterskill Falls* (1846; plate 40) and *Tree Trunk, Catskills* (9 July 1850; plate 41), are both *plein-air* oil sketches that Gifford probably executed while staying with the Scribners.[105]

By the end of the 1840s, other boarding houses serving artists and the more adventurous tourists had opened at the lower end of Kaaterskill Clove in the village of Palenville and at the upper end of the Clove in the village of Hunter. Something of the rapidity with which artists abandoned the Mountain House and colonized the villages of Kaaterskill Clove is suggested by Asher B. Durand's 10 and 24 September and 2 October 1848 letters to his son John.[106]

Durand's trip to the Catskills in September and October 1848 seems to have been occasioned by Thomas Cole's unexpected death in February 1848. In May 1848, William Cullen Bryant delivered a funeral oration for Cole at a memorial meeting of the National Academy of Design. Soon after that meeting, the prominent New York patron Jonathan Sturges commissioned Durand to paint a picture for Bryant that would commemorate Bryant's friendship with the artist. Durand spent the early summer of 1848 in the Adirondacks with John Casilear and John F. Kensett, but in early September the three artists traveled to Catskill where Durand and Casilear took rooms at the Mountain House from about 10 September until 23 September, when the hotel closed for the season. They then took lodgings at a boarding house in Palenville. On 24 September, Durand wrote his son that "there have been nine artists stopping here, two of whom still remain. [Köllner] the German and an amateur Englishman by the name of Metcalf." In the same letter he wrote, "The Clove where we now are is [rich in] beautiful wildness, beyond all we have met with heretofore, altho' extremely difficult of access." Durand and Casilear remained in Palenville until early October. The following March, Durand delivered *Kindred Spirits* to Bryant (fig. 14). *Kindred Spirits* draws on the geography of Kaaterskill Clove but does not represent an actual view. The foreground ledge seems to be based on a rock formation known as Church's Ledge. The lower of the middleground waterfalls is based on Fawn's Leap, located on the south side of Kaaterskill Clove just below the confluence of Lake and Kaaterskill Creeks (fig. 15).[107]

Durand returned to the Clove in August or early September 1849 and stayed in the village of Tannersville at a boarding house operated by John Rusk. When he arrived, he found Casilear, Kensett, and David Johnson already there. They had been in the Catskills since late May or early June and at Rusk's since early July. These four artists stayed at Rusk's until late September or early October; the German artist John Volmering was staying at another boarding house next door.

Fig. 14. Asher B. Durand, *Kindred Spirits*, 1849. Courtesy New York Public Library.

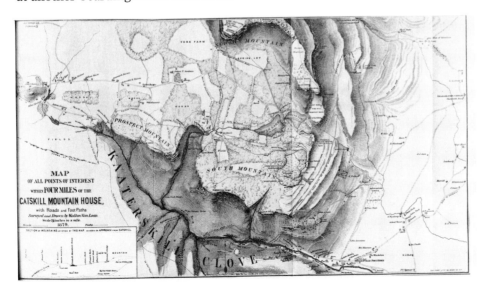

Fig. 15. Walton Van Loan, *Map of All Points of Interest within Four Miles of the Catskill Mountain House*, 1879. Courtesy Greene County Historical Society.

Kensett's oil studies of Kaaterskill Falls and the Clove were as well received at the spring 1850 exhibition at the National Academy of Design as Durand's *Kindred Spirits* had been in 1849.[108] By the following spring, landscape painters throughout the Northeast were aware of the inexpensive boarding houses and spectacular scenery in Kaaterskill Clove.

Durand returned to Rusk's in September 1850 accompanied by the Boston painter Christopher Pearse Cranch, and they were later joined by Jasper Cropsey.[109] Other artists working in the Clove by the mid-1850s included William Trost Richards, T. Addison Richards, Jervis McEntee (plate 42), the watercolorist William Rickarby Miller (plate 43), Walter Oddie, Benjamin Bellows Grant Stone, and Edmund Darch Lewis.[110] By 1857, the many landscape painters working in the Clove had become an attraction to be seen by tourists. Writing in *Appleton's Illustrated Hand-Book*, Richards informed potential visitors to the Catskills that Kaaterskill Clove was the "portion of the Catskills...most preferred by artists for study, and the inns at Palenville are often occupied by them, though they offer no inviting accommodation to the ease and comfort-loving tourist" (plate 44).[111]

Plate 42. Jervis McEntee, *Sketches of Home Scenery*, c. 1857. Courtesy Yale University Art Gallery.

Plate 43. William Rickarby Miller, *Catskill Clove*, 1856. Courtesy The Metropolitan Museum of Art.

Plate 44. Thomas Addison Richards, *Palenville*, July 1854. Courtesy Abernethy Library, Middlebury College.

Until after the end of the Civil War, most visitors to the Catskills stayed at the Mountain House and sought much the same experiences of the Falls and the sunrise as earlier tourists had. But the construction of new hiking trails and the development of less expensive accommodations in wilder areas west and south of the Mountain House suggest that artists and some tourists were developing a new taste for the experience of wildness—for the experience of hiking in the woods and up the neighboring mountains. Midcentury travel narratives and landscape paintings suggest that these visitors wanted something like the feeling of unmediated apprehension figured by the Indian in Cole's *Kaaterskill Falls*. But where earlier nineteenth-century writers and painters had identified this kind of experience with the evocative power of Kaaterskill Falls and the sea of clouds, midcentury writers and artists responded to the evocative power of more intimate and less obviously grand scenes.

This change is apparent in descriptions of the Catskills by John Burroughs and other midcentury essayists. While earlier writers had emphasized the major views and had represented them as evoking explicitly religious sentiments, midcentury writers focused on details of the larger scene and represented them as evoking a response that—though still moral—was less explicitly religious and doctrinal. The 1857 esssay by "E.B.M" on "Trees and Rocks at the Catskill Mountains" is typical of this new focus. The mosses and lichens that grow on the

Plate 45. Asher B. Durand, *Forest Scene in the Catskills*, c. 1855-60. Courtesy The Detroit Institute of Arts.

Fig. 16. John F. Kensett, *Waterfall in the Woods with Indians*, 1850. Courtesy Amon Carter Museum of Western Art.

> rocks of the Catskill Mountains . . . almost defy classification or description in their infinite variety. In the shadier places, and especially where the little streams creep through the crevices, the thick green mantle, layer upon layer, is not content to display its own richness, but nourishes a thousand kindred lives on its bosom, sprouting up like plants; these vary the dark hue of their bed, with greens, gay and sad, and bright, and yellow, or catch now and then a drop of the sweet water above them, and lean over to distill it into the fountain below. A day passed in these solitudes, far away from all thoughts of the artificial life of a great city, tends more to make gentle this rough nature of ours, than the essays of all the philanthropists or philosophers the world has produced.[112]

The development of this new taste is even more obvious in the work of the midcentury landscape painters. Where earlier artists had spent their time in the mountains making pencil drawings that were later worked up into finished oil paintings, these artists spent much longer periods of time in the mountains

Plate 46. Asher B. Durand, *Catskill Meadows in Summer,* 1861. Courtesy Wellesley College Museum.

Plate 47. E. and H. T. Anthony, *The Fawns Leap—Kauterskill Clove,* c. 1860-1870. Courtesy Greene County Historical Society.

Plate 48. John F. Kensett, *The Fawn's Leap,* 1859. Courtesy Mead Art Museum, Amherst College.

Plate 49. Charles Herbert Moore, *Mountain View,* 1860. Courtesy Indiana University Art Museum.

and produced closely observed oil sketches such as *Forest Scene in the Catskills* (plate 45) by Durand and *Tree Trunk, Catskills* (plate 41) by Gifford. These studies were then used in the production of larger studio works. Sometimes studio paintings were of familiar subjects such as Kensett's painting based on the geography of Kaaterskill Falls (fig. 16). More often, however, these artists painted unidentifiable forest interiors such as *Catskill Meadows in Summer* (plate 46) by Durand or developed new subjects such as the waterfall Fawn's Leap (plate 47) and Hunter Mountain. Located in Kaaterskill Clove near the confluence of Wild Cat and Kaaterskill Creeks, Fawn's Leap was painted by many midcentury artists including Durand (fig. 14), Kensett (plate 48), Charles Herbert Moore (plate 49), and John William Hill (plate 50). Located atop the Catskill plateau to the west of Kaaterskill Clove, Hunter

Plate 50. John William Hill, *Fawn's Leap, Catskill, New York*, 1868. Courtesy Kennedy Galleries, Inc.

Mountain was painted by Gifford (plate 92), T. Worthington Whittredge (plate 51), and McEntee (plate 109). Whether they painted old subjects, new subjects, or unidentifiable forest interiors, however, midcentury painters placed a new emphasis on close observation of particular natural details. Like everyone who visited the Catskills, they were aware of the familiar views. But like the tourists attracted to the new hiking trails, they were often most interested in the infinite variety of local plant life, the complicated structure of particular rocks, or the play of light as it fell through the forest canopy (plate 52).

Just as the development of mountain tourism in the 1820s had depended on the existence of sellers and consumers of landscape experiences, the reorganization of mountain tourism in the mid nineteenth century reflected changes in the experiences offered by operators of tourist accommodations and those sought by potential visitors. Charles L. Beach built new hiking trails and local residents turned their homes into inexpensive boarding houses because artists and other visitors wanted more trails and cheaper lodgings. In turn, the existence of these trails and boarding houses attracted more visitors who had learned to desire the experiences these amenities made possible.

The Catskills did not play as crucial a role in the development of the new taste for the experience of nature as they had played in the popularization of mountain scenery. By the 1840s and 1850s, too many people had learned to

Plate 51. Thomas Worthington Whittredge, *Autumn, Hunter Mountain, Catskills*, 1866. Courtesy D. Wigmore Fine Art, Inc.

appreciate mountains, the national transportation system had become too extended, and too many new resorts had opened for any one resort to dominate public consciousness in the way the Catskills had for a few years in the 1820s and 1830s. Moreover, neither in the Catskills nor in the newer resorts did the increasing popularity of hiking and other forms of nature appreciation simply replace the earlier taste for impressive views. Tourists who hiked or fished also enjoyed scenery. By the end of the Civil War, however, the organization of mountain tourism in the Catskills and the newer resorts became fragmented as some entrepreneurs catered to the needs of tourists who wanted to be in the woods, while others served those who wanted little more than comfortable accommodations and picturesque views.

By 1865, the rapid development of the national economy and the concomitant growth of cities had made it possible for many Americans to take traveling vacations. Many if not most Americans with the means and desire to travel had learned to appreciate mountain scenery and to enjoy being in the woods. The development of new resorts in Maine, the Green Mountains of Vermont, the Adirondacks in Upstate New York, and Yosemite in California, as well as the popularity of inexpensive stereographic and engraved views of these resorts, evidence the extent to which both kinds of landscape taste had become characteristic of the American middle and upper classes (plate 53). But despite the development of newer resorts, the Catskills continued to attract large numbers of visitors. Indeed, because of their accessibility to New York City, the Catskills began to draw increasing numbers of less wealthy tourists who had neither the time nor the money to visit more remote environments. By the middle of the 1870s, so many tourists were vacationing in the Catskills that painters and writers largely abandoned them. But that is another story.[113]

Plate 52. Thomas Worthington Whittredge, *I Come from Haunts of Coot and Hern*, n.d. Courtesy Trinity College.

Plate 53. Winslow Homer, *Under
the Falls, Catskill Mountains*, 1872.
Courtesy Kennedy Galleries, Inc.

1. Convenient introductions to the history of landscape taste are John Brinckerhoff Jackson, "The Meanings of 'Landscape,' " *Kulturgeographi* 88 (1965): 47-50 and E. H. Gombrich, "The Renaissance Theory of Art and the Rise of Landscape," in E. H. Gombrich, *Norm and Form* (London: Phaidon, 1966), 107-121. More general discussions of the social construction of individual experience can be found in Peter L. Berger and Thomas Luckmann, *The Social Construction of Reality* (Garden City, NY: Doubleday & Co., 1967) and Rom Harré, *Personal Being* (Cambridge, MA: Harvard University Press, 1984).

2. On the geographical origins of seventeenth- and eighteenth-century immigrants to North America, see D. W. Meinig, *The Shaping of America* (New Haven: Yale University Press, 1986) and Bernard Bailyn, *The Peopling of British North America: An Introduction* (New York: Alfred A. Knopf, 1986). On settlement patterns in the North American colonies, see John R. Stilgoe, *Common Landscape of America, 1580-1845* (New Haven: Yale University Press, 1982) and William Cronon, *Changes in the Land: Indians, Colonists, and the Ecology of New England* (New York: Hill & Wang, 1983).

3. On the Exodus from Egypt, see especially *Deuteronomy*, chapters 8, 29, and 32; and *Psalms*, 78 and 106-107. Concerning Christ's temptation, see *Matthew* 4:1-12; *Mark* 1:9-12; and *Luke* 4:1-14. Concerning the adaptation of biblical imagery by New England ministers, see Perry Miller, "The Errand Into the Wilderness," in Perry Miller, *Errand Into the Wilderness* (Cambridge, MA: Harvard University Press, 1956), 1-15, and the editor's introduction and the reprinted sermons in A. W. Plumstead, ed., *The Wall and the Garden* (Minneapolis: University of Minnesota Press, 1968).

4. Petrarch's account of his ascent of Mont Ventoux is translated in Ernest Cassirer, Paul Oskar Kristeller, and John H. Randall, Jr., eds., *The Renaissance Philosophy of Man* (Chicago: University of Chicago Press, 1949), 35-46.

5. On the history of landscape taste in Europe and England, see Clarence J. Glacken, *Traces on the Rhodian Shore* (Berkeley: University of California Press, 1967); Marjorie Hope Nicolson, *Mountain Gloom and Mountain Glory* (Ithaca, NY: Cornell University Press, 1959); D. G. Charlton, *New Images of the Natural in France* (Cambridge: Cambridge University Press, 1984); Andrew Wilton, *Turner and the Sublime* (London: British Museum Publications, 1980); and Keith Thomas, *Man and the Natural World* (New York: Pantheon Books, 1983).

6. The best brief analysis tracing the relationship between the development of the market economy and the history of landscape taste is Dieter Groh and Rolf-Peter Sieferle, "Experience of Nature in Bourgeois Society and Economic Theory: Outlines of an Interdisciplinary Research Project," *Social Research* 47 (1980): 557-581. On the concept of objectification, I have been most influenced by the writings of Michel Foucault. See especially *The Order of Things: An Archaeology of the Human Sciences* (New York: Vintage Books, 1975).

7. Jackson, "The Meanings of 'Landscape,' " 47. Most of Jackson's evidence is drawn from examples given in the *Oxford English Dictionary*.

8. Although a number of historians, including Jackson, "The Meanings of 'Landscape' " and Gombrich, "The Renaissance Theory of Art and the Rise of Landscape," suggest that the taste for natural landscape developed after and from the taste for painted landscapes, I know of no effort to trace this historical process in any detail. The most fully developed effort along these lines is John Barrell's provocative chapter on "The Idea of Landscape in the Eighteenth Century" in his *The Idea of Landscape and the Sense of Place 1730-1840* (Cambridge: Cambridge University Press, 1972), 1-62. Suggestive information can also be found in Elizabeth Wheeler Manwaring, *Italian Landscape in Eighteenth-Century England* (New York: Oxford University Press, 1925) and Christopher Hussey, *The Picturesque: Studies in a Point of View* (London: G. P. Putnam's Sons, 1927).

9. William Gilpin, *Remarks on Forest Scenery*, vol. 2 (London: R. Blamire, 1791), 166, cited in Edward J. Nygren, "From View to Vision," in Edward J. Nygren, ed., *Views and Visions: American Landscape before 1830* (Washington, D.C.: The Corcoran Gallery of Art, 1986), 18.

10. On Catskill geology, see John Lyon Rich, *Glacial Geology of the Catskill* (Albany: the University of the State of New York, 1935) and John H. Thompson, ed., *The Geography of New York State* (Syracuse: Syracuse University Press, 1966). Early nineteenth-century descriptions can be found in Horatio Gates Spafford, *A Gazetteer of the State of New-York* (Albany: H. C. Southwick, 1813), 9; Thomas F. Gordon, *Gazetteer of the State of New York* (Philadelphia: Collins, 1836), 6-7; and David Haskel and J. Calvin Smith, *A Complete Descriptive & Statistical Gazetteer of the United States of America* (New York: Sherman & Smith, 1847), 110.

11. Ives Goddard, "Delaware," in Bruce C. Trigger, ed., *Northeast* (Washington, D.C: Smithsonian Institution Press, 1978), 213-214. *Northeast* is volume 15 in the indispensable *Handbook of North American Indians*, edited by William C. Sturtevant.

12. T. J. Brasser, "Mahican," in Trigger, ed., *Northeast*, 200.

13. In addition to Goddard, "Delaware," and Brasser, "Mahican," see Robert J. Rayback, "The Indian," in Thompson, ed., *Geography of New York State*, 113-120; Jesse V. V. Vedder, *Official History of Greene County* (n.p.: Greene County Board of Supervisors, 1927), 22; and, especially, Allan W. Trelease, *Indian Affairs in Colonial New York: The Seventeenth Century* (Ithaca, NY: Cornell Univeristy Press, 1960).

14. E. B. O'Callaghan, ed., *The Documentary History of the State of New York*, vol. 1 (Albany: Weed, Parsons, & Co., 1849-1851), 746, quoted in D.W. Meinig, "The Colonial Period, 1609-1775," in Thompson, ed., *Geography of New York State*, 138. Oliver A. Rink, *Holland on the Hudson: An Economic and Social History of Dutch New York* (Ithaca, NY: Cornell University Press, 1986), 258, cites Adriaen Van Der Donck's seventeenth-century estimate that a 1656 outbreak of smallpox killed almost ninety percent of the Indians living in the Hudson Valley. Johnson's map was published in O'Callaghan, *Documentary History of the State of New York*, vol. 4, 1090.

Colonial and later accounts often refer to the Munsee-speaking Indians living on the west bank of the river in the area of modern Esopus Creek as Esopus Indians. The language and cultural traditions of the Esopus seem to have been closely related to the language and cultural patterns of the Mahicans who lived to their north. Tribal ranges were variable, and it is not clear either that the sharp distinction between Munsee- and Mahican-speaking Indians suggested by their assignment to separate twentieth-century ethnographic categories corresponds to seventeenth-century reality, or that the area of Catskill Creek was always controlled by Munsee-speaking tribes. The important point is that at the time of European settlement, Catskill Creek was a boundary area separating two Indian language groups and was only occasionally visited by either. The fact that the area was heavily used by neither group is suggested both by the relative absence of archaeological sites and by the subsequent pattern of Dutch settlement. Although one might think that the Dutch and other settlers would have tried to stay away from land used by the Indians, colonists generally preferred land that Indians had already partially cleared and planted. The fact that relatively few seventeenth-century Dutch settled in the area of Catskill Creek suggests that there had been little previous development in the area. Concerning the preference of European settlers for land already partially cleared, see Cronon, *Changes in the Land*, 90.

15. Rink, *Holland on the Hudson;* Meinig, "The Colonial Period," 121-128; and Raymond J. O'Brien, *American Sublime: Landscape and Scenery of the Lower Hudson Valley* (New York: Columbia University Press, 1981), 53-58. One of the most interesting contemporary accounts is Bartlett B. James and J. Franklin Jameson, eds., *Journal of Jasper Danckaerts 1679-1680* (New York: Charles Scribner's Sons, 1913), 196-228.

16. Meinig, "The Colonial Period," 128-139, and Walter Allen Knittle, *Early Eighteenth-Century Palatine Emigration* (Philadelphia: Dorrance, 1937). The Palatines began to arrive in 1709.

17. Adolf B. Benson, ed., *The America of 1750: Peter Kalm's Travels in North America* (New York: Wilson-Erickson Inc., 1937), 331, 343, 614-618, 626. On the survival of Dutch culture in the Valley, see also Jedidiah Morse, *The American Geography; or, A View of the Present Situation of the United States of America* (London: John Stockdale, 1792), 250-252, 258-259, and Washington Irving, "[A Voyage up the Hudson River in 1800]," *Miscellaneous Writings*, vol. 2 of *The Complete Works of Washington Irving* (Boston: Twayne Publishers, 1981), 344-345. On the effect of the manorial system on emigration, see Dixon Ryan Fox, *Yankees and Yorkers* (New York: New York University Press, 1940); David M. Ellis, *Landlords and Farmers in the Hudson-Mohawk Region 1790-1850* (1946; reprint, New York: Octagon Books, 1967), 5-15; Patricia U. Bonomi, *A Factious People: Politics and Society in Colonial New York* (New York: Columbia University Press, 1971), 179-228; and Michael Kammen, *Colonial New York: A History* (New York: Charles Scribner's Sons, 1975), 179-180.

18. *Dear Old Greene County* (1915; reprint, Cornwallville, NY: Hope Farm Press, 1986), 122-125; Vedder, *Official History of Greene County*, 39-40; Meinig, *The Shaping of America*, vol. 1, 125; Roderic H. Blackburn, "Dutch Arts and Culture in Colonial America," *Antiques* 130, July 1986, 140-141. A twentieth-century map showing the specific location of the van Bergen patent is reprinted in Bernard Bailyn, *Voyagers to the West: A Passage in the Peopling of America on the Eve of the Revolution* (New York: Alfred A. Knopf, 1986), 578. The Marten van Bergen house was torn down in 1862.

19. On the changing cultural significance of roads and fences in colonial and early nineteenth-century America, see Stilgoe, *Common Landscape of America*, 21-24, 111-115, 128-132, 188-192. Except for a few comments in Danckaerts's diary, there is little written record of how the Hudson Valley Dutch experienced the natural environment. Much of the written evidence that does exist is discussed in O'Brien, *American Sublime*, 69-75.

20. Vedder, *Official History of Greene County*, 42-44.

21. David M. Ellis, *New York, State and City* (Ithaca, NY: Cornell University Press, 1979), 84-95; Alf Evers, *The Catskills: From Wilderness to Woodstock* (1972; reprint, Woodstock, NY: The Overlook Press, 1982), 129-179; Charles Rockwell, *The Catskill Mountains and the Region Around* (1867; reprint, Cornwallville, NY: Hope Farm Press, 1973), 52-106.

22. Ellis, *New York, State and City*, 96. Timothy Dwight, *Travels in New-England and New-York*, vol. 3 (New Haven, CT: Timothy Dwight, 1821-1822), 237. See also Fox, *Yankees and Yorkers*, 176-223; Ellis, *Landlords and Farmers*, 16-66; and D. W. Meinig, "Geography of Expansion, 1785-1855," in Thompson, ed., *Geography of New York State*, 140-196. In *The Old New York Frontier* (New York: C. Scribner's Sons, 1901), Francis W. Halsey makes the telling observation that at the New York Constitutional Convention of 1821 a majority of the delegates had either emigrated from Connecticut or were sons of fathers who had.

23. Population figures come from Ellis, *Landlords and Farmers*, 31; Timothy Dwight, *Travels in New-England and New-York*, vol. 4, 15; Spafford, *Gazetteer of the State of New-York* (1813), 78; and Horatio Gates Spafford, *A Gazetteer of the State of New-York* (Albany: B. D. Packard and Troy: The Author, 1824), 208-209.

24. Information in this paragraph derives from the *Hampshire Gazette*, 1 April 1801, cited by John B. McMaster, *History of the People of the United States from the Revolution to the Civil War*, vol. 2 (New York: D. Appleton & Co., 1883-1913), 572; Clark Brown, "A Topographical Description of Catskill, in the State of New York," Massachusetts Historical Society *Collections* 9 (1804): 114, 118; Dwight, *Travels in New-England and New-York*, 15; Spafford, *Gazetteer of the State of New-York* (1813), 78; and Spafford, *Gazetteer of the State of New-York* (1824), 208.

25. Ellis, *Landlords and Farmers*, 72, explains that New England farmers settled the hilly lands "partly because the river bottoms had already been settled by [the] Dutch and . . . partly because they had become accustomed to hill farming. . . . Hill land was dry. It did not need draining, as was often the case with valley land. The higher land was more free from the dreaded 'swamp fevers.' In general, it was easier to clear since the level lands were more heavily timbered and were covered with underbrush and fallen trees. The scythe and the sickle were fully as effective on hilly as on level ground. Finally, the rich vegetable mould covered the highlands as well as the bottom land. Pioneers could not foresee that much of the land they were clearing would not be able to compete with more fertile lands under conditions of commercial agriculture." Pot and pearl ashes were used in the manu-

facture of soap and gunpowder. On the growth of New York City, see Robert G. Albion, *The Rise of New York Port, 1815-1860* (1939; reprint, Boston: Northeastern University Press, 1984), 1-15, 55-94.

26. On shipbuilding in Athens, see Spafford, *Gazetteer of the State of New-York* (1813) and Vedder, *Official History of Greene County*, 19-28.

27. On the Susquehanna Turnpike, see Brown, "Topographical Description of Catskill," 119; Dwight, *Travels in New-England and New-York*, vol. 4, 176-177; Spafford, *Gazetteer of the State of New-York* (1813); and A. T. Goodrich, *The North American Tourist* (New York: A. T. Goodrich, 1839), 37. An 1802 map showing the route of the turnpike from the village of Catskill to the Bataviakill is reprinted in Roland Van Zandt, *The Catskill Mountain House* (New Brunswick, NJ: Rutgers University Press, 1966), 18.

28. On the Little Delaware Turnpike, see Evers, *The Catskills*, 306-310, 351, 353.

29. Grandson of the prominent Baptist minister and historian Isaac Backus, Andrew Backus (1790-after 1879) left Catskill after a few months. By October 1815, he had settled in the even newer village of Columbus, Ohio. Andrew Backus was the first cabinetmaker to settle in Columbus and quickly became one of the city's most prominent citizens. Andrew Backus's letter to his father is in the Backus Papers, John Hay Library, Brown University, Providence, Rhode Island. I have added punctuation and capitalization.

30. The word *clove* derives from the Dutch *klove* meaning a rocky cleft or fissure, a gap, or a ravine. The Dutch noun derives from the same Teutonic root as the English verb *to cleave*. In his 1828 *American Dictionary of the English Language,* Noah Webster noted that the "word, though properly an appellative, is not often used as such in English; but it is appropriated to particular places that are real clefts, or which appear as such; as, the *Clove* of Kaaterskill, in the State of New-York." *American Dictionary of the English Language* (New York: S. Converse, 1828), s.v. "clove."

31. On the tanneries, see "The Prattsville Tannery," *Hunt's Merchant's Magazine* 17 (August 1847): 156-163; Vedder, *Official History of Greene County*, 57-58, 94-96; Albion, *Rise of New York Port*, 187-189; Evers, *The Catskills*, 332-350; Ellis, *Landlords and Farmers*, 210-211; and the *Dictionary of American Biography*, s.v. "Edwards, Colonel William" and "Pratt, Zadock." On the Hunter Turnpike through Kaaterskill Clove, see Vedder, *Official History of Greene County*, 57-58, 92, and New York State Division of Historical and Anthropological Services,

*Cultural Resources Survey Report Subject: PIN
1123.09.122 Route 23a* (Albany: New York State
Museum, 1980), 9-13.

32. What has come to be known as the Erie Canal was
originally called the Great Western Canal to distinguish it
from the Great Northern Canal linking the Hudson River
with Lakes George and Champlain. Construction on both
canals began in 1817. The Champlain Canal was opened
in September 1823. The Erie Canal from Albany to
Rochester was opened in October 1823. The section
linking Rochester to Lake Erie was opened in October
1825. On the history of the canals, see Cadwallader
Colden, *Memoir, Prepared at the Request of a Committee
...at the Celebration of the Completion of the New
York Canals* (New York: W. A. Davis, 1825); Nobel
E. Whitford, *History of the Canal System of the State of
New York* (Albany: Brandow Publishing Co., 1906); and
George R. Taylor, *The Transportation Revolution
1815-1860* (New York: Rinehart & Company, Inc., 1951),
32-36, 77, 160-173, 196, 213. On the effect of the Erie
Canal on the middle Hudson Valley economy, see Albion,
Rise of New York Port, 88-89, and Ellis, *Landlords and
Farmers*, 127, 163.

33. Henry Edwin Dwight, "Account of the Kaatskill
Mountains," *The American Journal of Science and Arts* 2
(November 1820): 11-12. Youngest son of Timothy
Dwight (1752-1817), Henry Edwin Dwight (1797-1832)
graduated from Yale College in 1815. After graduation he
moved to Catskill, where he clerked in the store kept by
his older brother Benjamin Woolsey Dwight. Henry
Edwin Dwight later studied divinity at Andover
Academy and the University of Göttingen. He died in
New Haven in 1832. See Appleton's *Cyclopedia of Amer-
ican Biography*, s.v. "Dwight, Henry."

34. On the history of steam navigation on the Hudson,
see Taylor, *Transportation Revolution*, 56-61; Albion, *Rise
of New York Port*, 143-164; Donald Ringwald, *Hudson
River Day Line* (Berkeley: Howell-North Books, 1965);
and Erik Heyl, *Early American Steamboats*, vol. 2
(Buffalo, NY: Ansel Press, 1953-1969), 191.

35. On DeLabigarre, see "Excursions on our Blue
Mountains," Society for the Promotion of Agriculture,
Arts and Manufactures *Transactions* 1 (1794): 128-139,
172-197. Scientific analyses include Brown, "Topo-
graphical Description of Catskill"; S. L. Mitchell, "A
Sketch of the Mineralogical History of the State of New
York," *Medical Repository* 1 (1804); and D. W. Barton,
"Notice of the Geology of the Catskills," *The American
Journal of Science and Arts* 4 (1822): 249-251.

36. Spafford, *Gazetteer of the State of New-York* (1813),
330. The authors of this brief account claimed that the
site attracted "numerous parties in the summer," but,

given the evidence in Henry Dwight and other early
sources, most of these visitors were probably local residents up from the villages of the middle Hudson Valley.

37. Irving, "[A Voyage up the Hudson River in 1800],"
345. See also "The Catskill Mountains," first published
in *The Home Book of the Picturesque* (New York: G. P.
Putnam's, 1851), 71-78.

38. The quoted phrase is from the second paragraph of
"Rip Van Winkle." Irving's first trip to the Catskills is
described in his 9 July 1832 letter to his brother Peter
Irving. This letter is reprinted in Ralph M. Aderman,
Herbert L. Kleinfield, and Jenifer S. Banks, eds.,
Letters, vol. 2 of *The Complete Works of Washington Irving*
(Boston: Twayne Publishers, 1979), 709-710.

39. James Fenimore Cooper, *The Pioneers, or the
Sources of the Susquehanna; a Descriptive Tale* (1823;
reprint, Albany, NY: State University of New York
Press, 1980), 291-292.

40. Cooper, *The Pioneers*, 293.

41. On the popularity of *The Pioneers*, see Frank
Luther Mott, *Golden Multitudes: The Story of Best Sellers
in the United States* (New York: The MacMillan
Company, 1947), 305; James Franklin Beard, "Historical
Introduction," in Cooper, *The Pioneers*, xxxviii-l; and
James D. Wallace, *Early Cooper and His Audience* (New
York: Columbia University Press, 1986), 163-169.
Interest in *The Pioneers* was fanned by the remarkable
popular success of Cooper's previous novel, *The Spy*, and
by the pre-publication printing of excerpts from the novel
by Cooper's friend William L. Stone in the *New-York
Commercial Advertiser*. Pre-publication interest was so
intense that Cooper and his publisher printed a second,
corrected, edition *before* the 1 February 1823 publication
of the first American edition. Although no definite
figures exist, the combined editions were probably in
excess of five thousand copies. The first English edition
was of one thousand copies and was published on 26
February 1823. According to Beard, "Historical Introduction," xlii, "The distribution of 3,500 copies of *The
Pioneers* in New York City by noon on 1 February
1823—only hours after publication—was 'indeed
"something new" in the United States' as *Niles Weekly
Register* remarked on 8 February.... no previous American book, not even *The Spy*, had been so auspiciously
greeted. Booksellers quoted the early sales figures to
stimulate further sales; and newspaper notices of the
arrival of shipments—Philadelphia on February third,
Baltimore on the fifth, Washington on the seventh—
testified to a lively interest and a demand at times
outrunning supply. Copies were 'hourly expected' in
Boston on February seventh, and a new shipment replen-
ished a short supply on the seventeenth." The novel was

widely and favorably reviewed. Although Cooper was disappointed with the final sales figures, and although it never sold as well as *The Spy*, *The Pioneers* was one of the eight or nine most popular narratives published in the United States during the 1820s.

42. Later narratives that quote parts of Natty's description include "A Visit to the Catskills," *The Atlantic Souvenir* (Philadelphia: Carey, Lea & Co., 1828), 277; Robert Sands, "Association," in [William Cullen Bryant, Gulian C. Verplanck, and Robert Sands, eds.], *The Talisman* (New York: Elam Bliss, 1829); Thomas Sully, *Diary*, entry for 23 August 1829 (manuscript in Beinecke Library, Yale University, New Haven, CT); William Cullen Bryant, *American Landscape* (New York: Elam Bliss, 1830), 10; William Dunlap, *A Trip To Niagara* (New York: E. B. Clayton, 1830), 31-39; Willis Gaylord Clark, "Ollapodiana: Number Fourteen," *The Knickerbocker* 8 (1836): 72; T. Addison Richards, "The Catskills," *Harper's New Monthly Magazine* 50, July 1854, 150; Charles Lanman, *Adventures in the Wilds of the United States and British American Provinces*, vol. 2 (Philadelphia: John W. Moore, 1856), 171, 182; and Ernest Duvergier de Hausanne, *A Frenchman in Lincoln's America*, trans. Ralph H. Bowen, vol. 1 (Chicago: Donnelly, 1974), 129. Natty's entire description is quoted in [David Murdoch, ed.], *The Scenery of the Catskill Mountains* (New York: D. Fanshaw, [1846]). Other important guidebooks that quote all or part of Natty's description include T. Addison Richards, ed., *Appleton's Illustrated Hand-Book of American Travel* (New York: D. Appleton & Co., 1857), 146; Rockwell, *The Catskill Mountains and the Region Around*, 185-188; and Walton Van Loan, *Van Loan's Catskill Mountain Guide* (Catskill: Van Loan & Van Gordern, 1876), 13. Except for Rockwell, each of the guidebooks went through many annual editions.

43. DeWitt Clinton, diary entry for 23-24 August 1823 in the New-York Historical Society; Spafford, *Gazetteer of the State of New-York* (1824), 245; "Pine Mountain House," *New-York Mirror* 9, 31 August 1833; James Silk Buckingham, *America: Historical, Statistic, and Descriptive*, vol. 2 (London: Fisher, Son, & Co., 1841), 253; Evers, *The Catskills*, 351-365; and Van Zandt, *The Catskill Mountain House*, 28-42.

44. The *Catskill Recorder* for 13 August 1829 reported that the "number of visitors continues to increase. On Tuesday 103 passed through the village on their way to Pine Orchard. The number of visitors the past week can not fall much short of 600" (Bronck Library, Greene County Historical Society, Coxsackie, NY). The developers who built the hotel at Pine Orchard called it the Pine Orchard House, but from the time it was built the hotel was regularly referred to as the Catskill Mountain House. For example, the hotel is labeled the Catskill

Mountain House on the lithograph by Duponchel (1826), the engraving by John Rubens Smith (1830), and the engraving after Cole (1830). Both names were widely used throughout the 1830s. By the mid-1840s, the scrub pines that had given the site its name had died out, and the original name was abandoned. I will henceforth refer to the hotel at Pine Orchard as the Catskill Mountain House.

45. Individuals varied their routes, but most early nineteenth-century English and American tourists began or ended their trips in New York City. In the later 1820s and 1830s, the most common itinerary went from New York City north up the Hudson to West Point, the Catskill Mountain House, and Albany. From Albany it picked up the Erie Canal and headed west to Niagara Falls. From Niagara Falls the most adventurous tourists might follow the path of emigration southwest to the Ohio River. If they did not push on to the Ohio, they might descend the St. Lawrence River to Montreal. Those who went to Montreal usually returned to the United States by way of Lake Champlain, Lake George, and Saratoga. Less adventurous tourists often skipped Montreal and traveled from Niagara to Saratoga by way of the Erie Canal. From Saratoga, tourists would return to the Hudson River at Troy. From Troy they might either descend the Hudson or travel east either to Boston or the Housatonic or Connecticut River Valleys. Significant numbers of tourists did not begin to visit the White Mountains of New Hampshire until the 1840s. The Green Mountains of Vermont did not become a popular tourist destination until after the Civil War. For early nineteenth-century patterns of tourist travel in the United States, see Hans Huth, *Nature and the American: Three Centuries of Changing Attitudes* (Lincoln, NB: University of Nebraska Press, 1957), 1-128; Christopher Mulvey, *Anglo-American Landscapes: A Study of Nineteenth-Century Anglo-American Travel Literature* (Cambridge, England: Cambridge University Press, 1983), 135-208, and Bruce Robertson, "The Picturesque Traveler in the United States," in Nygren, ed., *Views and Visions*, 187-210.

46. Alexis de Tocqueville, *Democracy in America*, ed. Phillips Bradley, vol. 2 (1840; reprint, New York: Alfred A. Knopf, 1945), 78. Tocqueville was in the United States from May 1831 until February 1832.

47. Thomas Cole, "Essay on American Scenery," in John W. McCoubrey, ed., *American Art, 1700-1960: Sources and Documents* (Englewood Cliffs, NJ: Prentice-Hall, Inc., 1965), 98, 99. Emphasis added.

48. Thomas Cole, manuscript journal entry for 1 August 1836 as transcribed in Thomas Cole, *The Collected Essays and Prose Sketches*, ed. Marshall Tymm (St. Paul, MN: The John Colet Press, 1980), 141.

49. Cole, "Essay on American Scenery," 98, 109. Emphasis added.

50. Cole visited the Mountain House on 4 July 1835. In his journal he complained that "there was much company & as usual in such places few that enjoyed the magnificence that nature spread around them. . . . Some of the ladies were riding on headless and tailless Hobby horses that were propelled 'round by several industrious gentlemen. One party of men was engaged in the intellectual game of ninepins and half a dozen ladies & as many of the other sex were dancing in a long room, where there was a mangle in one corner, to the sound of something like a three-stringed fiddle. What a desecration of the place where nature offers a feast of higher[,] holier enjoyment! Alas that men should thrust their frivolities into the very face of the sublimest regions of the world! We turned away disgusted & sought pleasure where we were sure to find it pure[,] healthful & unalloyed." Cole, *Collected Essays and Prose Sketches*, 130.

51. The subject is identified by Cole in his journal entry for 5 July 1835. See Cole, *Collected Essays and Prose Sketches*, 130.

52. The quotation is from the notice Dunlap sent to the New-York *Evening Post*, 22 November 1825, 2. Dunlap retold the story in the *New-York Literary Gazette*, 10 December 1825, 219-220, and in his *History of the Rise and Progress of the Arts of Design in the United States*, vol. 2 (1834; reprint, New York: Dover Publications, 1969), 359-360. The most complete account of Cole's early work is Ellwood C. Parry III, "Thomas Cole's Early Career: 1818-1829," in Nygren, ed., *Views and Visions*, 161-186. Additional information can be found in Louis Legrand Noble, *The Life and Works of Thomas Cole*, ed. Elliot Vesell (Cambridge, MA: Harvard University Press, 1964) and John K. Howat, "A Picturesque Site in the Catskills: The Kaaterskill Falls as Painted by William Guy Wall," Honolulu Academy of Arts *Journal* 1 (1974): 16-29, 63-65.

53. The most detailed reviews appeared in the *New-York Review and Atheneum Magazine* 2 (1826). In the January issue (153), the reviewer singled out *Caaterskill Upper Fall, Catskill Mountains* for special praise: "This is a view of part of the upper falls in the Kattskill mountains; and is the picture which attracted the attention of [John Trumbull, the president of our Academy,] and by that means brought into public view the uncommon talent of Mr. Cole. Though not a more perfect picture than the lake scene noticed in our last number, it is more splendid, more brilliant, more poetical. The artist had more difficulties to surmount, and, as he has surmounted them, has evinced more skill. We will call the attention of the spectator to the depth into which the water is rushing —to the rocks—to the autumnal foliage of the forest, so bright, so true, and so harmonious; and then direct his eye to the distant mountain, from where the wind is whirling the mist-cloud, and scattering it abroad into the heavens. This beautiful composition evinces in the painter the true poetical feeling of the sublime."

54. The commission is discussed in Cole's 6 July and 20 November 1826 letters to Wadsworth. The surviving Cole-Wadsworth correspondence is to be found in J. Bard McNulty, ed., *The Correspondence of Thomas Cole and Daniel Wadsworth* (Hartford, CT: The Connecticut Historical Society, 1983).

55. Howard S. Merritt, ed., "Correspondence Between Thomas Cole and Robert Gilmor, Jr.," The Baltimore Museum of Art *Annual* 2 (1967): 43-44.

56. The mill dam and observation platform are not mentioned in James Pierce's "A Memoir on the Catskill Mountains with Notices of their Topography, Scenery, Mineralogy, Zoology, Economical Resources, &c.," *American Journal of Science and Art* 6 (1823): 86-97. The fact that Pierce does not mention them suggests that they did not exist at the time he visited the site. The earliest located written description of the observation platform is in Joseph Story's 29 June 1825 letter to William Fettyplace. According to Story, there is "a small, rude house of entertainment, erected on the brow of the precipice which overlooks the falls." Story's letter appears in Joseph Story, *The Life and Letters of Joseph Story*, ed. William Wetmore Story, vol. 1 (Boston: Little & Brown, 1851), 452. The pencil drawings by Cole (plate 13) and Hilson (fig. 7) are the earliest known visual representations of the observation platform. Neither are dated, but both were probably drawn between 1825 and 1829. On Silas Scribner and his sawmill, see Evers, *The Catskills*, 362-363, 489.

57. *Stony Gap, Kaaterskill Clove* is a twentieth-century title. The painting is a copy, with variations, of the 1826 *View in the Clove* (private collection), which Cole sold to the New York collector Henry Ward. Parry, "Thomas Cole's Early Career," 174.

58. Ibid., 172.

59. Cole's dissatisfaction with the view is discussed in Gilmor's previously cited 1 August 1826 letter to Cole. Instead of a view of the Mountain House, Gilmor received the *Sunrise in the Catskills* (private collection) reproduced as figure 45 in Joseph Czestochowski, *The*

American Landscape Tradition (New York: E. P. Dutton, Inc., 1982).

60. Howard Merritt, *Thomas Cole* (Rochester, NY: Memorial Art Gallery of the University of Rochester, 1969), 24-25; Parry, "Thomas Cole's Early Career," 174.

61. On Wall, Marsiglia, and Ward, see the entries in the ensuing catalogue section.

62. Henry Inman is supposed to have worked in the Catskills from a very early period, but the earliest Catskill work of his I know is the oil painting *Trout Fishing in Sullivan County, New York* (Munson-Williams-Proctor Institute, Utica, NY), which is undated but has been assigned to the early 1840s. Daniel Huntington began to summer in the Catskills in the late 1830s. The earliest located Catskill scene by Huntington is the 1837 oil painting *Rondout Kill, Afternoon* (Baltimore Museum of Art).

63. Among the important pre-1840 painters of American scenery who did little or no work in the Catskills are John Barralet, George Beck, Thomas Birch, Alvan Fisher, Francis Guy, Henry Cheever Pratt, Joshua Shaw, and William Winstanley. On these artists, see the biographies and reproductions in Nygren, ed., *Views and Visions*. The numerous paintings by Thomas Doughty that now carry a Catskill title are either based on views in the western Catskills near the Delaware River or are generalized landscapes without direct relationship to a particular site. These images are discussed in the artist's entry on Doughty.

64. On patronage, see Neil Harris, *The Artist in American Society: The Formative Years, 1790-1860* (New York: Simon and Schuster, 1970), 98-107, 275-282, and Lillian Miller, *Patrons and Patriotism: The Encouragement of the Fine Arts in the United States, 1790-1860* (Chicago: University of Chicago Press, 1960).

65. James Kirke Paulding, *The New Mirror for Travellers; and Guide to the Springs* (New York: G. C. Carvill, 1828), 144.

66. Goodrich, *North American Tourist*, 34.

67. William L. Stone, "Ten Days in the Country," *New-York Commercial Advertiser*, 26 August, 3 and 25 September 1824.

68. The article appeared in the *Atheneum Magazine* (October 1825).

69. *The Atlantic Souvenir; A Christmas and New Year's Offering* (Philadelphia; Carey, Lea & Co., 1828); S. G. Goodrich, ed., *The Token; A Christmas and New Year's Present* (Boston: S. G. Goodrich, 1828); [Bryant et al., eds.], *The Talisman*. The literary annuals were published late in the year and, as their titles suggest, were marketed as Christmas and New Year's presents. They were among the most widely distributed literary books published in the United States in the early nineteenth century and included pieces by many of the most important writers of the period. For example, William Cullen Bryant's well-known sonnet, "To Cole the Painter Departing for Europe," was published in the 1829 issue of *The Talisman*. Many of Hawthorne's best-known early short stories were first published in *The Token*. Concerning the annuals, see Ralph Thompson, *American Literary Annuals & Gift Books: 1825-1865* (New York: W. Wilson Co., 1936).

70. From 1824 until its expansion in the mid-1840s, the hotel could accommodate about two hundred people a night (fourteen hundred a week). The fact that guests rarely stayed more than two or three nights is suggested both by the early travel narratives, which almost never describe a longer stay, and by the previously cited newspaper article in the *Catskill Recorder*. In order to accommodate five hundred new guests a week, the average stay would have had to have been less than three nights.

71. For accounts of wealthy visitors who left after only two or three nights, see Capt. Basil Hall, *Travels in North America in the Years 1827 and 1828* (Edinburgh: Cadell and Co., 1829), 93-97; Robert E. Moody, ed., *The Papers of Leverett Saltonstall*, Massachusetts Historical Society Collections 83 (1981): 44-48; and Tyrone Power, *Impressions of America, 1833-1835*, vol. 1 (London: Bentley, 1836), 426-431. Harriet Martineau, *Retrospect of Western Travel*, vol. 1 (London: Saunders & Otley, 1838), 63, reported that some guests thought the charges were too high. I do not mean to suggest the hotel was inexpensive. In this early period as throughout the nineteenth century, it was expensive to stay at the hotel at Pine Orchard. Operating expenses and therefore charges were high because furnishings and supplies—like the guests—had to be hauled up the escarpment from the village of Catskill. My point is that cost alone does not explain why the average stay of early nineteenth-century tourists was so short.

72. For examples, see the previously cited accounts by Timothy Dwight and Horatio Gates Spafford.

73. For examples, see Capt. Basil Hall and James Stuart, *Three Years Travel in North America* (Edinburgh: R. Cadell, 1833), 424-428. The previously cited account by Harriet Martineau is an exception to this generalization.

74. [Grenville Mellen], "Catskill, A Journal of the Grand and Glorious," in Goodrich, ed., *The Token,* 117. This essay was published without an identified author. Mellen is identified as the author in Thompson, *American Literary Annuals & Gift Books,* 459-460.

75. Willis Gaylord Clark, "Ollapodiana. Number Twenty," *The Knickerbocker* 10 (August 1837): 171-172. Reprinted in Lewis Gaylord Clark, ed., *The Literary Remains of the Late Willis Gaylord Clark* (New York: Burgess, Stringer, & Co., 1847).

76. In 1867, the Reverend Charles Rockwell compared the ascent of the Mountain House road with the pilgrimage pictured in Thomas Cole's series of paintings titled the *Voyage of Life:* "there is one place upon the road where the ascending weary ones enjoy more exquisite pleasure, for a moment, than at any other point in all that mountain region. It is at a turn in the road where the Mountain House stands; suddenly, before and above the traveller, revealed in perfect distinctness, column, capital, window, rock, people,—all apparently only a few rods distant. There too the road is level, and the traveller rejoices in the assurance that the toilsome journey is at an end, when suddenly, like the young pilgrim in Cole's 'Voyage of Life,' he finds himself disappointed in his course. The road that seemed to be leading directly to that beautiful mansion upon the crag just above him turns away, like the stream that appeared to be taking the ambitious young man directly to the shadowy temple of fame in the clouds; and many a weary step must be taken over a steep, crooked road before the traveller can reach the object of his journey." Rockwell, *The Catskill Mountains,* 180-181.

77. The Enoch Wood & Son transfer-printed earthenware plate *Catskill House, Hudson* is described and reproduced in Ellouise Baker Larsen, *American Historical Views on Staffordshire China,* 3d ed. (New York: Dover Books, 1975), 15, 309.

78. The two volumes of John Howard Hinton, *The History and Topography of the United States* (London: Simpkin & Marshall, 1832) included twelve engravings after Cole. The only other Catskill image was *The Falls of Cattskill, New York.* All twelve of these engravings seem to have been based on small paintings or pencil drawings Cole either carried with him to Europe or worked up after he arrived in London. Although obviously related to both the 1825 *Caaterskill Upper Fall, Catskill Mountains* bought by Trumbull and the 1826 *Kaaterskill Falls* painted for Wadsworth, the unlocated source for the engraving was a third version of the view from the cavern. On Cole's work for *The History and Topography of the United States,* see his 13 July 1832 letter to Wadsworth in McNulty, ed., *Correspondence of Thomas Cole and Daniel Wadsworth,* 56-57, and Henry H. Glassie,

"Thomas Cole and Niagara Falls," *New-York Historical Society Quarterly* 58 (1974): 91.

79. The Jackson plate is reproduced in Raymond Beecher, "Staffordshire Earthenware With Local Scenes," *Greene County Historical Journal* 9 (Winter 1985): 36; Parsons's lithograph, Boutelle's painting, and the lithograph by Stone are reproduced in Van Zandt, *The Catskill Mountain House,* 56, 57, and 181.

80. Cole's sketch is reproduced in Edgar P. Richardson, *American Romantic Painting* (New York: E. Weyhe, 1944), 96.

81. Smillie's engraving is reproduced in Morris Bishop, "The Journeys of Samuel J. Parker," *New York History* (1964): 146. Another exception is William Bennett's *Catskill Mountains,* published in *The New Mirror,* 9 September 1843. Bennett's engraving shows a farmer with three cows descending the road from the hotel.

82. [Mellen], "Catskill, A Journal of the Grand and Glorious," 124-125.

83. Alcide d'Orbigny, *Voyage Pittoresque dans les Deux Amériques,* vol. 1 (Paris: L. Tenré, 1836), plate 61 (facing page 483). The popularity of d'Orbigny's volume is discussed in the artist entry for Boilly.

84. Theodore Dwight, *The Northern Traveller* (New York: G. & C. Carvill, 1828).

85. The most influential eighteenth- and nineteenth-century analyses are Edmund Burke, *A Philosophical Enquiry into the Origin of Our Ideas of the Sublime and Beautiful,* ed. James T. Boulton (Notre Dame, IN: University of Notre Dame Press, 1968); Immanuel Kant, *Critique of Judgement,* trans. J. H. Bernard (New York: Hafner Press, 1951); and John Ruskin, *Modern Painters I,* vol. 3 of *The Complete Works of John Ruskin* (Library Edition), ed. E. T. Cook and Alexander Wedderburn (London: George Allen, 1903-1912). On the history of the concept, see Samuel Monk, *The Sublime* (1935; reprint, Ann Arbor, MI: University of Michigan Press, 1960) and Nicolson, *Mountain Gloom and Mountain Glory.* The most useful recent analysis is Thomas Weiskel, *The Romantic Sublime: Studies in the Structure and Psychology of Transcendence* (Baltimore, MD: The Johns Hopkins University Press, 1976).

86. "A Visit to the Catskills," 280.

87. One of the disappointed visitors was the portrait painter Thomas Sully, who complained that "the prospect is solely that of magnitude and grandeur; being about 3000 feet above the level country, objects were diminished too much to be picturesque." Sully's comments are from the entry for 23 August 1829 in his unpublished *Diary.*

88. T. Addison Richards, "The Catskills," *Harper's New Monthly Magazine* 9, July 1854, 147. Richards went on to note that "though every body does the 'sunrise,' and every body rhapsodizes thereon, . . .it never has been and never can be looked, or talked, or scribbled up or down."

89. Henry Dwight, "Account of the Kaatskill Mountains," 11.

90. Pierce, "A Memoir on the Catskill Mountains," 92.

91. "A Visit to the Catskills," 280-281.

92. [Mellen], "Catskill, A Journal of the Grand and Glorious," 122.

93. Robert Sands, "Association," 206.

94. Among the many examples, see Power, *Impressions of America, 1833-1835,* vol. 1, 431; Buckingham, *America, Historical, Statistic, and Descriptive,* vol. 2, 256; Park Benjamin, "Catskill Mountain House," *The New World* (July 1843), reprinted in [Murdoch, ed.], *Scenery of the Catskill Mountains,* 19; and Lanman, *Adventures in the Wilds of the United States,* vol. 1, 177-178.

95. The quoted phrase is from Elizabeth Fries Ellet, "The Fourth at Pine Orchard," in [Murdoch, ed.], *Scenery of the Catskill Mountains,* 26.

96. Henry Dwight, "Account of the Kaatskill Mountains," 20.

97. Buckingham, *America, Historical, Statistic, and Descriptive,* vol. 2, 255-256.

98. Martineau, *Retrospect of Western Travel,* vol. 1, 62.

99. This is probably the painting exhibited at the 1828 exhibition of the National Academy of Design as *View of the Round-Top in the Catskill Mountains.*

100. Evers, *The Catskills,* 394-404; Van Zandt, *The Catskill Mountain House,* 28-44.

101. The renovation is most fully described in Van Zandt, *Catskill Mountain House,* 55-56. See also Talbot Hamlin, *Greek Revival Architecture in America* (1944; reprint, New York: Dover Publications, Inc., 1964), 261-262.

102. *The Scenery of the Catskill Mountains* was published anonymously. The editor is identified as Murdoch in Rockwell, *The Catskill Mountains,* 299. The original edition contained thirty-nine pages and was regularly reprinted. Three new entries were added in 1860. These additions are neither noted on the title page nor listed in the table of contents. The expanded edition was forty-nine pages in length and was regularly reprinted until the late 1870s.

103. Ellet, "The Fourth at Pine Orchard," 26-27.

104. Richards, *Appleton's Illustrated Hand-Book,* 144-148.

105. In a 6 November 1874 autobiographical letter to Octavius Brooks Frothingham now in the Sanford Gifford Papers on microfilm at the Archives of American Art, Gifford wrote that he took his first "pedestrian tours in the Catskill Mts." in 1846. The earliest dated images of the Catskills by Gifford are also dated 1846. In John I. H. Baur, ed., "The Autobiography of Worthington Whittredge, 1820-1910," Brooklyn Museum *Journal* (1942), 59, Whittredge identified Gifford as the artist who "found" Scribners. According to Whittredge, "many years ago," it was Gifford who "hunted up a little house in Kaaterskill Clove, in which lived a family of plain country folk, and, as the place was secluded and there were no boarders, he liked it and managed to obtain quarters there. This house, scarcely large enough to hold the family, was, nevertheless, for many summers the abiding place of a congregation of artists. The beds were few and it may truly be said that the best were the cheapest, for the most expensive were composed of straw, while the cheapest were of feathers. As may well be imagined, the table at this house was not very good. Gifford was no gourmet, but he had a commendable ambition to improve the cooking of the Catskills. To this end, he urged the immigration of some of the wives and sisters of those present, whose culinary gifts he was acquainted with. In due time they appeared upon the scene and, by their adroit direction, new dishes were served and the coffee was improved. But this experiment proved fatal in the end. Boarders came in flocks from the city, and Scribner's Boarding House had to be abandoned by the artists and new quarters found further on."

106. Durand's letters are in the Durand Papers at the New-York Public Library and on microfilm at the Archives of American Art.

107. Information in this paragraph derives from Durand's letters to his son and Kensett's 1 July 1848 letter to Noah Kellogg. Kensett's letter is in the Kensett papers on microfilm at the Archives of American Art (reel #N68-85). In his 2 October letter, Durand noted that "Kensett is not with us[,] he left for Ithaca on the day we arrived at Catskill and has not returned." The German painter was probably August Köllner (1813-1907). A pencil drawing by Köllner inscribed "Catskill Mountains, N.Y. 1841" is in the Karolik collection of the Museum of Fine Arts, Boston. One of the other nine artists was probably Sanford R. Gifford, who was working in Kaaterskill Clove from early September until at least the 22nd. Gifford's activities are documented by dated drawings in his 1848 sketchbook in the collection of the Vassar College Art Gallery. Related drawings are in another 1848 sketchbook which is on microfilm in the Sanford Gifford papers at the Archives of American Art (reel #688). For the commission of *Kindred Spirits*, see William Cullen Bryant II, "Poetry and Painting: A Love Affair of Long Ago," *American Quarterly* 22 (1970): 881-882.

108. For the reception of Kensett's 1849-1850 paintings, see the artist's entry in the catalogue section.

109. On Cropsey's 1850 visit to Rusk's, see the artist's entry.

110. The presence of McEntee, Oddie, Miller, and the two Richards is established by dated or datable paintings; that of Stone and Lewis is established by entries in Stone's diary cited in Catherine Campbell, "Benjamin Bellows Grant Stone: A Forgotten American Artist," *New-York Historical Society Quarterly* 62 (1978): 26.

111. Richards, *Appleton's Illustrated Hand-Book*, 147.

112. "E. B. M.," "Trees and Rocks at the Catskill Mountains," *The Crayon* 4 (September 1857): 281. A useful selection of relevant essays by Burroughs can be found in John Burroughs, *In the Catskills* (Boston: Houghton Mifflin Company, 1910).

113. For the history of Catskill Mountain tourism in the later nineteenth and twentieth centuries, see Evers, *The Catskills*, 461-736. See also, The Architectural League of New York and the Gallery Association of New York State, *Resorts of the Catskills* (New York: St. Martin's Press, Inc., 1979).

Figs. 17 & 18. Views of the Catskill Mountain House, photographs
by Dr. R. B. Kahn, June 1958.

Fig. 19. Site of the Cat kill Mountain Hou e, photograph by Erik
Borg, 1987.

Guide to the catalogue

The catalogue is in four parts: artist entries, a list of photographs, a list of ephemera, and a list of books.

I. The artist entries are arranged alphabetically by artist's name. The objects by which the artist is represented in the exhibit are listed immediately following the name, ordered by date of execution. In cases in which there are both a painter and an engraver for a given work, complete information for that work is listed under the painter's name.

II. Photographs are listed alphabetically by photographer or, in cases where the photographer is unknown, by publisher.

III. Ephemera are listed chronologically by date of execution.

IV. Books that contain engravings after works of listed artists are listed in the appropriate artist entries. This part of the catalogue lists all other books included in the exhibition. It is arranged chronologically by date of publication.

Illustrations of objects in the exhibition have been designated Plates and are placed throughout the essay and catalogue sections in numerical order. The essay is further illustrated by works not included in the exhibition. These have been designated Figures.

Height precedes width in the measurements.

In most cases, notes to artist entries do not give page citations either to standard artist dictionaries or to standard nineteenth-century exhibition indexes. These include Matthew Baigell, *Dictionary of American Art* (New York: Harper & Row, 1982); George C. Groce and David H. Wallace, *The New-York Historical Society's Dictionary of Artists in America, 1564-1860* (New Haven: Yale University Press, 1957); Mary Bartlett Cowdrey, ed., *American Academy of Fine Arts and American Art Union, 1816-1852*, 2 vols. (New York: The New-York Historical Society, 1953); Mary Bartlett Cowdrey, ed., *National Academy of Design Exhibition Records, 1826-1860*, 2 vols. (New York: The New-York Historical Society, 1943); Clark Marlor, *A History of the Brooklyn Art Association with an Index of Exhibitions* (New York: J. F. Carr, 1970); Maria K. Naylor, ed., *The National Academy of Design Exhibition Record, 1861-1900*, 2 vols. (New York: Kennedy Galleries, Inc., 1973); Robert F. Perkins, Jr., and William J. Gavin, III, eds., *The Boston Athenaeum Art Exhibition Index, 1827-1874* (Boston: MIT Press, 1980); Anna Wells Rutledge, ed., *Cumulative Records of Exhibition Catalogues: The Pennsylvania Academy of the Fine Arts, 1807-1870; The Society of Artists, 1800-1814; The Artist's Fund Society, 1835-1845* (Philadelphia: The American Philosophical Society, 1955); and National Museum of American Art, *The National Museum of American Art's Index to American Art Exhibition Catalogues from the Beginning through the 1876 Centennial Year*, 6 vols., compiled by James L. Yarnall and William H. Gerdts (Boston: G. K. Hall & Co., 1986).

CATALOGUE OF THE EXHIBITION

Plate 54. Thomas Worthington Whittredge, *Portrait of an Artist with an Easel*, 1861. Courtesy Irwin Goldstein, M.D.

UNKNOWN ARTIST

Active c. 1796

Sketch of a Sunken Hill Opposite Town of Katts Kill on the North River Belonging to Jacob Bogardus Esqr which event took place A:D: 1796

Watercolor on paper, c. 1796
11⅞ x 18¼ in.

Kennedy Galleries, Inc., New York
Plate 55

Sketch of a Sunken Hill is a scientific illustration. It was intended to illustrate the process by which Mr. Borgardus's hill sank. The farm of Jacob Bogardus was located on the west bank of Catskill Creek across from the village of Catskill.[1] What seems to be the "event" represented in the watercolor is described by Clark Brown in his 1803 "Topographical Description of Catskill, in the State of New York." According to Brown, "In 1797 several acres of a large hill, lying on the west of Catskill-creek, slid off all at once, carrying the cattle and sheep, which were on it, several rods, without injuring any of them. This opened a large bed of marl, which has been found to answer a good purpose for manure; within a few rods of the spot, vessels which draw ten feet of water can come with convenience."[2] The numbers on the image correspond to a glossary inscribed at the bottom of the sheet, which indicate the stages by which the hill slid and identify many of the details in the background.

The large building to the left is the Catskill Academy, which was organized in 1793 and built in about 1795.[3] In the late eighteenth century, the Hudson River was often referred to as the North River. The name originated among the Dutch, who called the Hudson the North River in order to distinguish it from the South or Delaware River, the only other major river in the New Netherlands. To give the most revealing view of the sunken hill, the unknown artist has turned his back on the Catskills. The background hills are on the east bank of the Hudson.

1. Vedder, *Official History of Greene County*, 46; *Dear Old Greene County*, 129.

2. "Topographical Description of Catskill," 112.

3. *Dear Old Greene County*, 241-242.

Plate 55. Unknown artist, *Sketch of a Sunken Hill Opposite Town of Katts Kill on the North River. . .*, 1796. Courtesy Kennedy Galleries, Inc.

Plate 56. Unknown artist, *The Steamboat Chancellor Livingston,* 1822. Courtesy Albany Institute of History and Art.

UNKNOWN ARTIST

Active 1822

The Steamboat Chancellor Livingston

Watercolor on paper, 1822
19¾ x 30¾ in.

Albany Institute of History and Art
Plate 56

Named after Robert Fulton's chief financial backer and partner, the *Chancellor Livingston* was the last steamer Fulton designed before his death. Launched in 1816, she was the largest and fastest Hudson River steamboat of her time. In 1817, the *Chancellor Livingston* made the passage from Albany to New York in the then-record time of eighteen hours. In November 1825, she was in the procession of boats celebrating the opening of the canal from Lake Erie to the Hudson River. This is the event commemorated in Anthony Imbert's and Felix Dupon-chel's large lithograph after Archibald Robertson's drawing of the *Grand Canal Celebration, View of the Fleet Preparing to Form in Line.*[1]

The *Chancellor Livingston* continued to make the New York-Albany run until 1827, when she was rebuilt and shifted to Long Island Sound. She was dismantled in the mid-1830s.[2]

1. The lithograph is found in Colden, *Memoir.*

2. Heyl, *Early American Steamboats,* vol. 2, 31-32. A detailed contemporary account can be found in John M. Duncan, *Travels Through Parts of the United States and Canada,* vol. 1 (New York: W. B. Gilley, 1823), 305-308.

UNKNOWN ARTIST

Active 1828

Catskill Mountain House

Engraving by W.H. Spencer, 1828
4½ x 7 in.
Originally published in the *Rural Repository 5*
(7 June 1828)

Mr. and Mrs. R. M. Decker
Plate 30

W. H. Spencer's engraving of the *Catskill Mountain House* is the most architecturally revealing of the early views of the hotel, although it misleadingly suggests that the 1825 addition extended to the edge of the Catskill escarpment. Unlike the engraving after Cole (plate 20) and the lithographs by Duponchel (plate 19) and John Rubens Smith (plate 10), Spencer's engraving exaggerates neither the size nor the elegance of the building. Together with the engraving after William Henry Bartlett (plate 61), it is the most detailed surviving image of the original plain columns, side staircases, dormers, catwalk, and rooftop flagpole. Unlike the engraving after Bartlett, Spencer's engraving shows the awkward placement of the public rooms beneath the front porch and reveals the narrowness of the original structure. The tree stumps in the left foreground suggest the newness of the building.

Spencer's engraving appeared in the 7 June 1828 issue of the magazine *Rural Repository*, which was published in the city of Hudson, New York. In an accompanying unsigned article, the editors described the new hotel and concluded by expatiating on the sublimity and religious significance of the view from the escarpment:

> To all who can adore the Creator in the wonderful variety and harmony of his works, this Establishment offers inducements, and holds forth advantages, equal, if not superior to any place of fashionable resort in our country.
>
> Here, as may be imagined, a prospect unrivalled in picturesque grandeur, greets the eye of the traveller—mountains, forests and vallies are stretched in their beauty before him; beneath and around him, the dashing of the waterfall gives music and life to the scene, while the Hudson, its fertile shores sprinkled with villages, and its silvery waves whitened by sails, gliding in the distance silently along, as if impelled by some fairy hand, is seen far below, winding its way toward the ocean; he gazes with delight on a landscape, whose flourishing farms and uncultivated wilds, mingling their attractions, form a combination of *natural* and *artificial* scenery, which is probably no where to be surpassed within the same space.

> The cares of business, the thousand petty vexations which are wont to disturb our peace, are here forgotten; the soul is expanded, and we only regret that all cannot participate with us [in] the raptures of the moment.
>
> What in nature so sublime! as, when all above is hushed to peace and glowing in undiminished brightness, to hear the echoing thunders roll beneath our feet, and contemplate without fear of harm, the vivid lightning flash and play among the misty clouds below?—'Tis then the mind of man, raised above the grovelling thoughts of sublunary things, soars in ecstacy [*sic*] aloft—

> *"And looks through nature, up to nature's God!"* [1]

1. The quotation is from the conclusion of Alexander Pope's "An Essay on Man" (Epistle IV, line 332).

UNKNOWN ARTIST

Active after 1839

Catskill Mountain House

Oil on canvas, after 1839
14 x 20 in.
Copy after William H. Bartlett

Kennedy Galleries, Inc., New York
Plate 11

Catskill Mountain House is an oil copy of an engraving after William Henry Bartlett published in *American Scenery* in 1839.

UNKNOWN ARTIST

Active after 1860

Sunnyside from the Hudson

Oil on canvas, after 1860
24$\frac{1}{16}$ x 34$\frac{1}{16}$ in.
Copied from an engraving in *Frank Leslie's Illustrated Newspaper*, 31 March 1860

Historic Hudson Valley, Tarrytown, New York
Plate 57

Copied from a print in *Frank Leslie's Illustrated Newspaper* of 31 March 1860, *Sunnyside from the Hudson* is a view looking north up the Hudson River Railroad tracks from a position just south of Washington Irving's home Sunnyside.[1] Irving bought his Hudson River estate in 1835. With the help of George Harvey, he transformed the existing structure into a rural cottage and moved into

it in October 1836. The Hudson River Railroad Company was incorporated by an act of the New York State legislature in the spring of 1846. Construction began in the fall of 1847, and service on the stretch of track in front of Sunnyside began on 29 September 1849 with the opening of the section connecting Manhattan with Peekskill. Service was extended to Poughkeepsie on 31 December 1849. The section linking Poughkeepsie with Albany was opened on 3 October 1851.[2]

The desirability of a railroad linking Manhattan with Albany had been noticed as early as 1833, but little was done to bring it about until 1845. Although the promoters of the railroad had originally considered building well east of the Hudson, they ultimately decided that a river route would both generate more traffic and be less expensive to build. In his 1846 *Report* advocating the adoption of the river route, the company's chief engineer John Jervis noted the existence of numerous country estates on the river, admitted that the proposed line would cross many of them, and tried to undercut expected complaints by anticipating them. According to

Plate 57. Unknown artist, *Sunnyside from the Hudson*, after 1860. Courtesy Historic Hudson Valley.

Jervis, few property owners would be seriously inconvenienced because much of the railroad would be built on land located below the high-water mark. Only a few currently valuable sections of land would have to be bought, and only a few trees would have to be cut down. More positively, Jervis was sure that many property owners would welcome the railroad, both because it would make it easier for them to get to Manhattan in the winter when the Hudson was frozen and because it would raise the value of their property. Indeed, according to Jervis, the introduction of the railroad would make Hudson River properties not only more valuable but also more attractive: "With a proper regard to the situation of the grounds, in locating the line, a well constructed Railroad along these situations should not be regarded as a material injury, but an ornament and convenience. A Railroad well fenced and operated by steam-power, will interfere with the retirement of these situations, little if any more than a steamboat passing down the river; the occasional passing of a train will give a lively variety to such situations, and make them more rather than less interesting to most persons."[3]

One cannot be sure how seriously to take Jervis's claim that the addition of the railway would add to the picturesque character of the Hudson valley. He himself seems to have doubted the plausibility of the argument and therefore closed this section of his *Report* by claiming that the railroad was necessary to the economic development of the state and that few if any property owners would want to stand in the way of progress. In the event, of course, many property owners did object. In an early history of the project, Jervis rather smugly recalled the debate over the two proposed routes: "At a future day it will be interesting to look over the discussions that arose on this question. To adopt the river route, was claimed in the style somewhat of the Spanish Don, to be a *desecration* of the river, marring its beauty, and subverting the purpose of the Creator."[4] According to his nephew Pierre M. Irving, Washington Irving was one of those who thought the railroad an "utter desecration" of the "beautiful shore." Pierre Irving reported that his uncle said he wished "he had been born when the world was finished" and complained that "if the garden of Eden were now on earth, they would not hesitate to run a railroad through it."[5] Like his good friend James Kirke Paulding and most of the other affected property owners, however, Irving ultimately accepted the establishment of the railroad as being in the public interest and adapted himself to its presence as best he could.[6]

The engraving that *Sunnyside from the Hudson* is copied from was published shortly after Irving's death and shortly before the beginning of the Civil War. In both the engraving and the oil copy, the foreground figures and especially Irving's "rural cottage" express the pastoral way of life and values that midcentury Americans associated with the nation's agricultural beginnings. The

steamboat and railroad evoke the increasingly industrialized reality of the nation's present and future. In *Sunnyside from the Hudson,* as in John F. Kensett's *View on the Hudson* (plate 106), there is no indication that industrialization might mar the rural scene. But where Kensett defused the potentially disruptive sublimity of the steamboat and railroad by keeping them at a distance—by putting them in the background and by making them almost disappear in the vastness of the encompassing landscape—the creator(s) of *Sunnyside from the Hudson* followed Jervis's lead and represented the steamboat and railroad as positive additions to the picturesque character of the scene. In the face of widespread anxieties provoked by industrial expansion and the movement of large numbers of persons from the country to the cities, *Sunnyside from the Hudson* offers the reassuring picture of the couple who walk the railroad causeway as if it were a promenade; rather, it is a reassuring picture of a railroad causeway *as* a promenade.[7]

1. Joseph T. Butler, *Sleepy Hollow Restorations: A Cross-Section of the Collections* (Tarrytown, NY: Sleepy Hollow Restorations, Inc., 1983), 205.

2. Henry Varnum Poor, *History of the Railroads and Canals of America* (New York: John H. Schultz & Co., 1860), 259-260; Thomas C. Cochran, *Railroad Leaders, 1845-1890* (Cambridge, MA: Harvard University Press, 1953), 22-26.

3. John B. Jervis, *Report on the Hudson River Railroad* (New York: J. F. Trow & Co., 1846), 21.

4. [John B. Jervis], "The Hudson River Railroad, A Sketch of Its History," *Hunt's Merchants' Magazine* (March 1850): 6.

5. Pierre Monroe Irving, *Life and Letters of Washington Irving*, vol. 4 (New York: G. P. Putnam, 1864), 37.

6. The railroad company paid Irving thirty-five hundred dollars because, as they put it in a letter to him, he was "more seriously invaded by this necessary work, in respect to derangement of rural taste and retirement, than . . . any other proprietor on the whole line of the road below the Highlands." Quoted in ibid., 39. Paulding seems to have expressed the position of most of the property owners when he wrote Gouverneur Kemble (another property owner and another of Irving's good friends): "I am of [the] opinion—though it goes against my own particular feelings—that both the interests of the public and those of the Company require the Rail Road to be carried along the edge of the river. I have read Jervis's Report, and though I don't think much of his taste in the picturesque, I think him perfectly right in his general conclusions, and shall submit, like a true patriot, to be annoyed for the good of the Public, though no compensation I can expect to receive will prevent me from wishing it had pleased Providence to render the other route the most advantageous." The letter is printed in Ralph M. Aderman, ed., *The Letters of James Kirke Paulding* (Madison, WI: University of Wisconsin Press, 1962), 471.

7. On the attitudes of nineteenth-century Americans towards industrialization, see Leo Marx, *The Machine in the Garden: Technology and the Pastoral Ideal in America* (Oxford: Oxford University Press, 1964) and John Kasson, *Civilizing the Machine: Technology and Republican Values in America, 1776-1900* (New York: Penguin Books, 1976). See also the exhibition catalogue by Susan D. Walther, *The Railroad in the American Landscape* (Wellesley, MA: Wellesley College Museum, 1981).

WILLIAM ADAMS OF GREENFIELD

1798-1865

Cattskill Mountain House, U.S.

Pink transfer-printed earthenware plate
Staffordshire, England, after c. 1834
10⅜ in. diameter

Private Collection
Plate 58

The Staffordshire potter William Adams took over the direction of the family business at the time of his father's death in 1829. He had traveled in the United States in 1821-1822 and again in 1825. *The Cattskill Mountain*

House, U.S. is one of the so-called "Tunstall Views" which were produced at the new works Adams opened in Tunstall about 1834. The *Cattskill Mountain House, U.S.* was produced in black and brown as well as in pink. The back is marked "Adams," with an eagle surmounting a bar joining two cornucopias filled with flowers and fruit. The name of the view is within the enclosure formed by the cornucopias, eagle, and bar. The scene derives from the 1831 engraving after Thomas Cole's *View of the Cattskill Mountain House, N.Y.,* although the designer of the plate has replaced the pedestrian couple and horseman in the engraving with two well-dressed women.[1]

1. Larsen, *American Historical Views on Staffordshire China*, 3d ed., 141-142, 144, 325. On the technology and history of transfer-printed earthenware, see the entry for Enoch Wood.

Plate 58. William Adams, *Cattskill Mountain House, U.S.,* after c. 1834. Private collection.

Plate 59. James Bard, *The Hudson River Steamboat Francis Skiddy*, 1859. Courtesy The Hudson River Museum of Westchester.

JAMES BARD

1815-1897

The Hudson River Steamboat Francis Skiddy

Oil on canvas, 1859
36 x 64 in.

The Hudson River Museum of Westchester;
Anonymous gift, 1958
Plate 59

The son of an English-born laborer, James and his twin brother John Bard were born in New York City on 4 October 1815. Although neither Bard seems to have received any formal training, by the early 1830s they were in the business of painting steamboat and—occasionally—sailing ship portraits. Early examples of their work were always in watercolor and were usually signed by both brothers. The earliest known oil is of the steamboat *Trojan* (Mariners Museum, Newport News, Virginia) and is dated 1845. After 1845, the Bards usually worked in oil. John Bard withdrew from the partnership in 1849 and died in 1856. James Bard continued painting

steamboat portraits until 1890. His last known work is a pencil sketch dated 1892. He died in White Plains, New York, in 1897.[1]

Like painters of human portraits, the Bards generally worked on commission. Most of their works were ordered by steamboat builders or operators. In either case, businessmen who ordered paintings from the Bards would have thought of the canvases not as art—not as objects of aesthetic interest—but as a means of documenting and advertising the products of their boat yards or the assets of their steamboat lines. Prior to the twentieth century, steamboat portraits by the Bards hung in boat yard and steamboat ticket offices—not in exhibitions of art.[2]

Businessmen who commissioned paintings by the Bards expected that the brothers would work quickly, cheaply, and accurately. Nineteenth-century sources suggest that James Bard, after the breakup of his partnership with John, could produce as many as four finished oil portraits a month. In the 1860s, the going rate for one of these oils was twenty or twenty-five dollars.[3] According to one anonymous nineteenth-century source, James Bard "made drawings of almost every steamer that was built at or owned around the port of New York, the total number of these productions being about 4000."[4] Staggering as this total seems, the speed with which Bard worked and the modesty with which he was paid suggest that it may be accurate.

The early watercolors done by the two brothers seem to have been done freehand, but the later watercolors and oils—especially those done by James Bard alone—were products of meticulous craft. According to the author of James Bard's only known obituary, Bard began a painting by going to the boat yard, where he "would measure the boat to be pictured from end to end, and not a panel, stanchion or other part of the vessel, distinguishable from the outside, was omitted, each portion was measured and drawn to scale." After he had measured the boat, Bard would produce a mechanical scale drawing of it. He would then transfer this plan to a canvas on which he would paint over an already prepared ground. Bard used much thicker paint on the boat than he did on the foreground or background so as to make the boat seem to ride on its setting. Once the structural elements of the boat were in place, Bard used still thicker paint to fashion architectural details such as flag poles, fenders, posts, and rails.[5]

Although the Bards did work for all of the major steamboat builders and operators, they seem to have been most regularly employed by the Collyer brothers (George, Thomas, and William). The *Francis Skiddy* was designed and built by George Collyer in his New York City boat yard in 1849. Because of problems with her engines, she was not put into full service until June 1852. She began service as a day boat on the New York-Albany run. Three hundred twenty-two feet long and thirty-eight feet wide, she was one of the largest and best-appointed boats of her time. She was also one of the fastest. On 30 June 1852, she covered the distance from New York to Albany in the record time of five hours and twenty-three minutes. This record was not surpassed until after the Civil War.[6]

The *Francis Skiddy* was built with three decks but, as she was designed to be a day boat, only the first of these was divided into cabins. In 1856, cabins were added to the previously open second and third decks, and the *Francis Skiddy* was transferred to the New York-Troy night line. On the night of 21 November 1861, she collided with the schooner *W. W. Reynolds* off Blue Point (two miles below Poughkeepsie). As often happened, the *Skiddy's* boiler exploded. Three crewmen were killed by the explosion, and four passengers were fatally scalded. After this accident, she was repaired and returned to the night line. The *Francis Skiddy* stayed on the night line until 5 November 1864, when she wrecked by stranding at Van Staat's Landing (four miles below Albany).

1. A. J. Peluso Jr., *J. & J. Bard: Picture Painters* (New York: Hudson River Press, 1977), 3-19. This is the one indispensable source of information on the Bards. Other useful sources include Jean Lipman and Alice Winchester, *The Flowering of American Folk Art* (New York: Viking Press, in cooperation with the Whitney Museum of American Art, 1974); and Mariners Museum (Newport News, Virginia), *Catalog of Marine Prints and Paintings*, 3 vols.(Boston: G. K. Hall, 1964).

2. Peluso, *J. & J. Bard*, 23-24. The only time either of the Bards is known formally to have exhibited any of his paintings was in 1842 when James exhibited two at the Fifteenth Annual Fair of the American Institute of the City of New York. See ibid., 7. On the American Institute, see Sean Wilentz, *Chants Democratic: New York City & the Rise of the American Working Class, 1788-1850* (New York: Oxford University Press, 1984), 151-152, 271-272. The American Institute had been founded in 1827 by a group of local New York craftsmen. By 1842, the annual fair had become a popular event attended by tens of thousands of visitors. The Fair gave New York craftsmen and artisans a chance to exhibit their work to a mass audience.

3. Peluso, *J. & J. Bard*, 23.

4. The passage is to be found on page 6 of the *Marine Journal* for 29 August 1889. It is quoted in ibid., 85.

5. The obituary was published in the *Seaboard Magazine* for 1 April 1897. It is quoted by Peluso on page 86. On the evolution of Bard's style, see ibid., 85-96.

6. On George Collyer, see ibid., 21, and Ringwald, *The Hudson River Day Line*. On the *Francis Skiddy*, see vol. 1 of George W. Murdock's manuscript *Steamboat Collection* (Print Room, New-York Historical Society) and Heyl, *Early American Steamboats*, vol. 3, 149-151.

WILLIAM HENRY BARTLETT

1809-1854

The Two Lakes and the Mountain House on the Catskills

Engraving by J. C. Bentley, 1838
4¾ x 7⅛ in.

The Hudson River Museum of Westchester
Plate 37

Catterskill Falls from above the Ravine

Engraving by J. T. Willmore, 1838
4¹³⁄₁₆ x 7⅛ in.

The Hudson River Museum of Westchester
Plate 28

Catterskill Falls from below

Engraving by E. Benjamin, 1838
4½ x 7 in.

McKinney Library, Albany Institute of History and Art
Plate 29

Village of Catskill, Hudson River

Engraving by J.C. Bentley, 1839
4½ x 7 in.

McKinney Library, Albany Institute of History and Art
Plate 60

View from the Mountain House, Catskill

Engraving by R. Brandard, 1839
4½ x 7 in.

McKinney Library, Albany Institute of History and Art
Plate 61

American Scenery, with text edited by Nathaniel Parker Willis and engravings after William Henry Bartlett, was serially published in London. The first numbers appeared in 1838. The last appeared in 1842. It was the most widely distributed and influential volume of American landscape views published in the nineteenth century.[1]

In 1840, N. P. Willis[2] was one of the best-known writers in America. An anecdote indicates his popularity: a commercial gentleman "guessed that Goethe was the N.P. Willis of Germany."[3] Willis's work was first published in his father's *Boston Recorder* while he was still in school at Andover. During his college years at Yale, he developed a national reputation as a poet. He began editing major journals immediately upon graduation, and at the age of twenty-three founded his own *American Monthly Magazine.* After the magazine failed, he formed a partnership with George Pope Morris, editor of the *New York Mirror.* Willis was sent abroad as a foreign correspondent. He was widely known in Europe as well as in America, and many of his weekly columns, though published in America, were read in England. While in Europe, he was introduced to William Henry Bartlett and engaged by the London publisher George Virtue to select and edit the text for *American Scenery.*

William Henry Bartlett was born and raised in London, England. At the age of thirteen, he was apprenticed to the architect and antiquarian John Britton. As an apprentice, Bartlett assisted with the drawings for

Plate 60. William Henry Bartlett, *Village of Catskill, Hudson River,* 1839. Courtesy Albany Institute of History and Art.

Britton's *Cathedral Antiquities of England* (1814-1832) and *Picturesque Antiquities of English Cities* (1828-1830). After completing his apprenticeship, Bartlett contracted to illustrate a book by Dr. William Beattie on *Switzerland* (1836). Bartlett's drawings of Swiss scenes made his reputation, and in September 1836 Virtue hired him to produce the illustrations for a projected volume of American scenes. Bartlett traveled to the United States in late 1836 and remained there for much of 1837. Working in sepia and gouache, Bartlett sketched his way up the Hudson, through the New England states, as far west as Niagara Falls, and south to the Natural Bridge in Virginia. Bartlett restricted himself to drawing the views the same size as they would appear in the engravings so that they could be engraved with accuracy. In 1837, Bartlett returned to England. *American Scenery* contains two engravings after Thomas Doughty and 125 after Bartlett.

Almost immediately upon publication, painters began copying Bartlett's engravings. Among the American and European painters who copied Bartlett engravings were Victor DeGrailly, Thomas Chambers, Edmund Coates, and James Burt. Other engravers, including Currier and Ives, borrowed from Bartlett, sometimes reproducing the image exactly, and the Bartlett scenes were used in designs for transfer-printed earthenware as well. Bartletts were re-engraved to illustrate gift books and periodicals such as *Godey's Lady's Book* and the *Ladies' Companion*. Some of the engravings were reused to illustrate Bartlett's posthumously published *History of the United States of North America* in 1856, and in 1883 a Boston publisher, Estes and Lauriat, produced *Mountain, Lake and River: A Series of Twenty-five Steel Line Engravings from Designs by W.H. Bartlett and Others.*

1. On both *American Scenery* and Bartlett, see Mary Bartlett Cowdrey, "William Henry Bartlett and the American Scene," in *New York History* (1941): 388-400, Mary-Ellen Earl, *William H. Bartlett and His Imitators* (Elmira, NY: Arnot Art Gallery, October 1966), and Alexander M. Ross, *William H. Bartlett: Artist, Author, and Traveler* (Toronto: University of Toronto Press, 1973).

2. On Willis, see Henry A. Beers, *Nathaniel Parker Willis* (Boston: Houghton Mifflin, 1885). Also see the *Dictionary of American Biography*, s.v. "Willis, Nathaniel Parker."

3. *Dictionary of American Biography*, s.v. "Willis, Nathaniel Parker."

Plate 61. William Henry Bartlett, *View from the Mountain House, Catskill*, 1839. Courtesy Albany Institute of History and Art.

J. WETHERED BELL

Active 1869-1873

Catskill Mountain House

Pencil, white highlights, on pale green paper in sketchbook, c. 1869-1873
5⅛ x 7⅛ in.

The Hudson River Museum of Westchester
Plate 62

Little is known about J. Wethered Bell. In 1869, Bell exhibited an oil painting and a watercolor at the St. Louis Agricultural and Mechanical Association. The watercolor was of *Ohio Scenery,* and the exhibition catalogue described it as "one of the best of the young artist's productions." The sketchbook owned by The Hudson River Museum, labeled "Travel Sketchbook," is dated 1871. It includes images of Cowingo, Maryland, New York City, Rhode Island, Boston, the White Mountains, Quebec City, Montreal, Lake Champlain, the Adirondacks, Saratoga, and the Catskills. The sketchbook ends with the Catskill scenes. In 1873, Bell exhibited four Hudson Valley and Catskill scenes at the Brooklyn Art Gallery in Cincinnati, Ohio.[1]

1. Exhibition information derives from the *National Museum of American Art's Index to American Art Exhibition Catalogues.*

Plate 62. J. Wethered Bell, *Catskill Mountain House,* c. 1869-1873. Courtesy The Hudson River Museum of Westchester.

ALPHONSE BOILLY

1801-1867

2. Chute de Cattskill

Line engraving, 1836
5¼ x 7 in.

Mr. & Mrs. R. M. Decker

3. Cattskill Mountain House

Line engraving, 1836
5⅜ x 7 in.

The New-York Historical Society
Plate 63

Alphonse Boilly was the youngest son of the French painter and engraver Louis-Leopold Boilly. According to Asher B. Durand's son John, Boilly *fils* apprenticed in Asher B. Durand's studio in the years before Durand gave up engraving to become a full-time painter of oils. In his single passing reference to M. Boilly (the "M." may stand for Monsieur), John Durand refers to him as a stipple engraver, although his only known works are line engravings. Surviving correspondence between Boilly and Asher B. Durand reveals that Boilly returned to Paris by the late fall of 1834. In 1866, eight of his etchings were exhibited at the French Etching Club in New York.[1]

Both *2. Chute de Cattskill* and *3. Cattskill Mountain House* were published in a volume edited by Alcide Dessalines d'Orbigny entitled *Voyage Pittoresque dans les Deux Amériques* (1836).[2] D'Orbigny's book was an anthology of travel narratives. It included translations into French of narratives by a wide range of explorers including Columbus, Las-Casas, Magellan, and Humboldt. The anthology proved popular and was reprinted in 1841; it was also translated into German, Portugese, and Italian. A revised edition, published in Paris in 1853, was reprinted in 1854, 1859, and 1867.

Boilly borrowed the design of his engravings from the two engravings after Thomas Cole (plates 20 and 26) published in J. H. Hinton's 1832 *History and Topography of the United States.*

1. The letters are in the Asher B. Durand Papers in the manuscript collection of The New York Public Library and on microfilm at the Archives of American Art. The basic source of information is Emmanuel Bénézit, *Dictionaire Critique et Documentaire des Peintres, Sculpteurs, Dessinateurs, et Graveurs* (Paris: Librairie Gründ, 1976). See also John Durand, *The Life and Times of A. B. Durand* (New York: Charles Scribner's Sons, 1894), 94.

2. Alcide Dessalines d'Orbigny, ed., *Voyage Pittoresque dans les Deux Amériques* (Paris: L. Tenré, 1836).

Plate 64. James Renwick Brevoort, *Harvest Scene with Storm Coming Up*, c. 1863-1867. Courtesy The Hudson River Museum of Westchester.

JAMES RENWICK BREVOORT

1832-1918

Harvest Scene with Storm Coming Up

Oil on canvas, c. 1863-1867
32 x 48 in.

The Hudson River Museum of Westchester; Gift of the estate of Mrs. Florence Eickemeyer, 1941
Plate 64

The landscape painter James Renwick Brevoort was born in Yonkers, New York, and raised on his father's farm in Williamsbridge and Fordham, New York. He began drawing as a child and at eighteen began to study architecture as an assistant to his cousin, the prominent New York architect James Renwick. After completing a four-year program, he received a certificate in architecture from New York University in 1854. Even before completing his architectural degree, however, Brevoort began taking classes with the painter Thomas Seir Cummings at the National Academy of Design. He first exhibited at the National Academy of Design in 1856,

was elected an Associate in 1861, and became a full member of the Academy in 1863. In 1873, Brevoort auctioned more than 150 of his landscapes and moved to Europe. He lived in Europe for seven years before returning to New York in 1880. He died in Yonkers in 1918.[1]

Exhibition records indicate that Brevoort spent the fall of 1861 in the Catskills. Whether he returned in subsequent years is unclear. Brevoort did some work in Kaaterskill Clove, but, unlike earlier American landscape painters, he favored the lowland scenery between the Hudson and the mountains.[2] He appears to have spent most of his time in the Catskills in the area of Leeds. Located on Catskill Creek northwest of the village of Catskill, Leeds had a number of boarding houses and became a popular resort for artists in the years following the Civil War. Among others, George Inness stayed there between 1868 and 1870 (plate 99), and Winslow Homer was a regular visitor in the mid-1870s.

Like earlier artists, Brevoort gave geographically specific titles to many of the landscapes he did in the Catskills. Uninterested in the close observation of rocks and trees or the representation of mountains or wilderness, however, Brevoort indicated his break with the older landscape tradition by describing his paintings as scenes not of the Catskills, but of Leeds. Inness adopted a similar strategy when he began to paint scenes of the area.

The first Catskill painting Brevoort is known to have exhibited was a view *Near Leeds* which he showed at the Brooklyn Art Association in December 1861 and which was auctioned by Leeds & Co. on 23 December 1862. In 1862, Brevoort exhibited *On Catskill Creek* at the Brooklyn Art Association, the *Old Bridge at Leeds* at the National Academy of Design, and *Near Leeds, N.Y.* at the Artist Fund Society in New York. He exhibited *After the Shower, near Leeds, New York* at the Brooklyn Art Association in December 1863 and again at the Utica Mechanics Association in 1864. In 1871, he exhibited *Vicinity of Leeds* at both the National Academy of Design and the Brooklyn Art Association. Other paintings with Leeds or Catskill titles were included in the 1873 auction.

One of Brevoort's largest located paintings, *Harvest Scene with Storm Coming Up*, was given to The Hudson River Museum by the artist's daughter. The title is supposed to be that given by the artist. The painting is not dated but is signed "James Brevoort NA" (indicating his status as a National Academician) and, therefore, dates from after 1863. If the title was indeed given by the artist, the painting cannot date from later than 1867, when Henry Tuckerman praised Brevoort's *Harvest Scene with Storm Coming Up* as showing "advancing power and a fine management of light."[3] Despite the prominent reference in Tuckerman, no painting titled *Harvest Scene with Storm Coming Up* is listed in any of the nineteenth-century exhibition records.

Harvest Scene with Storm Coming Up seems to be a view of the main Catskill escarpment from the Kiskatom Plains. If this identification is correct, the foreground body of water is Kaaterskill Creek, and the mountain at the right rear is the northeastern face of High Peak. Palenville and the entrance to Kaaterskill Clove would be hidden behind the clump of trees in the right middleground. The Kiskatom Plains are a few miles southwest of the village of Leeds.[4]

In *Harvest Scene with Storm Coming Up*, as in his other paintings from this period in his career, Brevoort was primarily interested in the play of light on domesticated fields and rural buildings. Many of Brevoort's paintings do not contain human figures, but almost all contain evidence of man's presence—a distant farmhouse or a section of rail fence, for example. As in George Inness's paintings of the area around Leeds, Brevoort's paintings of Leeds represent man encompassed but not threatened by the vastness of the natural world. The farmers in *Harvest Scene with Storm Coming Up* are hurrying to harvest their hay before it is ruined by the coming storm. But although the approaching storm is a momentary inconvenience, the water it carries will revivify the parched fields visible in the foreground.

1. Biographical information derives from the artist dictionaries and Sutherland McColley, *The Works of James Renwick Brevoort, 1832-1918: American Landscape Painter* (Yonkers, NY: The Hudson River Museum, 1972).

2. The 1873 auction included two mountain views—*Haines' Ravine, Catskill* and *A Ravine in the Catskills*.

3. Henry Tuckerman, *The Book of the Artist* (1870; reprint, New York: James F. Carr, 1967), 567.

4. McColley, *Works of James Renwick Brevoort*, xv, suggested that the subject was in the Catskills near Leeds. The more specific location cited here was suggested to me by Mr. Kenneth Van Vechten Parks of Catskill, New York.

ALBURTUS D. O. BROWERE

1814-1887

Catskill, New York

Oil on canvas, 1849
34 x 44 in.

The Brooklyn Museum; Dick S. Ramsay Fund, 40.881
Plate 65

The son of the well-known sculptor John Henri Isaac Browere, Alburtus Del Orient Browere was born in Tarrytown, New York, and received rudimentary training from his father. He first exhibited at the National

Academy in 1831. The young painter enjoyed a good deal of early success. In 1832, he was awarded a silver medal for having the "Best Oil Painting" at the American Institute of the City of New York. In 1841, he received a premium award and a silver medal from the National Academy of Design for his large historical work, *Canonicus and the Governor of Plymouth*. Throughout the 1830s, Browere exhibited many genre paintings, including illustrations after Washington Irving's Knickerbocker *A History of New York* and "Rip Van Winkle" at the Apollo Association, at the American Art Union, and at the National Academy of Design.

Henri Browere died in 1834. He left behind large debts which were assumed by his son. Alburtus Browere married in 1835, and he and his wife had the first two of their eight children by 1840. Under mounting financial pressure, the Broweres moved from New York City to Catskill in 1840 or 1841. In Catskill, Browere found work first as a clerk in a drug store and later as a painter of buggies, surreys, and signs. Except for two fruitless trips to California in search of gold (1852-1856 and 1858-1861), Browere spent the rest of his life in Catskill.[1] Despite his lack of success as a prospector, he made enough money from the sale of the canvases that he continued to paint and as a sign painter to buy a small frame house on the Palenville turnpike about one mile west of Catskill.[2]

One of Browere's most effective paintings, *Catskill, New York* seems to be a view from the north side of Catskill Creek looking south across the creek to West Catskill. A wharf runs out into the Creek, Hoponose Hill (Hopp's nose) rises in the center, and a bit of the Catskills are visible at the rear. Browere has emphasized the bucolic character of the scene by using the road and middle-ground trees to hide the drawbridge across Catskill Creek.[3]

MF

1. Paintings of California scenes by Browere are in the M.H. De Young Memorial Museum in San Francisco, the Oakland Museum, and the Carnegie Institute Museum of Art.

2. Information in these paragraphs derives from artist dictionaries and exhibition records as well as from Roscoe P. Conkling, "Reminiscences on the Life of Alburtis [sic] Del Orient Browere," *Los Angeles County Museum of Art Quarterly* 8 (Spring 1950): 2-6; Mabel P. Smith with Janet R. MacFarlane, "Unpublished Paintings by Alburtis [sic] Del Orient Browere," *Art in America* 46 (Fall 1958): 68-71; and an unpublished typescript by Browere's great-grandson Charles G. Wright, *Alburtus D.O. Browere 1814-1887, A Genre Painter of the Hudson River School and Resident of Catskill, N.Y. 1840-1887*, a copy of which is on deposit at the Greene County Historical Society in Coxsackie, New York.

3. The bridge appears in the woodcut *Northwestern View of Catskill* in John Barber and Henry Howe, *Historical Collections of the State of New York* (New York: Tuttle, 1842), 184.

Plate 65. Alburtus D. O. Browere, *Catskill, New York*, 1849. Courtesy The Brooklyn Museum.

ANDREW FISHER BUNNER

1841-1897

Two Sketches: "Below Fawn's Leap, Catskill Mountains" and "Above the Bridge"

Pencil on paper, 31 July 1866
13¹³⁄₁₆ x 9⅞ in.

The Corcoran Gallery of Art; Gift of Kate Bunner

Kaatskill Creek near the Falls

Pencil on paper, 1 August 1866
13¹³⁄₁₆ x 9¹³⁄₁₆ in.

The Corcoran Gallery of Art; Gift of Kate Bunner
Plate 66

Three Sketches: "Lake in the Catskills, Fog Rising, Morning," "Lake in the Catskills, Morning, High Peak," and "In the Kaatskill Clove"

Pencil on pale blue paper, 1 and 2 August 1866
13¹³⁄₁₆ x 9¹³⁄₁₆ in.

The Corcoran Gallery of Art; Gift of Kate Bunner
Plate 67

Two Sketches: "Kaatskill Fall" and "In the Kaatskill Clove"

Pencil on white paper, 2 August 1866
13⅞ x 9¹³⁄₁₆ in.

The Corcoran Gallery of Art; Gift of Kate Bunner

Plate 66. Andrew Fisher Bunner, *Kaatskill Creek near the Falls*, 1 August 1866. Courtesy The Corcoran Gallery of Art.

Three Sketches: "Catskill Mountains, Round-Top in the Distance," "Catskills Looking North from Palenville," and "Round Top, Catskills, from the Road to Bracketts"

Pencil on paper, 4 August 1866
13¹³⁄₁₆ x 9⅞ in.

The Corcoran Gallery of Art; Gift of Kate Bunner
Plate 68

The landscape painter Andrew Fisher Bunner was born, raised, and spent most of his adult life in New York City. He exhibited two pen drawings at the American Institute of the City of New York in 1857. The fact that he does not seem to have exhibited any other works until the spring of 1865 suggests that for at least part of this time he was in the Union Army. Bunner was a member of the American Water Color Society and exhibited annually at the National Academy of Design from 1865 to 1870 and again from 1879 to 1896. He spent at least some of the years between 1870 and 1879 in Europe. In 1875, Bunner exhibited six paintings at the Chicago Interstate Industrial Exposition. Three of these paintings were of German or Swiss scenery, and Bunner listed his address as Munich. All known pencil drawings by Bunner were donated by his widow to The Corcoran Gallery of Art in 1902. Forty-three of the seventy-four sketchbook-style sheets document an 1866 sketching trip through Columbia, Greene, and Ulster Counties. Some of the sheets contain two or even three finely observed and

highly finished drawings. The ensemble is an impressive record of a summer of intense labor.[1]

Like other artists who spent the summer or autumn in the Clove, Bunner was amassing drawings that he would work up into finished paintings over the winter. In the spring following his 1866 trip to the mid Hudson Valley, Bunner exhibited paintings of *Esopus Creek* and a scene *In the Catskill* at the National Academy of Design.

Although none of the sheets contain any information as to who if anyone Bunner was traveling with, they reveal that he spent the summer moving from one mid Hudson Valley village to another. The earliest drawings date from early June, when Bunner was in the area of the Columbia County city of Hudson. Bunner remained in Columbia County until late July, at which time he crossed the Hudson into Greene County. The earliest of Bunner's fifteen Greene County views was done in Kaaterskill Clove on 31 July. By 3 August he had been up to the Kaaterskill Falls and had already made his way back down the Clove to Palenville. By 8 August he was in the picturesque Ulster County town of West Hurley. It seems that except for trips to the neighboring towns of Shandakan and Marbletown, Bunner stayed in West Hurley until September or October.

Plate 67. Andrew Fisher Bunner, *Three Sketches: "Lake in the Catskills, Fog Rising, Morning," "Lake in the Catskills, Morning, High Peak," and "In the Kaatskill Clove,"* 1 and 2 August 1866. Courtesy The Corcoran Gallery of Art.

Plate 68. Andrew Fisher Bunner, *Three Sketches: "Catskill Mountains, Round-Top in the Distance," "Catskills Looking North from Palenville," and "Round Top, Catskills, from the Road to Bracketts,"* 4 August 1866. Courtesy The Corcoran Gallery of Art.

All of Bunner's surviving drawings are precisely detailed, but the Greene County views are especially so. In large part this seems to be the result of his decision to squeeze multiple views onto a restricted surface. Unlike the Greene County views, almost all of the Columbia and Ulster County views are drawn one to a sheet. The fact that Bunner's sheets became increasingly crowded during his stay in Kaaterskill Clove—culminating in a two-sided sheet containing six views—suggests that his decision to put multiple views on one sheet was motivated not by aesthetic considerations, but by the fact that he was running out of blank paper.

Although it seems that Bunner's immediate motive for leaving the Clove so quickly was because he had run out of paper, he could easily have gone—or could even have sent—to the village of Catskill for a new sketchbook; his strikingly short visit thus seems to have resulted from some other circumstance. Perhaps, like George Inness, Winslow Homer, and a number of other post-Civil War artists who worked in the Catskills but avoided the Clove and the area around the Mountain House, Bunner was put off either by the number of tourists or the familiarity of the often-painted sites.

1. The most important source of biographical information on Bunner is Richard Koke, *American Landscape and Genre Paintings in the New-York Historical Society,* (New York: New-York Historical Society, 1982), 91. Koke based his short account on obituaries published in the New York *Times* and *Tribune.* Although Bunner's 1866 tour of the mid Hudson region may have been the first time he had visited Greene or Ulster Counties, he had been to Columbia County before. In the spring of 1866, he had exhibited a view of *Clavarack Creek, Columbia Co., N.Y.* at the National Academy of Design.

FREDERIC EDWIN CHURCH

1826-1900

Sunset, Hudson River (Scene on Catskill Creek, New York)

Oil on canvas, 1847
21½ x 29¾ in.

Washington County Museum of Fine Arts, Hagerstown, Maryland
Plate 69

The Van Vechten House, Catskill, New York

Oil on canvas, 1847
22⅛ x 30¼ in.

New York State Office of Parks, Recreation and Historic Preservation, Olana State Historic Site
Plate 70

Morning, Looking East over the Hudson Valley from the Catskill Mountains

Oil on canvas, 1848
18 x 24 in.

Albany Institute of History and Art; Gift of Catherine Gansevoort Lansing
Plate 31

Above the Clouds at Sunrise

Oil on canvas, 1849
27¼ x 40¼ in.

The Warner Collection of the Gulf States Paper Corporation, Tuscaloosa, Alabama
Plate 32

Mill, near Catskill, New York

Oil on paperboard, c. 1865
14 x 24 in.

Cooper-Hewitt Museum, Smithsonian Institution's National Museum of Design
Plate 71

Plate 69. Frederic Edwin Church, *Sunset, Hudson River,* 1847.
Courtesy Washington County (MD) Museum of Fine Arts.

Plate 70. Frederic Edwin Church, *The Van Vechten House,
Catskill, New York,* 1847. Courtesy New York State Office of
Parks, Recreation and Historic Preservation, Olana State
Historic Site.

The landscape painter Frederic Edwin Church was
born in Hartford, Connecticut, in 1826. The son of a
well-to-do businessman, Church exhibited an early
interest in landscape painting. Although Church's parents
were distressed by their son's desire to become a painter,
they bowed to his wishes and in May 1844 arranged for
him to study with Thomas Cole. In 1844, Cole was living
in Catskill and was generally recognized as the most
important painter of landscapes working in the United
States. Church was the first pupil he had ever accepted.
Church moved from Hartford to Catskill in early June
1844 and lived and studied with Cole for two years.
During these years, Church seems to have become
especially close to Cole's son Theodore, who appears in
numerous of Church's early pencil drawings and in his
1844 oil *Twilight among the Mountains* (Olana State
Historic Site). Church returned to Hartford by the fall of
1846 but promptly left again in order to set up a studio in
New York City. His talent was quickly and widely recognized. In 1847, he sold at least four paintings to the
American Art Union. In 1849, he sold eight paintings to

Plate 71. Frederic Edwin Church, *Mill, near Catskill, New York*, c. 1865. Courtesy Cooper-Hewitt Museum.

the Art Union and was elected an Associate member of the National Academy of Design. In 1850, he sold eight more paintings to the Art Union and became a full member of the National Academy. He was then twenty-three years old.

Surviving pencil drawings establish that Church returned to the Catskills in September 1847 and October 1848.[1] From 1849 until 1860, Church traveled the Northeast United States and South America in search of scenery more spectacular and less well known than the Catskills. He does not seem to have done any work in the Catskills during this time. In the months preceding his marriage in June 1860, Church and his fiancée decided to make their home in the Hudson Valley. They bought property on a large hill on the east bank of the Hudson River just north of the village of Catskill. Church seems to have remained friendly with the Coles during the 1850s, because he and his bride lived with them during the summer of 1860 while they awaited the completion of their new home across the river. The Churches moved into their cottage in September 1860. By 1867, Church had enlarged his local holdings, and, by 1870, he had begun to build the mansion his wife dubbed Olana. Church and his family moved into Olana in 1872; he died there in 1900.[2]

1. These drawings are in the collection of Olana State Historic Site, Hudson, New York.

2. Theodore L. Cuyler, "A Sabbath on the Catskills," in [Murdoch, ed.], *Scenery of the Catskill Mountains*, 48; Tuckerman, *Book of the Artists*, 373-376; David C. Huntington, *The Landscapes of Frederic Edwin Church* (New York: George Braziller, 1966), 21-34, 114-125; Franklin Kelly and Gerald L. Carr, *The Early Landscapes of Frederic Edwin Church, 1845-1854* (Fort Worth, TX: Amon Carter Museum, 1987), 1-4, 31-51.

JOHN H. COCKS

c. 1849-1938

The Stage Coach in the Catskills

Oil on canvas, 1880
36 x 38 in.

George Walter Vincent Smith Art Museum, Springfield, Massachusetts
Plate 72

John H. Cocks was born in Manhattan but spent most of his early years in Brooklyn. As a young man, he exhibited genre scenes at the Brooklyn Art Association in 1872 and 1875 and annually from 1877 to 1880. In 1880, one of his genre paintings, *The Arrival*, was hung in the annual exhibition of the National Academy of Design. In the catalogue to this exhibition, Cocks is listed as living at 119 St. James Street, Brooklyn. *The Stage Coach in the Catskills*, dated 1880, seems to be a depiction of the arrival of a stagecoach in the Greene County village of Cairo. Although one cannot be sure, it seems likely that *Stage Coach in the Catskills* is the painting that appeared in the 1880 NAD exhibition.[1]

On the right side of the stagecoach are the words "Cairo East." Cairo is a small village located near the juncture of Catskill Creek and the Shingle Kill, about six miles upstream from Leeds and about ten miles upstream from the village of Catskill. Like many of the smaller villages in the general area of the Mountain House, Cairo had been relatively unaffected by antebellum tourism. By 1880, however, the village had begun to attract a significant number of summer visitors. By that time, city people who boarded in Cairo were likely to have been more concerned with the cost of their lodgings, the quality of the food, and the coolness of the breezes than with the sublimity of the scenery. Cairo became even more popular in 1882 when it became the northern terminus for Charles Beach's Catskill Mountain Railway.[2]

In *The Stage Coach in the Catskills*, Cocks depicts the arrival of a new group of summer visitors. The house on the left seems to be a boarding house. The stagecoach driver—probably a local resident—ignores everything that goes on between the two groups of summer visitors. The three girls in the yard eye the new arrivals. The man on the stage eyes the girls in the yard as one of his companions reaches her arm around him in a possessive gesture.

Although all six of the young people are outwardly calm, the extravagant movements both of the pictorially central horses and of the two birds in the lower right-hand corner suggest that their demeanor is a mask concealing passions that they either already feel or at least hope to feel before the end of their vacations. Unlike the

Plate 72. John H. Cocks, *The Stage Coach in the Catskills*, 1880. Courtesy George Walter Vincent Smith Art Museum.

tourists in Cole's *A View of the Two Lakes and Mountain House, Catskill Mountains, Morning* (plate 77) or George Harvey's *Catskill Mountain House* (plate 24), none of the young people in Cocks's painting seem to have traveled to the Catskills to experience the wilderness or God's presence in the landscape. Indeed, although the village of Cairo lies almost in the shadow of Black and North Mountains, Cocks has chosen to show neither of them. Like the young people in his painting, he appears to have been interested not in what T. Addison Richards called the "romance of American scenery," but in romance, plain and simple. While staying in Cairo, these young people might fish or go for an occasional walk in the woods, but what they most want is the adventure of love. They came to court.

Cocks moved from Brooklyn to Plainfield, New Jersey, in 1888. According to his only known obituary, he worked both as a sculptor and as an illustrator for *Harper's* and *Scribner's* magazines. He died in Plainfield in 1938.[3]

1. The G. W. V. Smith Museum acquired the painting from its principal benefactor, G. W. V. Smith, who bought it at the Abbe sale held in Springfield, Massachusetts, on 3 November 1922.

2. On the changing focus of mountain tourism in the years following the Civil War see Evers, *The Catskills*, 481-487, 510-519, 532-560, and the essays by Elizabeth Cromley, Betsy Blackmar, and Neil Harris in The Architectural League of New York, *Resorts of the Catskills*.

3. Cocks's obituary appeared in *The [Brooklyn] Eagle*, 29 January 1938. I would like to thank Dr. Clark Marlor of Brooklyn for bringing this obituary to my attention.

SARAH COLE

1805-1857

A View of the Catskill Mountain House

Oil on canvas, 1848
15⅛ x 23⅜ in.

Albany Institute of History and Art
Plate 36

The youngest child of James and Mary Cole and the sister of the landscape painter Thomas Cole, Sarah Cole was born in Lancashire, England. In 1818, James Cole moved his family to the United States, first to Philadelphia, then west to Steubenville, Ohio. Of his seven sisters—he had no brothers—Thomas seems to have been closest with Sarah, who was the only sibling younger than himself. After the failure of his business in 1822, James Cole moved his family to Pittsburgh and then to New York City in late 1824. Thomas and Sarah followed their parents to New York City in April 1825.

Cole family papers in the Albany Institute of History and Art suggest that Sarah Cole lived in New York City for most of the rest of her life, although she seems to have spent time in Baltimore. After her brother's death on 11 February 1848, she traveled to Catskill, New York, in order to be with his widow. Although we do not know when she started to paint, surviving exhibition records suggest that she did not begin to show her work until the fall of 1848. Thomas Cole did not leave his family in a very secure financial position; it therefore seems possible that Sarah Cole began to exhibit more out of need than ambition. She exhibited at the National Academy of Design (1848, 1850-1852), the Maryland Historical Society (1849), and the American Art Union (1848-1852). All of the exhibited works were landscapes. Sarah Cole died in Catskill, New York, in 1857.[1]

A View of the Catskill Mountain House and a view of *Mount Aetna* are the only currently located works by Sarah Cole. Both descended through the Cole family and are now in the collections of the Albany Institute of History and Art. Both are copies of paintings by her brother. The back of the canvas of the first of these is inscribed "A View of the Catskill Mountain House copied from a picture by T. Cole by S. Cole, 1848."

Like Sarah Cole's copy, Thomas's original is a view of the Mountain House from the road. The two works are virtually identical in size. The handling and coloring of Sarah's copy are comparatively crude. Thomas's original (in a private collection) is not dated, but it shows the Mountain House as it appeared after Charles L. Beach's renovation of the front facade and therefore dates from after 1845. Thomas Cole's painting descended in the Beach family until it was sold to the present owner in 1952.[2]

1. The best source of biographical information is Chris Petteys, et al., *Dictionary of Women Artists: An International Dictionary of Women Artists Born before 1900* (Boston: G. K. Hall, 1985). Supplemental information can be found in Dunlap, *History of the Rise and Progress*, 351-359; Noble, *Life and Works of Thomas Cole*, 4-5, 32, 248; " 'Thomas Cole Is No More': A Letter from John Falconer to Jasper Cropsey February 24, 1848," *The American Art Journal* 15 (1983): 74-76; " 'The Brushes That He Painted With That Last Day Are There...': Jasper F. Cropsey's Letter to his Wife, Describing Thomas Cole's Home and Studio, July, 1850," *The American Art Journal* 16 (Summer 1984): 78-82; and Parry, "Thomas Cole's Early Career," in Nygren, ed., *Views and Visions*, 162-167.

2. Thomas Cole's original (oil on canvas, 15 x 23 inches) is signed, lower center, "TC." It is not dated. The back of the canvas is marked "Edward Descheaux." Thomas Cole's painting is described but not illustrated in the exhibition catalogue *Thomas Cole (1801-1848): One Hundred Years Later* (Hartford, CT: The Wadsworth Atheneum, 1948), where it is listed as item 13. It is reproduced as figure 96 in Richardson, *American Romantic Painting*. Concerning Beach's renovation of the Mountain House, see Van Zandt, *The Catskill Mountain House*, 54-57, and Evers, *The Catskills*, 400-402. I would like to thank Professor Ellwood C. Parry III of the University of Arizona and Christine Robinson of the Albany Institute for sharing information included in this entry.

THOMAS COLE

1801-1848

Lake of Dead Trees—Catskill

Pencil on paper, c. 1825
6¾ x 10¼ in. (irregular)

The Detroit Institute of Arts; Founders Society Purchase, William H. Murphy Fund

Study for Lake with Dead Trees

Pencil on paper, c. 1825
6¼ x 9 in.

Alexander Gallery, New York

Study for Catskill Lake (Lake with Dead Trees)

Oil on composition board, c. 1825
7 x 11 in.

Alexander Gallery, New York

Lake with Dead Trees (Catskill Lake)

Oil on canvas, 1825
27 x 34 in.

Allen Memorial Art Museum, Oberlin College; Gift of Charles F. Olney
Plate 12

Plate 73. Thomas Cole, *Falls at Catskill*, c. 1828-1829. Courtesy Albany Institute of History and Art.

Double Waterfall—Kaaterskill Falls

Pencil, charcoal, black and white crayon on paper,
c. 1825-1826
16½ x 14⅝ in.

The Detroit Institute of Arts; Founders Society Purchase,
William H. Murphy Fund
Plate 13

Kaaterskill Falls

Pencil on paper, c. 1825-1826
14 x 10⅜ in. (irregular)

The Detroit Institute of Arts; Founders Society Purchase,
William H. Murphy Fund

Falls of the Kaaterskill

Pencil, charcoal, black and white crayon on paper,
c. 1825-1826
14⅛ x 17⅞ in. (irregular)

The Detroit Institute of Arts; Founders Society Purchase,
William H. Murphy Fund

Falls of Kaaterskill (Landscape, Catterskill Fall, Catskill Mountain)

Oil on canvas, 1826
43 x 36 in.

The Warner Collection of the Gulf States Paper
Corporation, Tuscaloosa, Alabama
Plate 2

View from the Top of Kaaterskill Falls

Oil on canvas, 1826
31⅛ x 41⅛ in.

The Detroit Institute of Arts; Founders Society Purchase,
Dexter M. Ferry, Jr., Fund
Plate 14

Stony Gap, Kaaterskill Clove

Oil on panel, c. 1826
17⅞ x 25⅜ in.

Joslyn Art Museum, Omaha, Nebraska;
Mr. and Mrs. Edwin S. Miller Bequest Fund, 1951
Plate 15

Scene from "Rip Van Winkle"
Pencil and ink on paper, n.d.
9⁵⁄₁₆ x 13¹⁄₁₆ in.

Albany Institute of History and Art

Rip Van Winkle

Pencil and ink on paper, n.d.
7½ x 12¼ in.

Albany Institute of History and Art
Plate 8

View in the Catskills
Pencil on paper, n.d.
11⁵⁄₁₆ x 17½ in. (irregular)

The Detroit Institute of Arts; Founders Society Purchase,
William H. Murphy Fund

Rocky Conglomerate, South Mt. Catskill

Pencil on paper, n.d.
8⅜ x 10⅝ in. (irregular)
Inscribed: "From South Mountain"

The Detroit Institute of Arts; Founders Society Purchase,
William H. Murphy Fund

Plate 74. Thomas Cole, *Distant View of Round Top, Catskill Scenery*, c. 1833. Courtesy Albany Institute of History and Art.

Memorandum of Mists Rising after a Thunderstorm from the Catskill Mountain

Pen and brown ink over pencil on paper, n.d.
8¼ x 12¾ in.

The Detroit Institute of Arts; Founders Society Purchase, William H. Murphy Fund

Catskill Mountain House

Pencil on paper, c. 1827
10⅛ x 14⅛ in. (irregular)

The Detroit Institute of Arts; Founders Society Purchase, William H. Murphy Fund

Autumn in the Catskills

Oil on canvas, 1827
18⅝ x 25⁷⁄₁₆ in.

Arnot Art Museum, Elmira, New York
Plate 16

North Lake and Catskill Mountain House

Oil on canvas, c. 1827-1829
28½ x 36½ in.

Alexander Gallery, New York

Falls at Catskill

Lithograph, c. 1828-1829
(Drawn on stone by Cole, probably printed by Anthony Imbert)
10½ x 8½ in.

Albany Institute of History and Art
Plate 73

Kaaterskill Falls

Engraving by Fenner, Sears & Company, 1831
4¼ x 6¹⁄₁₆ in.

Originally published in J.H. Hinton, ed., *The History and Topography of the United States*, vol. 2 (1832)

Mr. and Mrs. R. M. Decker
Plate 26

View of the Cattskill Mountain House, N.Y.

Engraving by Fenner, Sears & Company, 1831
5¼ x 4¼ in.

Originally published in Hinton, ed., *The History and Topography of the United States*, vol. 2

Mr. and Mrs. R. M. Decker
Plate 20

Distant View of Round Top, Catskill Scenery

Oil on canvas, c. 1833
17 x 25 in.

Albany Institute of History and Art
Plate 74

North Mountain and Catskill Creek

Oil on canvas, mounted on wooden panel, 1838
28 x 38 in.

Yale University Art Gallery; Gift of Anne Osborn Prentice
Plate 75

Plate 75. Thomas Cole, *North Mountain and Catskill Creek*, 1838. Courtesy Yale University Art Gallery.

Plate 76. Thomas Cole, *Study for A View of the Two Lakes and Mountain House, Catskill Mountains, Morning*, c. 1844. Courtesy Hirschl & Adler Galleries, Inc.

Study for a View of the Two Lakes and Mountain House, Catskill Mountains, Morning

Oil on canvas, c. 1844
8¾ x 10¾ in.

Hirschl & Adler Galleries, Inc., New York
Plate 76

A View of the Two Lakes and Mountain House, Catskill Mountains, Morning

Oil on canvas, 1844
36¼ x 54 in.

The Brooklyn Museum; Dick S. Ramsay Fund, 52.16
Plate 77

Long Dock or Catskill Landing on Hudson River

Pencil on paper, 1847
6⅜ x 10½ in.

Albany Institute of History and Art
Plate 78

Palenville, Clove Valley, Catskill Mountains

Pencil and ink on paper, c. 1847
7¹⁄₁₆ x 11¼ in.

Albany Institute of History and Art; Gift of Florence Vincent Cole

The only son and next-to-youngest child of a woolen manufacturer, the landscape painter Thomas Cole was born in Bolton-le-Moor, Lancashire, England, in 1801. After the failure of his father's business, Cole learned to engrave as an apprentice to a maker of calico print designs. In the spring of 1818, the Coles sailed from Liverpool for Philadelphia and arrived on 3 July 1818. Cole quickly found work as a wood engraver and remained in Philadelphia; his parents departed for Steubenville, Ohio, the following September. In January 1819, Cole made a brief trip from Philadelphia to Saint Eustatius in the West Indies. The following autumn, he joined his family in Steubenville, where his sisters had opened a girls' school and his father had begun to manufacture wallpaper. In addition to mixing paints, designing wallpaper patterns, and cutting the woodblocks used to print wallpaper, Cole received some training in the use of oil paints from an itinerant portrait painter in Steubenville and began to offer instruction in both drawing and painting. In February 1822, he left Steubenville to make his fortune as an itinerant painter of portraits. The family wallpaper manufactory failed in the fall of 1822; Cole's family then moved to Pittsburgh, where his father began to manufacture floor cloth. Cole moved from Ohio to Pittsburgh in the spring of 1823. While living with his family in Pittsburgh, Cole made careful pencil drawings along the banks of the Monongahela and painted a few landscapes and portraits.

In November 1823, Cole moved back to Philadelphia and received permission to study in the Pennsylvania Academy of the Fine Arts. There, he gained a firsthand acquaintance with the landscapes of the Philadelphia artists Thomas Birch and Thomas Doughty. Cole moved from Philadelphia to New York City in April 1825. He made his first trip to the Catskills late the following summer, and his work was "discovered" by Col. John Trumbull, William Dunlap, and Asher B. Durand in late October. Cole first exhibited at the American Academy of Fine Arts in December 1825. The following May he helped found the National Academy of Design and exhibited both at the first exhibition of the new National Academy and at the older American Academy.

Cole spent the summer and early fall of 1826 in the Catskills. He may have returned to the area during the summer of 1827 or 1828, but it seems doubtful. If he did return, it was for no more than a brief visit. On 1 June 1829, Cole left New York for what turned into a three-and-a-half-year residence in Europe. Between 1825 and his departure for Europe, Cole painted numerous views of the Catskills, including *Lake with Dead Trees (Catskill Lake)* (1825; plate 12), *Falls of Kaaterskill (Landscape, Catterskill Fall, Catskill Mountain)* (1826; plate 2), *View from the Top of Kaaterskill Falls* (1826; plate 14), *Stony Gap, Kaaterskill Clove* (c. 1826; plate 15), and *Autumn in the Catskills* (1827; plate 16).[1]

Cole returned to New York in November 1832. He returned to the Catskills the following June and every year thereafter until 1836.[2] In 1836, Cole bought the John A. Thompson estate located just northeast of the village of Catskill, married a local girl named Maria Bartow, and became a permanent resident of the village. Except for his 1841-1842 trip to Europe, Cole lived in Catskill until his death in February 1848.

When Cole first visited the Catskills in the late 1820s, he painted at least two views of the mountains as seen from Catskill Creek east of the village of Catskill, but he had been most interested in the wilder scenery in the area of the Mountain House and in the surrounding Cloves.[3] After 1832, almost all of Cole's paintings of the Catskills are of the view from Catskill Creek. Indeed, by the late 1830s, he seems to have to come to rely on the ready marketability of his views of the Catskills from Catskill Creek as a way of subsidizing his other work.

Cole returned to the subject in 1833 when he painted the oil sketch *Catskill Scene* (Kennedy Galleries), *View on Catskill Creek* (The New-York Historical Society), and the large composition *Catskill Scenery* (The Saint Louis Art Museum). The oil sketch *Distant View of Round Top, Catskill Scenery* (plate 74) is closely related to the *View on Catskill Creek* and probably dates from about the same time. The following year Cole painted *View on Catskill Creek, New York* (1834; The New-York Historical Society), and in 1837 he painted his largest version of the scene (thirty-nine by sixty-three inches)—*View on the Catskill, Early Autumn* (The Metropolitan Museum of Art). Both *Catskill Scene* (1833) and *Distant View of Round Top, Catskill Scenery* (c. 1833) remained in Cole's studio until his death, and he seems to have used them in the composition of the 1838 *North Mountain and Catskill Creek* (plate 75).[4] Cole continued to work variations on the theme in the 1840s, when he painted *Sunset in the Catskills* (1841; Museum of Fine Arts, Boston), *Mill Dam on the Catskill Creek* (1843; private collection), *Settler's Home in the Catskills* (1843; Hirschl & Adler Galleries), *River in the Catskills* (1843; Museum of Fine Arts, Boston), and *Catskill Creek* (1845; The New-York Historical Society). Frederic Church worked his own variation on his teacher's theme in his *Sunset, Hudson River (Scene on Catskill Creek, New York)* (plate 69).

Although Cole rarely painted the mountain top after 1829, he continued to visit the area around the Mountain House and the Cloves.[5] The only major view of the mountain top he painted after 1829 was the magisterial *A View of the Two Lakes and Mountain House, Catskill Mountains, Morning* (1844), which he sent to the National Academy of Design in May 1845. Like William H. Bartlett's 1838 *The Two Lakes and the Mountain House on the Catskills* (plate 37) and Jasper Cropsey's 1855 *Catskill Mountain House* (Minneapolis Institute of Arts), Cole's painting is a view from Sunset Rock looking south.

Plate 77. Thomas Cole, *A View of the Two Lakes and Mountain House, Catskill Mountains, Morning,* 1844. Courtesy The Brooklyn Museum.

Reviews of the painting were mixed. According to the reviewer in *The Anglo-American,* "The scene is singularly romantic, particularly that of two lakes near the summit of a lofty mountain, and the white vapor here and there running in lines and apparently cutting portions of the hills off from the rest: and the diminished vallies in the back ground well express the elevation of the mountain house, but the scene loses some of its beauty from the quantity of wood which monopolises the canvass. This however is not the artist's fault."[6] The reviewer in *The New World* took a rather different approach: "Cole's *A View of the Two Lakes and Mountain House, Catskill Mountains, Morning* is the best he has placed on the Academy's walls this season; but it has not enough of his peculiar merit to satisfy an admiration which has dreamed itself into enthusiasm over his *Voyage of Life.* The mountains are somewhat mannered, and the whole is slightly painted. But his boldness and vigor are here apparent, as well as his wondrous skill at amassing the details, for it is a subject which not another member of the Academy could, with impunity, venture to handle."[7]

Plate 78. Thomas Cole, *Long Dock or Catskill Landing on Hudson River,* 1847. Courtesy Albany Institute of History and Art.

1. The compositional history and iconography of these paintings are discussed in the essay. The most important nineteenth-century sources of information on Cole are Dunlap, *History of the Rise and Progress*, vol. 2, 350-367; William Cullen Bryant, *Funeral Oration, Occasioned by the Death of Thomas Cole* (New York: D. Appleton & Co., 1848); Noble, *Life and Works of Thomas Cole*; and Tuckerman, *Book of the Artists*. The most complete account of Cole's early career is Parry, "Thomas Cole's Early Career," in Nygren, ed., *Views and Visions*, 160-187. Useful supplemental material is in John K. Howat, "A Picturesque Site in the Catskills," 16-29, 63-65.

2. This date is established by the sheet inscribed "Catskill. Sunset after a showery day. June 14, 1833" in a sketchbook Cole began in Italy in 1832 (Detroit Institute of Arts #39.566 and on microfilm at the Archives of American Art).

3. Cole's earliest known paintings of the Catskills from Catskill Creek are *Near Catskill Village* (1827; private collection) and the *View near Catskills* (1828-1829; Kennedy Galleries). The first is reproduced in Merritt, *Thomas Cole*, Figure 10 (64). The later is reproduced as plate 136 in Parry, "Thomas Cole's Early Career," 185.

4. The close relationship between the two sketches and the Yale painting was pointed out by David Steinberg in his article "Thomas Cole's *North Mountain and Catskill Creek*," Yale University Art Gallery *Bulletin* 39 (Winter 1986): 24-29.

5. Some of these visits are described in Cole, *Collected Essays and Prose Sketches*.

6. *The Anglo-American* 5 (26 April 1845): 21.

7. *The New World* 10 (10 May 1845): 297.

JASPER FRANCIS CROPSEY

1823-1900

View in the Catskills

Pencil on tan paper, 5 July 1850
4^{15}/$_{16}$ x 9^{15}/$_{16}$ in.

Verso inscribed: "Outline of Catskill Mountain July 5, 1850"

Newington-Cropsey Foundation

View of the Catskill Mountain House from Old Mountain Road

Pencil on tan paper, 22 June 1852
8^{7}/$_{8}$ x 11^{3}/$_{16}$ in.

Newington-Cropsey Foundation
Plate 79

Plate 79. Jasper Francis Cropsey, *View of the Catskill Mountain House from Old Mountain Road*, 22 June 1852. Courtesy Newington-Cropsey Foundation.

Plate 80. Jasper Francis Cropsey, *Pine on South Mountain, Catskill*, 16 October 1855. Courtesy Newington-Cropsey Foundation.

Pine on South Mountain, Catskill

Pencil on buff paper, 16 October 1855
11⅜ x 9 in.

Newington-Cropsey Foundation
Plate 80

Tree – Probably on South Mountain

Pencil on tan paper, 16 October 1855
11⅛ x 9 in.

Newington-Cropsey Foundation

Three Sketches: Hudson Valley from the Catskills; Catskill Mountain House; Tree

Pencil on buff paper, c. 1850-1855
10⅞ x 8½ in.

Newington-Cropsey Foundation

Catskill Creek

Oil on canvas, c. 1850
18⅜ x 27¼ in.

National Museum of American Art,
Smithsonian Institution

The stretcher is inscribed "Catskill Creek, Autumn, J. F. Cropsey 1850" and carries an American Art Union label.
Plate 81

Tree Study

Oil on canvas, 1855
15 x 11 in.

Newington-Cropsey Foundation
Plate 82

Jasper F. Cropsey was born on his father's farm at Rossville, Staten Island, New York, on 18 February 1823. In 1837, he was apprenticed to a Manhattan architect. He completed his apprenticeship in 1842. Although Cropsey quickly found work as an architect, he just as quickly abandoned it in order to pursue a career as a painter of landscapes. The first oil painting he is known to have exhibited was an untitled landscape shown at the 1842 exhibition of the American Institute of the City of New York. He first exhibited at the National Academy of Design in 1843 and was elected an Associate in 1844. Cropsey was in Europe from May 1847 to the summer of 1849 and again from 1856 to 1863. He was elected a full member of the National Academy of Design in 1851. In 1866, Cropsey bought forty-five acres in Warwick, New York, where he built himself a twenty-nine-room mansion he called Aladdin. The view north from Aladdin was of Mounts Adam and Eve with the Catskills in the distance. The expense of building and maintaining Aladdin eventually exceeded Cropsey's income, and in 1884 the house and furnishings were taken by creditors. After the sale of the Warwick mansion, Cropsey moved to a cottage in Hastings-on-Hudson, New York. He lived in Hastings until his death in 1900.

As one would expect of a midcentury landscape painter living in New York City, Cropsey visited the Catskills often. Surprisingly, however, he painted relatively few views of the area. Cropsey's first recorded trip to the Catskills was in the summer of 1844, when he drew scenes on Rondout, Esopus, and Goodbeer-Kiln Creeks in Ulster and Sullivan Counties.[1] In the fall of 1844, Cropsey exhibited a *View on Esopus Creek* at the American Art Union. The following spring, he exhibited at least three Catskill scenes—*Twilight, View in Sullivan County, View on Esopus Creek,* and a view of the *New-York and Saugherties White Lead Works, on Esopus Creek,*

Saugherties, New-York—at the National Academy of Design. This last painting was listed as being owned by James McCullough and seems to have been the original for the colored lithograph of the McCullough lead mill published by John Endicott. It seems probable that the painting of McCullough's mill was a commission which Cropsey used to support his two 1844 trips to the area.[2]

Cropsey was most active in the Catskills in the years between his two trips to Europe. He may have made a brief visit to the area of the Mountain House in late August 1849,[3] but his next well-documented visit was in early July 1850. On 2 July or—probably—3 July, Cropsey traveled from New Jersey to the village of Catskill, where he stayed with Thomas Cole's widow Maria, visited the late artist's studio, and made a few quick sketches before departing for Staten Island on 5 July. The tone of Cropsey's 7 July letter to his wife suggests that he had not met Mrs. Cole previously and that the trip had been intended as a sort of pilgrimage to the haunts of a departed master.[4] Whatever Cropsey's motives for his July visit, he returned for a somewhat longer stay the following September. From information contained in his 24 September letter to his wife, we know that Cropsey traveled from New York to Catskill on Friday, 21 September. In Catskill, Cropsey stayed with the Reverend Louis Legrand Noble, who was already at work on his biography of Thomas Cole. Cropsey spent Saturday visiting Catskill friends. Indeed, his letter makes clear that he liked the people so much that he was thinking of renting a house in town. On Sunday, Cropsey went to Episcopal services, had lunch, and left for John Rusk's boarding house in Kaaterskill Clove. At Rusk's he found the artist Christopher Pearse Cranch and learned that Asher B. Durand had been at Rusk's until the previous week and was expected back shortly.[5] Although we do not know how long Cropsey actually stayed at Rusk's, he closed his letter by telling his wife that he would probably leave on Saturday, 29 September.

Cropsey began his 24 September letter by giving his wife an extended description of the Clove. This description makes clear that this was Cropsey's first visit to the area and that his wife had never seen it. Cropsey's letter begins,

My dear Mary
I arrived here last evening about 6 oclock from Catskill, I say here, that is I am in the great ravine which breaks the continuity of the chain. It is south of the Mountain House about 1 mile, and is a very wild and picturesque gorge; down it rushes the cauterskill creek, which when swollen by heavy rains is a furious stream, could you but see the great rocks that have been twirled over and over, and the immense trunks of trees that have been bourn on its surface, you would think it not only furious but terrible, nature or rather the author of nature, however, has shut it up within its bounds,

which are high and everlasting hills, and here it must roar and tumble and answer the purposes of the great author. It is on this stream dear Mary that Mr Kensett made those beautiful studies which were in the exhibition, that one which you admired so much, today I have seen its original, but that prettyness which Mr K. gave it is scarcely in the original.[6] It is wild and grand and has almost a soul, so much has the Creator displayed his handy work in it. Mr K. "Catskill Picture" which you remember in the exhibition is from this place. But now I dislike the picture more than ever because he has so changed it from the original and deprived it of its greatest features viz. sublimity. But dear, I have scarce time to write in this critical, descriptive, and analectic manner, so I will give you other matter.[7]

Cropsey produced at least two Catskill landscapes in the months following this trip. At the fall 1850 exhibition of the American Art Union, he showed a painting of *Catskill Creek* (plate 81), now owned by the National Museum of American Art. The geographical subject of the painting is uncertain and may be a composite. The background peak seems to be Round Top as seen from North Mountain.[8] At the spring 1851 exhibition of the National Academy of Design, Cropsey showed a painting of a storm in Kaaterskill Clove. This was probably the melodramatic *Storm in the Wilderness* now in the collections of The Cleveland Museum of Art.[9] Cropsey is known to have returned to the Catskills in late June 1852 (plate 79), in September or October 1853, and in mid-October 1855 (plate 80).[10] By late December 1855, he had completed at least three major paintings of scenes associated with the Mountain House: a view of the *Catskill Mountain House* commissioned by his Chicago patron James Edgar; a view of the *Falls of the Kauterskill* commissioned by his New York patron P. R. Strong, and a view of *Catskill Mountain* commissioned by another Chicago collector named E. H. Sheldon. The first of these paintings is now in the collections of The Minneapolis Institute of Art. The other two are currently unlocated. Although it is impossible to establish when Cropsey started these works, his account book shows that all of them were finished in the late fall of 1855.[11] Cropsey left on his second European trip in June 1856. Although he later painted numerous views of the Catskills as seen from the area of Aladdin or from the east bank of the Hudson, he does not seem to have completed any other paintings of the well-known views associated with the Mountain House.[12]

Plate 81. Jasper Francis Cropsey, *Catskill Creek*, c. 1850. Courtesy National Museum of American Art, Smithsonian Institution.

1. On 24 May Cropsey did a pencil drawing of *James McCullough's Leadmill on the Esopus Creek Saugerties Ulster Co. N.Y.* (The Corcoran Gallery of Art). On 26 June he did a pencil drawing of a *Scene on Goodbeer-Kiln Creek Sullivan Co.* (Newington-Cropsey Foundation). On 27 July he did a pencil drawing of *A View on the Roundout [sic] near naponock Uls. Co. N.Y.* (Newington-Cropsey Foundation). Cropsey seems to have left the area sometime after he did the Rondout Creek drawing, but he returned in September with a letter from the dealer John P. Ridner introducing him to Asher B. Durand. On this letter, see *Jasper F. Cropsey 1823-1900* (Washington, DC: National Collection of Fine Arts, 1970), 64.

2. *Jasper F. Cropsey 1823-1900*, 63-64.

3. Cropsey returned from Europe in late July or early August 1849. He quickly left New York on a sketching trip to the White Mountains. He returned to New York by way of Vermont, Lakes Champlain and George, and the Hudson River. The Museum of Fine Arts, Boston owns an indistinctly dated pencil drawing of the *Catskill Mountain House* (#54.1623) which is related to the 1855 oil painting in the Minneapolis Institute of Art. The last two digits of the date are partly illegible, but the date seems to be 28 August of 1848, 1849, 1868, or 1869. Cropsey was still in Europe in 1848, and both 1868 and 1869 seem too late. If the drawing is indeed from 1849, then Cropsey must have made a *very* brief stop on his trip from New Hampshire back to New York. The only sources of information concerning this trip are Cropsey's pocket diary for 1849 (owned by the Newington-Cropsey Foundation) and a few dated pencil drawings.

4. This letter has been published as "'The Brushes That He Painted With That Last Day Are There...': Jasper F. Cropsey's Letter to his Wife Describing Thomas Cole's Home and Studio, July, 1850," 78-82.

5. Cranch had arrived at Rusk's on Friday, 14 September and did not finally leave until mid-October. Durand had arrived earlier in September and also stayed until mid-October. Information on their stay is to be found in Leonora Scott Cranch, *The Life and Letters of Christopher Pearse Cranch* (Boston: Houghton Mifflin Co., 1917), 179, Asher B. Durand's letters to his daughter Caroline (18 September 1850) and his son John (4 and 9 October 1850), and John Durand's 7 October 1850 letter to his father. The various Durand letters are all in the Durand Papers owned by the New York Public Library and on microfilm in the Archives of American Art.

6. At the spring 1850 National Academy of Design exhibition, Kensett showed a *Study of Rocks*, two works titled *Study from Nature*, and a painting of *Catskill Mountain Scenery*. None of these paintings are currently located.

7. Jasper Cropsey to Mary Cropsey, 24 September 1850, from a xerox supplied to the author by the Newington-Cropsey Foundation, Hastings-on-Hudson, New York.

8. The American Art Union Catalog described *Catskill Creek* as being "27 x 18 [inches]. An autumnal scene. The trees are nearly stripped of their foliage. Beyond the water rise hills, and in the sky are drifting clouds."

9. William S. Talbot makes this identification in both his dissertation, *Jasper F. Cropsey 1823-1900* (New York: Garland Publishing Inc., 1977), 88-89, and in the exhibition catalogue *Jasper F. Cropsey 1823-1900*, 73. In the 1851 NAD exhibition catalogue, the painting is listed as number 6, *The Cove*. We know that this title refers to a view of the Clove because of the detailed description of the painting in the *New York Tribune*, 21 April 1851, 5. This review was first noticed by Talbot, who used it and a similar description in Tuckerman, *Book of the Artists*, 539, to identify *The Cove* with both *Clove—A Storm Scene in the Catskill Mountains* (60 x 48 in.), which Cropsey sold to Tibbits in 1856, and *Storm in the Wilderness*. Although Talbot's identification still seems probable, it should be noted that in an 1865 list of paintings left in England, Cropsey listed a "48 x 60" painting titled *The Storm in the Catskill Mountains*. It is possible that this reference is to a different—now unidentified—painting, that Cropsey painted a second version of his original, or that he reacquired the 1851 painting sometime after its 1856 sale to Tibbits. A related, undated wash drawing now known as *Catskill Creek in Storm* is in the Museum of Fine Arts, Boston (#54.1663).

10. Both the Museum of Fine Arts in Boston and the Newington-Cropsey Foundation own pencil drawings of the Catskill Mountain House dated 22 June 1852. The Newington-Cropsey Foundation also owns a 25 June 1852 letter from Cropsey to his daughter Mary in which he explains that he and her mother had returned from the Catskills on the 24th. The 1853 visit is documented by a comment in Cropsey's 25 September 1853 letter to his student B. B. G. Stone and by his pencil drawing of the *Home and Studio of Thomas Cole, Catskill, New York*, which is inscribed 1853. Cropsey's letter to Stone is quoted in Campbell, "Benjamin Bellows Grant Stone," 26. Cropsey's drawing is reproduced in Kenneth W. Maddox, *An Unprejudiced Eye: The Drawings of Jasper F. Cropsey* (Yonkers, NY: The Hudson River Museum,

1979), 45. The 1855 visit is documented by the two 16 October 1855 pencil drawings included in this exhibition, the 16 October 1855 pencil drawing *Note to Summit of North Mt Catskill* in the Museum of Fine Arts, Boston, and the 17 October 1855 pencil drawing *Note to Catskill Falls*, also in the Museum of Fine Arts, Boston.

11. Cropsey's account book is in the Newington-Cropsey Foundation. *The Crayon* for 5 December 1855 (361) noted that "Mr. Cropsey, in addition to various studies from Nature made the past summer, has painted a view on the Catskills, taken from North Mountain, embracing the mountain-house and the lakes of the vicinity. The light of the picture is that of the early part of the day, and the character of the foliage autumnal. It is one of his most pleasing works. The picture is the property of a gentleman of Chicago." P. R. Strong exhibited the *Falls of the Kauterskill* at the National Academy of Design in 1859. *The Catskill Mountain House* was exhibited at the Chicago Exhibition of Fine Arts in 1859 and at the Northwestern Fair (Chicago) in 1863. Curiously, both times it was listed as being owned not by James Edgar, but by E. H. Sheldon. I have not found any exhibition record of the *Catskill Mountain* commissioned by E. H. Sheldon. Number 223 in Maria Cropsey's catalog *Of the Collection of Oil Paintings and Water Colors by the Gifted American Artist, the Late Jasper F. Cropsey* (New York: Silo Art Galleries, 1906) is an oil painting of *Kauterskill Falls*.

12. The only other Catskill title to appear in nineteenth-century exhibition records is *Vernon Valley, with Mountains Adam and Eve, and the Catskill Mountains in the distance, New Jersey* exhibited at the Northwestern Fair (Chicago) in June 1865, the Utica (New York) Art Association in 1866, and the Pennsylvania Academy of the Fine Arts, also in 1866. The 1861 painting that has acquired the title *Sunset after a Storm in the Catskills* (Newington-Cropsey Foundation) is a composition done while Cropsey was in England. The central mountain may be modeled on Chocorua in New Hampshire or Sugarloaf in southern New York, but the painting does not seem to be of the Catskills.

Plate 82. Jasper Francis Cropsey, *Tree Study*, 1855. Courtesy Newington-Cropsey Foundation.

NATHANIEL CURRIER AND JAMES MERRITT IVES

1813-1888, 1824-1895

Scenery of the Cattskill. The Mountain House

Colored lithograph, after 1857
9 x 12½ in.

New York State Museum, Albany
Plate 25

Nathaniel Currier founded his own lithography company in 1834 in New York City after a Boston apprenticeship with the Pendleton Brothers. In 1857, the lithographer James Ives joined Currier's medium-sized establishment. After midcentury, Currier & Ives prints accounted for three-quarters of the American print market and were sold at prices ranging from six cents to three dollars. During the 1850s and 1860s, the most popular prints were historical events, whale fishing, and American scenery. Tastes changed in later years, and genre and sporting pictures became increasingly popular. The firm closed in 1907 after producing more than seven thousand different prints.

Currier & Ives were able to lead the American print market and make their lithographed prints so widely available for a combination of reasons. Under Ives's management, the company opened franchises in nearly every large American city. The firm produced and distributed a greater number of different prints than any of its competitors. Because they produced so many impressions of each print, they could sell them at a lower cost than could competitors.[1] The lithographs were printed in black ink and later colored by hand. The use of color attracted customers but increased cost. Currier & Ives reduced costs by hiring unskilled workers to add solid patches of watercolor to the black-line lithographs.

MF

1. The most complete sources for this material are Gale Research Corporation, *Currier & Ives: A Catalogue Raisonné* (Detroit, MI: Gale Research Corp., 1983), Peter C. Marzio, *The Democratic Art: Chromolithography* (Boston: David R. Godine, 1979), and Harry T. Peters, *Currier & Ives: Printmakers to the American People* (New York: New York Public Library, 1931). For a brief biographical summary see Baigell, *Dictionary of American Art*, 82-83.

FELIX O. C. DARLEY

1822-1888

Rip Van Winkle No. 2: Rip with the Children

Pen and ink and watercolor on paper, c. 1848
8⅞ x 10⅞ in.

Historic Hudson Valley, Tarrytown, New York

Rip Van Winkle No. 4: Rip's Return

Pen and ink and watercolor on paper, c. 1848
8⅞ x 10⅞ in.

Historic Hudson Valley, Tarrytown, New York
Plate 9

American Art Union, *Illustrations of Rip Van Winkle, Designed and Etched by Felix O. C. Darley, for the Members of the American Art-Union, 1848* **(New York: American Art Union, 1849)**

The Hudson River Museum of Westchester, Archives

The illustrator Felix Octavius Carr Darley was born in Philadelphia, where he first studied and worked. By 1843, his illustrations had appeared in *Godey's Lady's Book* and the *Democratic Review*. Darley moved to New York City in 1848 and was immediately hired by the directors of the American Art Union to design and etch a series of lithographs to illustrate a proposed edition of Washington Irving's "Rip Van Winkle." A copy of the *Illustrations of Rip Van Winkle* was to be distributed as a premium to every member of the Art Union. Darley completed the sixth and final lithograph in late 1848 or early 1849. According to an article in *The Literary World*, the Art Union intended to print twenty thousand copies.[1] Distribution began on 1 May 1849.[2]

Rip with the Children and *Rip's Return* are hand-colored pen drawings. Part of a complete set of six, they are either preliminary studies for the published engravings or, perhaps more likely, copies done after the completion of the commission. The coloring seems to be nineteenth century and is supposed to have been added by Darley. A related pencil drawing of *Rip's Return* is in the collections of The New-York Historical Society.

The *Illustrations of Rip Van Winkle* were so popular with both the reviewers and Art Union members that in 1849 the directors hired Darley to do a set of six illustrations for Irving's "The Legend of Sleepy Hollow." These two series made Darley's reputation, and he quickly became the most popular book illustrator in the United States. He was made an honorary member of the National Academy of Design in 1852 and was elected a member in 1853. In 1859, he married and moved to Claymont, Delaware, where he died in 1888.[3]

Like all of Darley's mature works, the *Illustrations of Rip Van Winkle* are line drawings with very little shading. Of the six drawings, reviewers were most impressed with *Rip's Return*. The reviewer in *The Literary World* wrote of it,

There is something of that sincerity of the Puritan in Mr. Darley's composition which we inherit from the gloomy earnestness of our English sires, and which is the strength of the American character. Look at the tragic figure of Rip Van Winkle . . . as he returns to his dilapidated roof and broken threshold, and gazes on the dog, which looked like his old companion, but unlike that friend, "snarled, showed his teeth, and passed on." The attitude, the accessories, the weeds and thistles keeping guard over the desolation, the sadly wondering tragic countenance, are not in the letter of the story, but a grandeur borrowed from the artist's genius.[4]

1. *The Literary World* 3 (11 November 1848): 812.

2. *The Literary World* 4 (7 April 1849): 319.

3. Koke, *American Landscape and Genre Paintings*, 242; Theodore Bolton, "The Book Illustrations of Felix Octavius Carr Darley," *American Antiquarian Society Proceedings* 61 (April 1951): 131-182; Frank Weitenkampf, "F. O. C. Darley, American Illustrator," *Art Quarterly* 10 (Spring 1947): 100-113.

4. *The Literary World* 3 (11 November 1848): 812. An English review that singles this illustration out for special praise is reprinted in *The Literary World* 5 (27 October 1849): 362.

THOMAS DOUGHTY

1793-1856

Catskill Falls

Engraving by George B. Ellis, 1828
4$\frac{1}{16}$ x 2$\frac{3}{4}$ in.

From *The Atlantic Souvenir* (1828)
Abernethy Library, Middlebury College, Middlebury, Vermont
Plate 27

The Anglers

Oil on canvas, 1834
27¼ x 34½ in.

The Parrish Art Museum, Southampton, New York; Littlejohn Collection
Plate 83

One of the first American painters to specialize in landscape, Thomas Doughty was born in Philadelphia. As a boy he was apprenticed to a tanner. After his apprenticeship, he started a leather business with one of his older brothers. Although he had little or no formal training as an artist, Doughty exhibited a landscape at the Pennsylvania Academy of the Fine Arts in 1816. He married in about 1817. In 1820, ignoring the advice of friends and family, Doughty abandoned his trade and became a full-time painter of landscape.

Doughty quickly became one of the most successful landscape painters working in Philadelphia. In 1822, Doughty exhibited at the Pennsylvania Academy for the first time since 1816. He exhibited at the Academy annually from 1822 until 1832 and was elected a full member in 1824. According to William Dunlap, when Thomas Cole arrived in Philadelphia from the west in 1824 and attended the annual Academy of the Fine Arts exhibition, his heart sank "as he felt his deficiencies in art, when standing before the landscapes of Birch and Doughty."[1] In the later 1820s, Doughty exhibited at Peale's Baltimore Museum, the American Academy of Fine Arts (New York), the National Academy of Design (New York), the Boston Museum, and the Boston Athenaeum. He was elected an honorary member of the National Academy of Design in 1827. In 1828 he moved from Philadelphia to Boston, where he opened a drawing school and studied lithography. Doughty returned to Philadelphia in the fall of 1830.[2]

Along with Thomas Cole, Doughty was the most prominent landscape painter working in the United States during the late 1820s and 1830s. Like Cole, Doughty supplemented his income by supplying publishers with landscape views suitable for engraving. The first of Doughty's designs to be engraved seems to have been a view of *Washington's Capitol*, which was published in A. R. Poole's *Picturesque Pocket Diary for 1823*. The following year, the Philadelphia publishers H. C. Lea & I. Carey used one of Doughty's paintings of the Fairmount waterworks as the frontispiece for *Philadelphia in 1824*. In the fall of 1825, Lea & Carey published the first (1826) annual volume of *The Atlantic Souvenir: A Christmas Book and New Year's Offering. The Atlantic Souvenir* was the first and one of the most successful of the annuals or gift books published in the United States between 1825 and the end of the century. A completely new edition was published every year until 1832, at

Plate 83. Thomas Doughty, *The Anglers*, 1834. Courtesy The Parrish Art Museum.

which time it was merged with *The Token* and became *The Token and Atlantic Souvenir*. Engravings after designs by Doughty appeared in *The Atlantic Souvenir* annually from 1826 to 1828 and in 1831, 1832, and 1835.[3]

Catskill Falls was published in *The Atlantic Souvenir* for 1828. It accompanied an article titled "A Visit to the Cattskills." It was also issued as the frontispiece to the third (1828) and subsequent editions of Theodore Dwight's *The Northern Traveller. Catskill Falls* is the earliest known engraving of Kaaterskill Falls from below. Unlike Cole's 1826 painting *Falls of Kaaterskill* (plate 2), Doughty's engraving is topographically accurate. He conceals neither the observation platform atop the Falls nor the presence of tourists. Cole presented the Falls as if they were deep in the wilderness; Doughty presented them as an awe-inspiring but nonetheless easily accessible —and safe—tourist attraction.[4]

Doughty moved from Philadelphia back to Boston in 1832. He remained in Boston until 1837, when he trav-

eled to England. He returned in 1838 to settle in New York, where he lived until he once again visited Europe in 1845.

Doughty seems to have visited the Catskills during the mid-1830s. But although there are numerous paintings by him dating from this period that now carry Catskill titles, none of them are of subjects associated with the Mountain House.[5] Moreover, despite the number of these paintings now carrying Catskill titles, the unlocated *Peep at the Catskill Mountain House* which Doughty sold to the American Art Union in 1849 is the only painting he ever exhibited with a Catskill title.[6] Doughty did exhibit numerous paintings with Susquehanna and Delaware River titles. *The Anglers* seems to be a scene along one of these rivers in the western Catskills.[7]

Doughty returned from Europe in 1848 and once again settled in New York City. Much of his late work is hastily sketched and lacks the shimmering tones characteristic of his best early work. He died in New York City in 1856.

1. Dunlap, *History of the Rise and Progress*, vol. 2, 359. Dunlap is paraphrasing an 1834 autobiographical statement he had solicited from Cole. The atmospheric landscape in the background of Cole's 1825 *Landscape with Figures and a Mill* (The Minneapolis Institute of Arts) may owe something to his experience of Doughty's work.

2. Biographical information on Doughty is taken from E. Anna Lewis, "Thomas Doughty," *Graham's Magazine* 45 (November 1854): 483-484; Tuckerman, *Book of the Artists*, 506-507; Howard N. Doughty, "Biographical Sketch of Thomas Doughty" (unpublished manuscript, National Museum of American Art, 1941); Frank Goodyear, Jr., *Thomas Doughty, 1793-1856: An American Pioneer in Landscape Painting* (Philadelphia: Philadelphia Academy of the Fine Arts, 1973); and Robert F. Looney, "Thomas Doughty, Printmaker," in Robert F. Looney, ed., *Philadelphia Printmaking: American Prints Before 1860* (West Chester, PA: Tinicum Press, 1973), 131-148.

3. On gift books, see Frederick Faxon, *Literary Annuals and Gift-Books* (Boston: The Boston Book Company, 1912); Frank Weitenkampf, "The Keepsake in Nineteenth-Century Art," *The Boston Public Library Quarterly* 4 (1952): 139-148; and, especially, Thompson, *American Literary Annuals & Gift Books*.

4. The fact that *Catskill Falls* is both the earliest known engraving of the site from below and topographically accurate suggests that Doughty had visited it. This conclusion is also suggested by the fact that engravings after Doughty of sites he could not have visited—such as the view of Athens, Greece, that appeared in *The Atlantic Souvenir* for 1827—usually credit another artist for the original drawing. Various editions of *The Atlantic Souvenir* included engravings after Doughty of Montmorenci Falls, Quebec (1826), Trenton Falls, New Jersey (1827), and Passaic Falls, New Jersey (1827). Thompson, *American Literary Annuals & Gift Books*, 42, notes that Doughty was paid fifteen dollars each for his sketches of Trenton and Passaic Falls.

5. Among the most important of these are *In the Catskills* (1836; Reynolda House, Inc., Winston-Salem, North Carolina), *In the Catskills* (1836; Addison Gallery of Art, Andover, Massachusetts), and *Near Little Point, Catskill Mountains* (c. 1840; Hunter Museum of Art, Chattanooga, Tennessee).

6. The *Bulletin of the American Art-Union*, 2 (April 1849): 27, describes it this way: "In the opening, between large trees and masses of foliage, which rise on each side of the foreground, appear the windings of a quiet stream, with banks well wooded, and bearing pleasure boats. In the distance rise a succession of hills, the more remote of which are blue and misty. The season is summer. A fisherman stands beside a piece of still water in the immediate foreground." This seems to be the same painting as the *Peep at the Catskills* that Tuckerman, *Book of the Artists*, 507, lists as one of Doughty's most memorable.

7. This suggestion was made by Goodyear in *Thomas Doughty, 1793-1856*.

FELIX DUPONCHEL

Active 1825-1826

Catskill Mountain House

Lithograph printed by Anthony Imbert, 1826
9¼ x 8¾ in.

New York State Library, Albany
Plate 19

Like many early New York City lithographers, next to nothing is known about Felix Duponchel. No other impressions of the *Catskill Mountain House* are known to exist. The only other currently located works by Duponchel are also lithographs printed by Imbert and are bound in Cadwallader C. Colden's *Memoir, prepared at the request of a committee of the Common Council of the City of New York, and presented to the mayor of the city, at the celebration of the completion of the New York Canals* (1825). Duponchel's lithograph of the *Catskill Mountain House* was the source for the transfer-printed earthenware plate *Catskill Mountain, Hudson* produced by Enoch Wood & Sons.[1] This would seem to be the earliest of numerous plates to represent the Mountain House. Duponchel may have been the engraver of the unsigned and undated, but compositionally related, Imbert lithograph of the *Catskill Mountain House* now in the collections of the Haines Falls Free Library, Haines Falls, New York.

Anthony Imbert (1794 or 1795-1834) is reported to have been born in Calais, France, to have been a lieutenant in the French navy, to have been captured by the British off Dover on 23 February 1810, and to have been a prisoner at Chatham until his release on 20 May 1814. Nothing is known about his activities between 1814 and his arrival in New York City in 1824 or 1825. Whatever the specific date of his arrival, Imbert had established his lithographic press by November 1825. Although he was not the first commercial lithographer in New York City, Imbert was the first to be commercially successful. Despite increasing competition from other lithographers, Imbert's business remained successful until his death in 1834.

Most of the artists Imbert employed between 1824 and 1826 are either known or thought to have been French. These include Edme Rousseau (active between 1824 and 1843, known to have been French) and C. Des Essart (probably French, and active in 1825). It therefore seems likely that Felix Duponchel was also French.[2]

Imbert printed at least two and probably three other lithographs of Catskill scenery. He is known to have printed the view of the *Catskill Mountain House* owned by the Haines Falls Free Library and the view of *Catskill Falls* from within the cavern drawn on stone by Gherlando Marsiglia (c. 1825-1831; plate 17). Imbert probably printed the frontal view of the *Falls at Catskill* drawn on stone by Thomas Cole (probably 1828-1829; plate 73). Only two impressions of the *Falls at Catskill* are known. Neither impression is signed or inscribed, but one of them bears the penciled notation, "Drawn on stone by Thomas Cole, N.A. and by him presented to T.S. Cummings. By T.S. Cummings to Jonathan Sturges Esq. April 5th, 1865." The belief that Imbert printed the *Falls at Catskill* is based on the fact that he is known to have printed the *Distant View of the Slides that Destroyed the Whilley Family*, drawn on stone by Cole in 1828 or 1829. The only known impression of the latter lithograph as well as the unannotated impression of the *Falls at Catskill* descended through the Cole family and are now in the collections of the Albany Institute of History and Art.[3]

Imbert was an ambitious publisher interested in printing books containing large numbers of lithographs.[4] The fact that he printed lithographs of both the White Mountains and the Catskills between 1826 and 1829 suggests that he was trying to put together a book on American scenery.[5] One imagines that he hoped to produce a book of lithographs and accompanying text to compete with more expensive volumes of aquatint engravings such as Joshua Shaw's *Picturesque Views of American Scenery* (1820) and William Guy Wall's *Hudson River Portfolio* (1821-1825). William Cullen Bryant and Asher B. Durand were to have a similar idea: New York City publisher Elam Bliss published the first number of their projected series of text with engraved views as *The American Landscape* in 1830. But Bryant and Durand were undercapitalized, and the project went no further. Much of the success of John H. Hinton's *The History and Topography of the United States* (1830-1832) was no doubt due to the engraved cityscapes and landscapes which—although barely integrated with the accompanying text and awkwardly distributed in poorly organized fascicles—were copiously spread throughout the volume. And of course, *American Scenery*, edited by Nathaniel Parker Willis with engraved views after William Henry Bartlett, was a phenomenal and long-lasting success when it was serially published between 1838 and 1842.

1. The plate is dark blue. Six and one-half inches in diameter, it is described and reproduced in Larsen, *American Historical Views on Staffordshire China*, 3d ed., 15, where it is listed as Enoch Wood & Sons #18. On transfer-printed earthenware, see the entry for Enoch Wood & Sons.

2. The information in this and the preceding paragraph derives from John Carbonell, "Anthony Imbert: New York's Pioneer Lithographer," in David Tatham, ed., *Prints and Printmakers of New York State, 1825-1940* (Syracuse, NY: Syracuse University Press, 1986). Carbonell mentions Duponchel twice but has nothing substantial to say about him or his work—except for the speculation that he was probably French.

3. The only other lithograph Cole is known to have drawn is *The Good Shepherd*, which he was working on at the time of his death in 1848. On Cole's lithographs, see entries 88-90 in Howard S. Merritt, *To Walk with Nature: The Drawings of Thomas Cole* (Yonkers, NY: The Hudson River Museum, 1982), 59-61, and Janet Flint, "The American Painter-Lithographer," in *Art & Commerce: American Prints of the Nineteenth Century* (Charlottesville, VA: The University of Virginia Press and the Boston Museum of Fine Arts, 1978), 126-132. I have condensed Flint's convincing argument in favor of her 1828-1829 date for *The Falls at Catskill*.

4. In 1826, Imbert published three numbers containing fifteen lithographs of Edme Rousseau's projected ten-part book with fifty lithographs on the *Lithographic Principles of Landscape Drawing*. In August and then October 1827, he published the first two numbers, each containing four lithograph views by Alexander Jackson Davis, of what was projected to be *Views of Public Buildings, Edifices, and Monuments, in the Principal Cities of the United States*. The one book-length project he completed was Colden, *Memoir*, which appeared in 1826 and which—depending on which copy one examines—contains more than thirty-five lithographs. Carbonell, "Anthony Imbert," 15-16, 24-25, 17-20, 39.

5. Carbonell, "Anthony Imbert," 20, mentions but does not reproduce, describe, or give a location for a hand-colored lithograph of Kaaterskill Falls drawn by John Robert Murray and published by Imbert.

ASHER B. DURAND

1796-1886

View in the Catskills

Oil on canvas, 1844
37¾ x 54 in.

Berry-Hill Galleries, New York
Plate 84

Catt's Kill, in the Clove

Engraving by Bobbett and Edmonds, 1851
11¼ x 8¼ in.

Originally printed in *The Bulletin of the American Art-Union* (June 1851). Reprinted in Henry Beckwith, ed., *The Home Book of the Picturesque* (1852)
Vedder Memorial Library, Greene County Historical Society, Coxsackie, New York
Plate 85

Landscape with Birches

Oil on canvas, c. 1855
24 x 18 in.

Museum of Fine Arts, Boston; Bequest of Mary Fuller Wilson
Plate 86

Forest Scene in the Catskills

Oil on canvas, c. 1855-1860
15 x 24 in.

The Detroit Institute of Arts; Gift of Mr. and Mrs. Harold O. Love
Plate 45

Plate 84. Asher B. Durand, *View in the Catskills*, 1844. Courtesy Berry-Hill Galleries.

Plate 85. Asher B. Durand, *Catt's Kill, in the Clove*, 1851. Courtesy Greene County Historical Society.

Catskill Meadows in Summer

Oil on canvas, 1861
17 x 24 in.

Wellesley College Museum; Gift of Mrs. Leeds A. Wheeler (Marion Eddy, Class of 1924)
Plate 46

In 1820, Asher Durand was commissioned to engrave Trumbull's *Declaration of Independence*, a popular image that made his reputation as an engraver and that caused his teacher and partner Peter Maverick to grow jealous and eventually to destroy their partnership. From 1820 until 1835, Durand was involved in a series of business ventures. Although none of these efforts were financially successful, his involvement in the New York art scene earned him other rewards. In 1826, Durand was elected by members of the New York Drawing Association to be one of the charter members of the National Academy of Design, and a year later he became one of the founding members of the Sketch Club.[1]

In the early 1830s, Durand began to paint portraits, genre scenes, and occasional landscapes. After a sketching trip to the Adirondacks with Thomas and Mrs. Cole in 1837 (he had visited the Coles in Catskill in the spring of the preceding year), and with the memory of encouragement from the recently deceased collector Luman Reed,[2] he began to specialize in landscape. Although he continued to paint and exhibit portraits and

genre scenes in subsequent years, by 1845 he was exhibiting landscapes almost exclusively.

Durand's earliest paintings of the Catskills, such as *View in the Catskills* (plate 84), are pastoral scenes done in Ulster County and near the Hudson River. His first well-documented trip to the area of the Mountain House was in the fall of 1848, when he and John Casilear spent two weeks at the Mountain House and another two weeks boarding in Palenville. Durand returned to the Clove in 1849 and spent more than a month at John Rusk's boarding house in Tannersville. He again returned to Rusk's in 1850. Dated pencil drawings in The New-York Historical Society establish that Durand returned to the Clove in 1857, 1858, 1864, 1865, and 1867.

Like Cole, Durand was deeply religious and wanted to allow nature, which he experienced as a manifestation of God, to represent itself. He wrote of his ideas on nature and painting in the famous nine "Letters on Landscape Painting" printed in *The Crayon* in 1855. According to Durand, the primary training a student needed was to go to nature, and, "if he is imbued with the true spirit to appreciate and enjoy the contemplation of her loveliness, he will approach her with veneration, and find in the conscientious study of her beauties all the great first principles of Art."[3]

Plate 86. Asher B. Durand, *Landscape with Birches*, 1855. Courtesy Museum of Fine Arts, Boston.

One of Durand's favorite subjects was the forest interior, such as *Landscape with Birches* (plate 86) or *Forest Scene in the Catskills* (plate 45), where he seemed to feel a special affinity for the trees. Of one of his forest interiors Henry Tuckerman wrote, "Its unexaggerated, simple, yet profoundly true expression, shows how the genuine artist can effect wonders without adventitious means. In another painter's hands it would prove but a sketch; in Durand's it becomes a landscape; and one of the most fresh and vigorous he has ever made."[4]

Yet Durand did not slavishly devote himself to the transcription of nature in such detail that he lost the poetic effect of the scene. *Catskill Meadows in Summer* (plate 46) not only effectively represents the trees and countryside, but Durand has imbued it with the sense of warmth and tranquility one feels in August. The editor of the *Knickerbocker* wrote,

> A more close delineation of nature no more makes a great painter than it does a great poet.... Bryant, in the true spirit of a poet, imbues his descriptions of nature with a human sentiment and feeling, and therefore appeals, and never in vain, to the thoughtful and contemplative soul. In this power Durand is eminent above all his contemporaries. Take his landscapes, those we mean that are the offspring of his own nature, which he has painted in the real spirit of love; those that convey his own character, if we may so speak, and which he has created in the midst of the tranquil quiet of his studio; and we shall find in these a deep and pervading *sentiment*, which appeals directly to the heart.[5]

MF

1. For biographical information, see John Durand, *The Life and Times of Asher B. Durand* (New York: Scribner's Sons, 1894); David B. Lawall, *Asher Brown Durand* (New York: Garland Publishing Co., 1977); and Tuckerman, *Book of the Artists*.

2. Thomas Cole to Asher Durand, 16 June 1836, Durand Papers, New York Public Library.

3. Asher Durand, "Letters on Landscape Painting, Letter I," *The Crayon* (3 January 1855): 2.

4. Tuckerman, *Book of the Artists*, 190.

5. "Editor's Table," *The Knickerbocker* 41 (January 1853): 78.

Plate 87. Charles Loring Elliott, *James Fenimore Cooper*, c. 1835-1851. Courtesy Historic Hudson Valley.

CHARLES LORING ELLIOTT

1812-1868

James Fenimore Cooper

Oil on canvas, c. 1835-1851
18 x 14 in.

Historic Hudson Valley, Tarrytown, New York
Plate 87

One of the best American portrait painters of the mid nineteenth century, Charles Loring Elliott was born in central New York State in 1812. In 1829 he moved to New York City, where he studied with the genre painter John Quidor. The following year, Elliott attempted an ambitious series of paintings illustrating scenes from Washington Irving's Knickerbocker's *History of New York*. From 1830 to 1839, Elliott supported himself as an itinerant portrait painter in central New York State. During these years he developed an unassuming style characterized by the use of neutral tones, which proved popular after his 1839 return to New York City. Elliott was elected an Associate of the National Academy of Design in 1845 and became a full member in 1846. His contributions to the 1846 National Academy of Design exhibition earned him much praise and established his reputation as New York's leading portrait painter.[1]

MF

1. In addition to biographical dictionaries, see Theodore Bolton, "Charles L. Elliott: An Account of his Life and Work," *Art Quarterly* 5 (1942).

Plate 88. Harry Fenn, *The Catskills: Sunrise from South Mountain*, 1873. Courtesy Kennedy Galleries, Inc.

HARRY FENN

1838-1911

The Catskills: Sunrise from South Mountain

Steel plate engraving by S.V. Hunt, 1873
8⅝ x 5¾ in.

Originally published in William Cullen Bryant, ed., *Picturesque America* (1872-1874)

Kennedy Galleries, Inc., New York
Plate 88

Sunset Rock

Wood engraving, 1873
12½ x 9¾ in.

Originally published in Bryant, ed., *Picturesque America*

The Hudson River Museum of Westchester, Archives
Plate 89

Harry Fenn was born in Surrey, England. Originally trained as an engraver, he began to paint before his 1857 immigration to the United States. Fenn remained in the United States until about 1863, when he returned to Europe to continue his studies in Italy. He returned to the United States by 1864 or 1865, at which time he began to work as a commercial illustrator. Almost all of his illustrations were landscapes. His drawings for John Greenleaf Whittier's *Snow-Bound* (1868) and *Ballads of New England* (1870) were well received, and he quickly became one of the most successful illustrators working in the United States. He was a charter member of the Salmagundi Sketch Club and a founder of the American Water Color Society (1866). Harry Fenn died at his home in Montclair, New Jersey, in 1911.[1]

The most lavish and the most popular late nineteenth-century illustrated guide to American scenery was *Picturesque America*, edited by William Cullen Bryant (plate 88) and serially published between 1872 and 1874. Every number contained articles on two or three United States environments. Every article contained about fifteen woodcuts and a single steel plate engraving. Fenn spent all of 1870 working on the project and did the drawings for twenty-five of the articles, including the one on the Catskills. The steel plate engraving titled *The Catskills: Sunrise from South Mountain* is a view from the

Sunset Rock.

and ragged, far out over the glen, and then falls in broken lines a scarred and frowning precipice.
The lines of the South Mountain and

Plate 89. Harry Fenn, *Sunset Rock*, 1873. Courtesy The Hudson River Museum of Westchester.

shoulder of South Mountain above (to the south of) the Mountain House. *Sunset Rock* is a view from Sunset Rock on South Mountain looking west up Kaaterskill Clove. Haines Falls is in the middle distance; Hunter Mountain is at the rear. The view is similar to Sanford Gifford's *Kauterskill Clove* (plate 38), but Fenn is more faithful to the actual geography of the site.

1. Obituary, *The New York Times*, Sunday, 23 April 1911; Sinclair Hamilton, *Early American Book Illustrators and Wood Engravers 1670-1870* (Princeton: Princeton University Press, 1958), 125-127; *M. and M. Karolik Collection of American Watercolors and Drawings, 1800-1875*, vol. 1 (Boston: Museum of Fine Arts, 1962), 156.

(G)EILMANN

Active 1851

Hudson River Railroad Passenger Station at Chambers Street, Frederick Hotel in Background

Wash drawing, 1851
21 x 18 in.

Museum of the City of New York, Prints and Photographs Department

Nothing is known about this artist.

By the 1840s, improvements in the size and design of steamboats had reduced the cost of shipping freight up and down the Hudson and had made passenger travel cheaper, faster, and more comfortable. Unfortunately, the Hudson was closed to steam navigation for three to four months every winter. The Hudson River Railroad Company was incorporated by an act of the New York State legislature in the spring of 1846. Construction began in the fall of 1847. Passenger service began on 29 September 1849 with the opening of the section connecting Manhattan with Peekskill; service was extended to Poughkeepsie on 31 December 1849. The section linking Poughkeepsie with Albany was opened on 3 October 1851.[1]

1. [Jervis], "The Hudson River Railroad, A Sketch of Its History," *Hunt's Merchants' Magazine* (March 1850): 155-163; Poor, *History of the Railroads and Canals of America*, 259-260; Thomas C. Cochran, *Railroad Leaders, 1845-1890* (Cambridge, MA: Harvard University Press, 1953), 22-26.

SANFORD ROBINSON GIFFORD

1823-1880

Kauterskill Falls

Oil on paper, 1846
15 x 10¼ in.

Alexander Gallery, New York
Plate 40

Tree Trunk, Catskills

Oil on paper, 9 July 1850
9½ x 14¾ in.

Private Collection
Plate 41

Kauterskill Clove

Oil on canvas, 1862
48 x 39⅞ in.

The Metropolitan Museum of Art; Bequest of Maria DeWitt Jesup, 1915
Plate 38

Scribner's Pasture, in the Catskills

Oil on canvas, c. 1863
8 x 18½ in.

The Dayton Art Institute; Gift of I. Austin Kelly, III, in memory of Ironton Austin Kelly
Plate 90

A Sketch from North Mountain, in the Catskills (The Catskill Mountain House)

Oil on canvas, 3 October 1865
9¾ x 18⅞ in.

Private Collection
Plate 91

A Sketch of Hunter Mountain, Catskills

Oil on canvas, 9 October 1865
10¼ x 17 in.

James D. Terra Collection, Terra Museum of American Art, Chicago, Illinois
Plate 92

Plate 90. Sanford Robinson Gifford, *Scribner's Pasture, in the Catskills*, c. 1863. Courtesy The Dayton Art Institute.

South Mountain—Catskills

Engraving by R. Hinshelwood, c. 1873
4⅜ x 7¹⁄₁₆ in.

Originally published in *The Ladies' Repository*

Vedder Memorial Library, Greene County Historical Society, Coxsackie, New York
Plate 93

Sanford Gifford was born near Saratoga Springs, New York, in July 1823. By January 1824, Gifford's father had moved his family to Hudson, New York, where he invested in an iron foundry. The foundry was successful, and the Giffords quickly became one of the wealthiest families in Hudson.

Sanford Gifford was educated at a private preparatory academy in Hudson. He entered Brown University in 1842 but left after three semesters. Gifford seems to have spent much of 1844 at home in Hudson. According to Worthington Whittredge, Gifford spent most of that year deciding what he wanted to do with the rest of his life:

This was no easy task. Betwixt his desire to please his father and at the same time to please himself, he found himself in doubt. At length, in no happy mood he started off one morning for the fields, and finally brought up on the top of Mount Merrino, a high hill to the south of Hudson, overlooking the river and with a clear view of the Catskill Mountains. Here he stretched himself in the shadow of a tree until, as he expressed it, he came to the conclusion that any of the pursuits which had been suggested were good enough for him, but that he was good for nothing for any of them. This was a step forward. Below him on the opposite side of the river lay the village of Catskill, its roofs and windows glistening in the sun. There was one house standing in the village which was in full view, around

which we may well believe there was a halo of light that morning which lighted up the path which he was to follow. This was the house and studio of Thomas Cole, the father of a long line of American landscape painters.[1]

Whittredge's account is sentimentalized but seems to be chronologically accurate. The earliest known works by Gifford are figure drawings—mainly of faces—dated August 1844. In 1845, Gifford moved to New York City, where he studied drawing and perspective with John Rubens Smith (plate 10). His earliest known landscape drawings date from the summer of 1845, when he made a tour of Saratoga, Lakes George and Champlain, Montreal, and Quebec.[2]

Although Gifford may have done some work in the area of the Mountain House during the summer of 1845, his first well-documented visit to the area was during the summer of 1846. In a 6 November 1874 letter to Octavius Brooks Frothingham, Gifford recalled,

During the summer of 1846 I made several pedestrian tours in the Catskill Mts., and the Berkshire Hills, and made a good many sketches from nature. These studies, together with the great admiration I felt for the works of Cole developed a strong interest in Landscape Art, and opened my eyes to a keener perception and a more intelligent enjoyment of nature. Having once enjoyed the absolute freedom of the Landscape Painter's life I was unable to return to portrait painting. From this time my direction in art was determined.[3]

Kauterskill Falls (plate 40) dates from one of these 1846 excursions and is the earliest of the currently located oil landscapes by Gifford. It is a topographically accurate view of the upper leap of Kaaterskill Falls. It shows the observation platform and refreshment stand operated by Peter Schutt, and it was probably done from just off the path that led from the platform to the cavern behind the upper leap of the Falls. The cavern is clearly visible in the right foreground.

In November 1846, Gifford registered for classes at the Antique School of the National Academy of Design. The first public exhibition of one of his paintings took place in the spring of 1847, when *Lake Scene, on the Catskill* (currently unlocated) was shown at the annual exhibition of the National Academy of Design. Gifford spent the summer and fall of 1847 in the Catskills and Adirondacks.[4] During the fall of 1847, he attended the Life School of the National Academy of Design, attended anatomy lectures at the Crosby Street Medical College, and sold a *View on the Kauterskill Creek* to the American Art Union. Gifford returned to the Catskills in September 1848. On this trip he worked both in Kaaterskill Clove and in the less developed Plattekill Clove to its south.[5] Gifford spent July 1849 in the eastern Catskills, and the following autumn he explored the East and West Branches of the Delaware River in the then rarely visited western Catskills.[6] In the winter of 1849, Gifford sold at least eight paintings to the American Art Union. The following spring, he was elected an Associate of the National Academy of Design, and four of his paintings were selected for its annual exhibition. Two of his paintings included in the 1850 National Academy of Design exhibition were *Kauterskill Clove, Catskill Mountains* and *Deep Hollow, Catskill Mountains*. Gifford returned to the Catskills in July 1850, when he painted the oil sketch inscribed *Tree Trunk, Catskills* (plate 41). In August 1850, he was working in the Shawangunk Mountains, which are located just south of the Catskills near the city of New Paltz, New York.

Until 1851, Gifford had been most active in the Catskills and upper New York State. During the 1850s, he traveled further afield and spent little time in the Catskills.[7] Gifford was elected a full member of the National Academy of Design in May 1854. In May 1855, he sailed from New York for England. He did not return to the United States until September 1857. Gifford did not spend much, if any, time in the Catskills in either 1858 or 1859.[8]

Gifford's best known and most powerful paintings date from the early and mid-1860s. Many of these are of Catskill subjects. Gifford returned to the Catskills in 1860 and spent July and August in Kaaterskill Clove. For much of this time he seems to have been boarding with George Brockett, whose farm was located on Kaaterskill Creek just above the waterfall known as Fawn's Leap.[9] Worthington Whittredge and Jervis McEntee were probably staying with Gifford at Brockett's.[10] The Civil War began in April 1860. Gifford was mustered into service with the Seventh Regiment of the New York State National Guard on 30 April 1861. His initial period of mobilization was brief, and he was back in New York by the end of May. Gifford spent July, August, and September 1861 in Kaaterskill Clove. Whittredge was with him in August and was probably with him in September as well.[11] Gifford returned to Kaaterskill Clove in October 1862 and, probably, in October 1863. He does not seem to have visited the area in 1864, but he returned to the Clove annually from 1865 to 1867.[12]

Plate 91. Sanford Robinson Gifford, *A Sketch from North Mountain, in the Catskills*, 3 October 1865. Private collection.

Although Gifford often stayed in Kaaterskill Clove and although many of his oil sketches from the 1860s are of subjects located in the Clove, most of his larger paintings of the Catskills are of views from the mountain top. Many of the most spectacular views on the mountain top are from the bare outcroppings on the south shoulder of South Mountain. Gifford's first three large paintings of the Catskills were all of Kaaterskill Clove as seen from South Mountain. Gifford's first large version of this view was *A Twilight in the Catskills—Kauterskill Clove* (currently unlocated), which he exhibited at the National Academy of Design in 1861.[13] According to the reviewer in *The Crayon*, *A Twilight in the Catskills—Kauterskill Clove* was "regarded as the most attractive [landscape] . . . in the exhibition. The point of view is well selected and the scene is well adapted to the hour at which we view it in the picture. The crimson glow of the clouds and the gloom of the deep gorge, enlivened by the stream which marks a pathway of light through it, present fine contrasts in color and chiaroscuro."[14] Gifford reworked the view from South Mountain in *Kauterskill Clove* (plate 38), which he completed in 1862. *Kauterskill Clove* was sold to Morris K. Jesup upon completion and was not exhibited until after Gifford's death. Gifford painted another version of the view in 1862-1863. Titled *Kauterskill Clove* (currently unlocated), this painting was sold to D. Willis James and was shown at the annual exhibition of the National Academy of Design in the spring of 1863.[15] In 1864, Lucia D. Pychowska described the subject of all three of the paintings:

the king of [Catskill] views is that obtained from the cliffs of the South Mountain overhanging the Clove. This vista has furnished sketches for two remarkable pictures painted by that rare artist and genuine son of Helios, S. R. Gifford. Looking toward the west is the rolling plateau of the Clove, with the far-away mountains beyond Hunter, the Parker and North Mountains, the openings to the Stony and Plattekill Cloves, Clum's Hill, and the silver thread of Haines's Fall. At the foot of the cliffs, more than a thousand feet below, lie Brockett's (classic ground for artists), the Clove road, Moore's Bridge, the Dog Fall, and the brawling Kauterskill. . . . The effects of light and shadow are such as we have never seen surpassed. This earth there seems made of gold or crimson lights, of gray seas of mist, or of every imaginable combination of beautiful hues.[16]

Kauterskill Clove is not a topographically accurate representation of the view from the cliffs along the southern flank of South Mountain. In adapting his pencil drawings and oil sketches, Gifford contrived a nonexistent central vantage point, widened the Clove so as to make it into a U-shaped valley, moved Haines Falls north into the center of the western end of the widened Clove, and added the lake nestled in the depths of the Clove.

Gifford returned to Kaaterskill Clove and the cliffs along the southern flank of South Mountain in the fall of 1863, but instead of concentrating his attention on the view west towards Haines Falls, he worked on the view east towards the Hudson River. In May 1864, Gifford exhibited *A Twilight in the Adirondacks* and *South Mountain—Catskills* at the annual National Academy of Design exhibition. According to the reviewer in *The Continental Monthly*, *South Mountain—Catskills*

presents a view doubtless well known to many of our readers. The far-away horizon, the winding Hudson with its tiny sails, the square dent where lies the lake in the Shawangunk range, the serrated ridges of the lower hills, the smoke from the lowlands outside the Clove, the shadowed, ridgy sides of the Round Top Mountain, the stunted pines of the South Mountain, so characteristically represented, the great rock overhanging the cliffs, and the whortleberry bushes and other low growth clustering about its base—all speak to us unmistakably of that very spot, and tell the story of the place as we scarcely thought it could have been told, yet so simply, so naturally, that the art of the artist is almost forgotten in actual enjoyment of the scene portrayed.[17]

Gifford returned to this subject in 1873, when he painted the large *View from South Mountain, in the Catskills* (St. Johnsbury Atheneum). The St. Johnsbury painting derives from an 1873 oil sketch (private collection), which was the immediate source for the engraving by R. Hinshelwood published in *The Ladies' Repository* (plate 93).[18]

Gifford's earliest known views of the Catskill Mountain House are pencil drawings done in August or September 1861. In 1862, Gifford developed these drawings into a moderately sized view of the *Catskill Mountain House* as seen from North Mountain. Gifford returned to this subject in 1865, when he executed a large number of pencil drawings and at least one oil sketch of the Mountain House as seen from North Mountain (plate 91). The amount of time Gifford spent on this subject in 1865 suggests that he was thinking of painting a large view of it, but no such large work was ever done.[19]

At the same time that he was working on the view of the Mountain House from North Mountain, Gifford was also producing pencil drawings and oil sketches of Hunter Mountain. Hunter Mountain is located on the Catskill Plateau just west of Haines Falls. It is visible in the background of many views of Kaaterskill Clove from South Mountain. Gifford painted *A Sketch of Hunter Mountain, Catskills* (plate 92) on 9 October 1865—just six days after he had painted *A Sketch from North Mountain, in the Catskills*. Worthington Whittredge's 1866 *Autumn, Hunter Mountain, Catskills* (plate 51) and Jervis McEntee's *Autumnal Landscape* (plate 109) adopted a similar vantage point and may have been based on drawings or oil sketches done at the same time. Over the winter of 1865-1866,

Plate 92. Sanford Robinson Gifford, *A Sketch of Hunter Mountain, Catskills,* 9 October 1865. Courtesy Terra Museum of American Art.

Gifford developed his drawings and oil sketches of Hunter Mountain into the large *Hunter Mountain, Twilight* (Terra Museum of American Art) which he exhibited at the National Academy of Design in May 1866.[20]

In May 1867, Gifford sailed from New York for England with the McEntees. He did not return to the United States until late September 1869. Immediately upon his return to the United States, Gifford joined the McEntees and Eastman Johnson at Scribner's Boarding House, which was located on Lake Creek between the outlet of South Lake and the top of Kaaterskill Falls (plate 90). Gifford accompanied the McEntees to the Catskills almost every year from 1871 until his marriage to Mary Canfield in June 1877. He did not visit the Catskills in 1877, but he returned in 1878 and 1879. During the 1870s, Gifford and the McEntees usually stayed at the Laurel House, located on Lake Creek between Scribner's Boarding House and the top of Kaaterskill Falls. During the 1870s, Gifford returned to many of the same sites he had painted in the 1860s and painted the St. Johnsbury *View from South Mountain, in the Catskills* as well as a number of large versions of Haines Falls from South Mountain. Sanford Gifford died in New York City in August 1880.[21]

1. John I. Baur, ed., "The Autobiography of Worthington Whittredge, 1820-1910," 56. The long account of Gifford in Whittredge's "Autobiography" derives from a memorial address Whittredge delivered after Gifford's death. This elegy was published as "Address by W. Whittredge" in *Gifford Memorial Meeting of the Century* (New York: The Century Association, 1880).

2. The most important sources of biographical information are Ila Weiss, *Sanford Robinson Gifford (1823-1880)* (New York: Garland Publishing, Inc., 1977) and Ila Weiss, "Reflections on Gifford's Art," in Alexander Gallery, New York, *Sanford R. Gifford* (New York: Alexander Gallery, 1986), unpaginated.

3. Gifford's letter is in the Sanford Gifford Papers on microfilm at the Archives of American Art. This letter is the most important single source of information concerning Gifford's early life and career.

4. A sketchbook including dated drawings from 1847 and 1848 (Vassar College Art Gallery) shows that Gifford spent early August in Ulster County, in the area of Marbletown and Hurley. He traveled north to the mountain top and the Kaaterskill Clove in late August and early September.

5. Gifford's itinerary is documented both by the previously cited 1847-1848 sketchbook in the Vassar College Art Gallery and by another early sketchbook (private collection) which is on microfilm in the Sanford Gifford Papers at the Archives of American Art (Reel #688).

6. Gifford's activities during the summer of 1849 are documented by dated drawings in an 1849 sketchbook in the Albany Institute of History and Art and an 1849-1850 sketchbook in the Vassar College Art Gallery.

7. The 1851 sketchbook (private collection) on microfilm in the Sanford Gifford Papers at the Archives of American Art (reel #688) shows that Gifford made a brief trip to Plattekill Clove in July 1851 but spent most of the 1851 season in the Adirondacks and on the Delaware River. Gifford spent most of the 1852 season on the Juniata and Susquehanna Rivers in Pennsylvania. He visited the Shawangunks in 1853, but he does not seem to have worked in the Catskills. The visit to the Shawangunks is documented by the pencil drawing inscribed "House of Abel Adams Ayres—Shawangunk, Oct 14th 1853" (Vassar College Art Gallery). Gifford spent the summer of 1854 in the White Mountains.

8. Gifford may have visited the Catskills in September 1858, but, if so, he did not stay long. He spent the summer and fall of 1859 in Nova Scotia, Maine, and New Hampshire.

9. This conclusion is drawn from the subjects of Gifford's 1860 drawings and from the 29 July drawing inscribed "Brocketts—View of Door." Drawings done in 1860 are on microfilm in the Sanford Gifford Papers at the Archives of American Art (Reel #688).

10. In his address to the Gifford Memorial Meeting, Whittredge noted that he had first met Gifford "on the Rhine" in June 1856. In his funeral address at the same meeting, McEntee noted that he had first met Gifford in the early fall of 1857, when they both tried to rent the same studio in the Tenth Street Studio Building. Gifford got the studio. The fact that Whittredge and McEntee gave two of the three addresses at the Memorial Meeting is an accurate reflection of the close friendship between the three artists. Throughout the 1860s and 1870s, the three often took summer and fall sketching excursions together. McEntee's presence in Kaaterskill Clove in late July 1860 is established by dated pencil drawings in The Corcoran Gallery of Art, the Albany Institute of History and Art, and the Yale University Art Gallery. Whittredge's presence in the Clove at the same time is suggested by an article titled "Domestic Art Gossip" published in *The Crayon* 7 (December 1860): 353, which noted that Gifford and Whittredge were working on "interesting studies from the Catskills."

11. On 7 August 1861, the landscape painter James Suydam wrote John Frederick Kensett, "Gifford and Whittredge are up in the Catskills." Suydam's letter is in the Kensett Papers on microfilm at the Archives of American Art (reel #N68-85). Gifford's 1861 sketchbook, on microfilm at the Archives of American Art (reel #688), contains a pencil drawing inscribed "Bear Trap" and dated 3 August 1861. The Mead Art Gallery of Amherst College owns a pencil drawing by Whittredge inscribed "Bear Trap," also dated 3 August 1861. The bear trap represented in both drawings is almost certainly the trap described in *Guide to Rambles from the Catskill Mountain House* (Catskill: J. Joesbury Book & Job Printer, 1863), 4: "To the north of this [North] lake, to those who have a desire to see mountain life, may be found a Bear Trap, in which Mr. Thorp—the 'Man of the Mountain'—caught three bears in the Fall of 1857, with the singular bait of dry codfish and honey."

12. Information in this paragraph derives from Gifford's sketchbooks in the Vassar College Art Gallery, the Albany Institute of History and Art, The Detroit Institute of Art, and the Sanford Gifford Papers on microfilm at the Archives of American Art.

13. In the 1861 National Academy of Design exhibition catalogue, the painting was listed as *A Twilight in the Catskills*. The complete title is given in *A Memorial Catalogue of the Paintings of Sanford Robinson Gifford, N.A.* (New York: The Metropolitan Museum of Art, 1881), where the painting is listed as #235 and described as being 27 x 54 inches.

14. "The National Academy of Design," *The Crayon* 8 (April 1861): 94. Additional reviews are cited in Weiss, *Sanford Robinson Gifford*, 225-226.

15. The painting bought by James is listed as #282 in the *Memorial Catalogue*, where it is described as being 48 x 38 inches. The painting bought by Jesup is listed as #276 in the *Memorial Catalogue*, where it carries the title *Kauterskill Falls*.

16. Lucia D. Pychowska, "Sketches of American Life and Scenery, II.—The Catskill Mountains," *The Continental Monthly* 5 (February 1864): 272-273. The fact that Pychowska knew only two paintings of the view by Gifford suggests that the unexhibited painting owned by Jesup was not widely known.

17. "An Hour in the Gallery of the National Academy of Design," *The Continental Monthly* 5 (June 1864): 686-687. The *Memorial Catalogue* describes *South Mountain—Catskills* as being 22 x 42 inches. *Memorial Catalogue* entries 317-319 are related oil sketches.

18. The oil sketch is reproduced as fig. 37 in the previously cited Alexander Gallery catalogue. The St. Johnsbury painting is 23 x 40 inches.

19. Some of the 1861 drawings are in the privately held 1861 sketchbook on microfilm at the Archives of American Art. Others are in the 1861 sketchbook at the Albany Institute of History and Art. The 1862 painting of the Mountain House (9⅜ x 18⅜ inches) is listed in the *Memorial Catalogue* as #278 and is now in the MacMurray Collection of Trinity College in Hartford, Connecticut. The oil sketch included in the current exhibition is almost certainly the painting listed in the *Memorial Catalogue* as #403. Adams Davidson Galleries in Washington, D.C., currently has an even smaller oil sketch of the Mountain House from North Mountain (6½ x 11 inches). This sketch was probably done at about the same time as the sketch included in the current exhibition and is probably *Memorial Catalogue* #481. Three other currently unlocated oil sketches of the Mountain House are listed in the *Memorial Catalogue* (#479, #480, and #482).

20. The most important pencil drawing is on page 15 of the 1865-1866 sketchbook at Vassar College. The oil sketch dated 9 October is *Memorial Catalog* #405. *Memorial Catalogue* #406 is another 1865 oil sketch of Hunter. A larger (11 x 18½ inches) oil sketch of Hunter is currently owned by William Vareika Fine Arts, Newport, Rhode Island.

21. Information in this paragraph derives from Gifford's previously mentioned sketchbooks, Jervis McEntee's manuscript diary, which is on microfilm in the Jervis McEntee papers at the Archives of American Art, and the previously cited book by Ila Weiss. Late versions of the view from South Mountain looking east include two paintings dated 1880 and titled *October in the Catskills*. One of these is in the collections of the Los Angeles County Museum of Art; the other is currently with James Maroney, Inc., in New York City.

Plate 93. Sanford Robinson Gifford, *South Mountain—Catskills*, c. 1873. Courtesy The Greene County Historical Society.

GEORGE HENRY HALL

1825-1913

The Turner's Shop, Palensville [sic], Catskill Mountain

Oil on canvas, 1880
35 x 47½ in.

Berry-Hill Galleries, New York
Plate 94

Best known as a painter of still life and genre, George Henry Hall was raised and probably born in Boston. He began exhibiting portrait paintings at the Boston Athenaeum in 1846. After visiting the 1849 exhibition of modern German paintings at the Düsseldorf Gallery in New York, Hall and his friend Eastman Johnson left the United States for the Academy in Düsseldorf. The first genre painting he exhibited was *Rubens and his Wife Hawking*, which he painted in Europe and sent back to the Boston Athenaeum in 1851. After a year in Düsseldorf, Hall traveled to Paris, where he remained for a year before moving to Rome. He lived in Rome until 1852 and then returned to New York. Hall began concentrating on his still life and genre work after 1852 and gradually stopped painting portraits. He was elected an Associate of the National Academy of Design in 1853. Hall traveled to Spain in 1860 and again in 1865 or 1866. He returned to New York in 1867 and was elected to full membership in the National Academy of Design in 1868. During the 1870s he maintained his studio in New York but made trips to Italy, Egypt, and Palestine. He died in New York City in 1913.[1]

Although we do not know when Hall first visited the Catskills, it must have been before 1865, the year that he exhibited a painting at the National Academy titled *In the Catskills-Portraits*. Hall became a seasonal resident of the area by 1867, when the local atlas identified him as the owner of a building on Kaaterskill Creek near the entrance to Kaaterskill Clove in the village of Palenville.[2] Hall moved nearly a mile upstream in 1871 and bought an old dry goods store from Elijah Trumpbour. Hall transformed this early nineteenth-century building into a large studio (plate 129). Located across Bristol Turnpike from Burger's Hotel and next to the bridge over the Kaaterskill Creek, Hall's studio commanded a view of the Dog's Hole Falls with the Clove beyond. At the same time that he rebuilt Trumpbour's store, Hall bought or built himself a small frame residence on a ledge behind Burger's Hotel. Distinguished by a flamboyant chimney covered in tiles that he had bought in Spain, Hall's studio quickly became a prominent local landmark and tourist destination. From 1876 until well into the twentieth century, Van Loan's *Catskill Mountain Guide* directed tourists to visit "the studio of the Artist Hall, with its old fashioned chimney outside of the house and then stop at Burger's Hotel to water your horses."[3] After he built his studio, Hall continued to winter in New York City and to travel abroad, but he seems to have spent nearly every summer and autumn in Palenville.

Hall exhibited *The Turner's Shop* at the National Academy of Design in 1880. It is set in Jim Barton's turning mill, the only turning mill in Palenville that had two lathes. By 1880, Barton would have been much older than the turner depicted, so it is likely that this craftsman was Barton's partner and son-in-law Charlie Post.[4]

With his vest hung above his workbench and his apron on, the turner stands with his back to his customers and to the viewer. We cannot see his face. He works while the other figures are at leisure. The other man in the picture is seated; we see his face in profile. His social position is ambiguous. That he is not wearing a jacket like the men in John Cocks's *Stage Coach in the Catskills* (plate 72) or the E. & H. T. Anthony stereograph *View from the top of the Kauterskill Fall, Looking down the Glen* (plate 34), suggests that he is not a typical middle- or upper-class tourist and that he did not enter the shop with the women. If he had, it would have been exceedingly rude for him to have sat down while they remained standing. A plausible explanation for his behavior is that he was already seated when the women came into the shop, rose to greet them, and returned to his seat at their urging. If this is so, then we must suppose that the seated man knows the turner, but the fact that he has the time to visit suggests that he is not a working man himself.

The young women are clearly tourists. They have come into the shop to purchase walking sticks. While the taller of the two women studies the artfully turned ornament, her companion makes eye contact with the seated man. The intimacy of their mutual gaze is visually echoed by the positioning of the walking sticks they carry: the stick he has resting in his lap extends to meet the base of the stick she holds in her left hand. The woman apparently finds the intimacy of the gaze somewhat unsettling, for she has reached out to her companion in a gesture that suggests a desire for emotional as well as physical support.

The three figures on the right are linked—walking stick to walking stick, hand to shoulder. But the turner stands apart. He is isolated both at the end of his workbench and by the fact that his back is to his customers and to us. The unused second lathe visually separates him from the figures to his right. The fact that we see his back instead of his face is the most visually striking element in the painting and can be described in two complementary ways. On the one hand, the turner has turned his back because he is alone in the way that all craftsmen are ultimately alone with their work: he has turned *towards* his work, and his back represents the commitment of the serious artisan. On the other hand, in turning towards his

Plate 94. George Henry Hall, *The Turner's Shop, Palensville [sic], Catskill Mountain*, 1880. Courtesy Berry-Hill Galleries.

work he has turned *from* his customers, and his dramatically turned back suggests some degree of hostility or resentment. It is likely that Hall's decision to paint the turner with his back turned and his face averted was influenced by historical events in Palenville.

When Hall first moved to Palenville in the late 1860s, the local economy was already becoming increasingly dependent on tourism. In the early nineteenth century, most Palenville residents had worked in the tanneries, the quarries, or as lumberjacks. Even after artists began to board in Palenville in the late 1840s, few residents had been completely dependent on tourism for their livelihood. By the late 1860s, most of the quarries had closed, the best timber had been cut, and the hemlocks necessary for tanning had become scarce. Most of the surviving tanneries and mills collapsed during the Panic of 1873. By the late 1870s, tourism was the major industry in Palenville, and many if not most Palenville residents had become financially dependent on the patronage of tourists.

The rapidity with which tourism grew is evidenced by the advertisements in Van Loan's *Catskill Mountain*

Guide. Prior to the 1870s, most tourists who visited the Catskills stayed on the mountain top. No one published a guide to boarding houses in the villages at lower elevations because there was not enough demand for such houses to warrant a guide. However, every edition of Van Loan's *Guide* since the first in 1876 included a boarding house directory. The 1878 boarding house directory for Palenville listed five houses with a total of 275 beds. The following year, the year Hall painted *The Turner's Shop*, the boarding house directory for Palenville listed twelve houses with a total of 458 beds.[5] Some of this increase was due to the opening of the Winchelsea, which seems to have been the first local hotel run by non-residents. Unlike locally owned establishments, which were advertised as "Houses," "Boarding Houses," or—in the case of Burger's—as a "Hotel and Boarding House," the Winchelsea was advertised as a "First-Class Summer Resort." Resorts like the Winchelsea were resented by the local citizens not only because they took business from locally owned establishments, but because they employed outsiders and frequently violated local liquor laws.[6]

By 1880, the local economy had become heavily dependent on the business of urban tourists whose wealth and drinking must have shocked the religiously and socially conservative residents. Residents who could remember the still recent days when Palenville had been a successful if small manufacturing center must have resented their increasing reliance on the patronage of city folk who saw them either as employees or as part of the picturesque scenery.

The turned back and averted face of the working figure in Hall's painting suggests the ambivalence that many late nineteenth-century Palenville residents must have felt toward the tourists they both needed and served. Moreover, whether the biographical Charlie Post who probably served as the model for the figure in the painting felt or was able to articulate this ambivalence, Hall is likely to have been acutely aware of it. In 1879-1880, when he painted *The Turner's Shop*, Hall was both an experienced world traveler who had spent years in Europe and a long-time local property owner. Unlike the women in his painting, he would have known Charlie Post and all the other local residents well. After all, he had already lived among them for at least thirteen years. And yet, of course, he was still the "Artist Hall," who came up from New York every summer. He was not a tourist, as were the women in *The Turner's Shop*, but neither was he a resident.

Hall's position in late nineteenth-century Palenville would have been like that of the ambiguous figure seated in the lower right-hand corner of *The Turner's Shop*. Neither obviously a tourist nor obviously a local resident, the seated figure both flirts with one of the tourists and seems to know the turner. Seated like an artist at his easel, he is both an observer of the little drama taking place in front of him and a participant in that drama. In the scene but not quite of it, the seated figure seems to be a surrogate for the artist: with his stick touching that of the woman at right and his attitude of familiarity with the turner, he is connected to but apart from both the tourists and the turner.

MF

1. The most useful biographical account is Bruce Chambers, "George Henry Hall, A Revised Biography," an unpublished manuscript in the Hall file at Berry-Hill Galleries, Inc. See also Lee M. Edwards, "George Henry Hall," in *Domestic Bliss: Family Life in American Painting, 1840-1910* (Yonkers, NY: The Hudson River Museum, 1986), 66.

2. F. W. Beers, *Atlas of Greene County, New York* (New York: F. W. Beers, A. D. Ellis, & G. G. Soule, 1867).

3. Van Loan, *Van Loan's Catskill Mountain Guide*, 9. An 1893 photograph of Hall at work in his studio is to be found in R. Lionel De Lisser, *Picturesque Catskills: Greene County* (1894; reprint, Cornwallville, NY: Hope Farm Press, 1983), 35. The building's history is traced in New York State Museum Division of Historical and Anthropological Services, *Cultural Resources Survey Report. Subject: PIN 1124.09.122*, 165-173, 184.

4. The turner is identified in Terrance DePietro, "Papers on Palenville" (Palenville, NY: Terrance Gallery, n.d.), an unpublished manuscript in the Hall file at Berry-Hill Galleries, Inc.

5. Unfortunately, the earliest such directory I have been able to locate is for 1878. Some of the increase in the number of beds listed may be due to the fact that houses that had not advertised in 1878 did so in 1879. Still, the spectacular rise in the number of advertised beds points both to the rapidly increasing scale of Catskill tourism and to the increasingly organized structure of the hospitality industry. The publication of Van Loan's *Guide* no doubt hastened the growth of local tourism, but the fact that the *Guide* was an immediate and long-lasting success suggests that the conditions necessary to the rapid growth of tourism were already present in 1876.

6. On the resentment residents felt toward summer visitors, see Evers, *The Catskills*, 483-484.

JAMES HAMILTON

1819-1878

Scene on the Hudson

Oil on canvas, 1845
38⅛ x 57⅛ in.

National Museum of American Art, Smithsonian Institution
Plate 95

The landscape and marine painter James Hamilton was born near Belfast, Ireland. In 1834, Hamilton's parents moved the family to the United States; they settled in Philadelphia. He first exhibited his work at the 1840 exhibition of the Artist Fund Society (Philadelphia); he exhibited both landscapes and marine scenes throughout the 1840s and early 1850s. Following his 1854 trip to Europe, he gradually stopped painting landscapes and concentrated his energies on the marine scenes for which he is now best known. In the mid-1840s, Hamilton exhibited a number of Hudson Valley views including *Scene on the Hudson* (plate 95), *Spuyten Tuyvil* [sic] *Creek, on the Hudson* (1846; American Art Union), *Landscape (Legend of the Hudson)* (1847; Pennsylvania Academy of the Fine Arts), and *Old Pines on Catskill Lake* (1848; American Art Union). Hamilton died in San Francisco in 1878.[1]

Scene on the Hudson represents two or perhaps three passages from Washington Irving's story "Rip Van Winkle." In the center foreground, Rip's eyes glaze over as he finishes a flagon of the mysteriously potent brew given him by Hendrik Hudson's men.[2] Beneath the arch of rock to Rip's left, Hendrik Hudson and his men are bowling. The middleground landscape was probably inspired by an earlier passage in the story where Rip rested from his fatiguing hike up the Catskill escarpment and looked out over the Hudson "moving on its silent

Plate 95. James Hamilton, *Scene on the Hudson*, 1845. Courtesy National Museum of American Art, Smithsonian Institution.

but majestic course, with the reflection of a purple cloud or the sail of a lagging bark here and there sleeping on its glassy bosom, and at last losing itself in the blue highlands."[3]

1. In addition to artist dictionaries and nineteenth-century exhibition records, see John Sartain, "James Hamilton," *Sartain's Union Magazine of Literature and Art* 10 (1852): 331-333, and Arlene Jacobowitz, *James Hamilton, 1819-1878: American Marine Painter* (Brooklyn: The Brooklyn Museum, 1966).

2. Hamilton inscribed the entire passage on the reverse of the canvas: "By degrees Rip's awe & apprehension Subsided. He even ventured, when no eye was fixed upon him, to taste the beverage, which he found had much the flavor of excellent Hollands. He was naturally a thirsty soul, and was soon tempted to repeat the draught. One taste provoked another, and he reiterated his visits to the flagon so often that at length his senses were overpowered, his eyes swam in his head, his head gradually declined, and he fell into a deep sleep."

3. Washington Irving, *The Sketch Book* (1819; reprint, New York: New American Library, 1961), 43.

GEORGE HARVEY

1801-1878

Early Twilight—Kaatskill Landing and Mountains from the East Bank of the Hudson River, N.Y.

Watercolor on paper, c. 1834-43
10 x 14¾ in. (sight)

Historic Hudson Valley, Tarrytown, New York
Plate 96

The Catskill Mountain House

Watercolor on paper, c. 1845-1850
9½ x 14 in.

Mrs. Judith Filenbaum
Plate 24

The Catskill Mountain House

Engraving by James Smillie, 1850
4¾ x 6¾ in.

New York State Library, Albany

Born in England, the watercolorist George Harvey traveled to the United States in 1820. By 1828, he had been elected an associate member of the National Academy of Design. By 1829, Harvey had settled in Boston, where he made his living as a painter of portraits in miniature. Harvey moved to Hastings-on-Hudson, New York, in 1834, and there designed and built himself a rural cottage. Harvey's cottage and its grounds so impressed his neighbor Washington Irving that Irving had Harvey help him design his home Sunnyside.

According to Harvey, it was his work as a landscape gardener that led him "more and more to notice and study the ever-varying atmospheric effects" of North America.[1] Harvey exhibited some of his "atmospheric landscapes" at the National Academy of Design in 1837 before returning to Europe in 1838. While in Europe, Harvey determined to have a set of his landscapes engraved. Like William Guy Wall's *Hudson River Port-folio* and William Henry Bartlett's *American Scenery* Harvey's *Atmospheric Landscapes* was to be published serially. His plan called for eight numbers, each of which was to contain five plates. The accompanying text was to be written by Harvey and revised by Washington Irving. By 1841, Harvey had acquired the patronage of Queen Victoria and enough financial backing to have four of the scenes engraved by the prominent engraver William J. Bennett. These engravings were published as *Harvey's Scenes in the Primeval Forests of America, at the Four Periods of the Year* (1841), which was designed to serve as a prospectus for the larger project. In order to drum up interest in the project, Harvey exhibited the full set of original atmospheric landscapes, impressions of the four engraved scenes, and a copy of the bound *Primeval Forest* in New York in both 1842 and 1843 and in Boston in 1844. Despite favorable reviews, Harvey was unable to secure additional financial support, and none of the *Atmospheric Landscapes* except the four plates in *The Primeval Forests* were ever engraved or published.

Early Twilight—Kaatskill Landing and Mountains from the East Bank of the Hudson River, N.Y. (plate 96) was

Plate 96. George Harvey, *Early Twilight—Kaatskill Landing and Mountains from the East Bank of the Hudson River, N.Y.*, c. 1834-1843. Courtesy Historic Hudson Valley.

to have been number thirty-five of the *Atmospheric Landscapes*. Another version of the scene, also in watercolor, is owned by the New-York Historical Society. The completed *Atmospheric Landscapes* was also to have included a second Catskill scene based on the unlocated watercolor *Morning Sky, Mountains, from near Kaatskill Village.*

The *Catskill Mountain House* (plate 24) dates from after the renovation of the Mountain House in 1845-1846. Engraved by James Smillie, it was published in the December 1850 issue of *Graham's Magazine* and reprinted in *Hudson River and Tappan Sea* (date unknown). Smillie's engraving of Harvey's watercolor is the unacknowledged source for the colored lithograph *Scenery of the Cattskill. The Mountain House* (plate 25), published by Currier & Ives. Unlike the vast majority of views of the Mountain House from the road, Harvey filled his foreground with an image of tourists *descending* from the hotel.[2]

1. George Harvey, *Harvey's Scenes in the Primeval Forests of America, at the Four Periods of the Year* (London: George Harvey, 1841), 9.

2. Koke, *American Landscape and Genre Paintings*, 94-95, 102; Donald Shelley, "George Harvey and His Atmospheric Landscapes of North America," *New-York Historical Society Quarterly* 32 (1948): 104-113; *The Knickerbocker* 18 (1841): 162-4; 20 (1842): 585; 23 (1844): 156-159; and 52 (1858): 436.

JOHN HEATEN (attributed)

1698-after 1745

The van Bergen Farm

Oil on cherry boards, American white pine battens,
c. 1733
18 x 87 in.

New York State Historical Association, Cooperstown, New York
Plate 3

Little is known about the artist John Heaten. English or of English descent, Heaten was active in Albany from 1730 until the mid-1740s. During this period, he married into a Dutch family, had children baptized in the Dutch church, and bought land in Albany.

Abraham Wendell was a prominent Albany merchant. About fifteen mid eighteenth-century Albany area portraits, including paintings of Abraham Wendell (Albany Institute of History and Art) and his brothers Johannes (dated 1737) and Philip, have been ascribed to the "Wendell limner." In a 17 August 1737 entry in his Day Book, Abraham Wendell wrote, "John Heaten I sent him 7 frames & Speckled Linne [linen] to Cover the Same for the Pictures I ordered." This entry was discov-

ered by the art historian Mary Black, who has ascribed all of the Wendell limner portraits to Heaten. It was Black who first noticed the stylistic similarities connecting these portraits with *The van Bergen Farm* and ascribed the latter to Heaten. In making this attribution, Black noted both that Heaten was one of the few limners active in the Catskill-Albany region in the 1730s, and that he painted William van Bergen and his wife in 1742. William was the son of Garret van Bergen, whose house is visible in the right background of *The van Bergen Farm.*[1]

1. Concerning the Wendell limner, see Mary Black, "Limners of the Upper Hudson," in Ian Quimby, ed., *American Painting to 1776: A Reappraisal* (Charlottesville, VA: University of Virginia Press, 1971), 217-249. Black describes her discovery of the Wendell Day Book entry in her article "Contributions Toward a History of Early Eighteenth-Century New York Portraiture: Identification of the Aetatis Suae and Wendell Limners," *American Art Journal* 12 (Autumn 1980): 30-31. Black ascribes *The van Bergen Farm* to Heaten in "Remembrances of the Dutch Homeland in Early New York Provincial Painting," in Roderic H. Blackburn and Mary Black, eds., *New World Dutch Studies: Dutch Arts and Culture in Colonial America, 1609-1776. Proceedings of the Symposium organized by the Albany Institute of History and Art, 2-3 August 1986* (Albany, NY: Albany Institute of History and Art, 1987), 129. Additional information concerning both Heaten and the van Bergen Farm can be found in Roderic H. Blackburn, "Dutch Arts and Culture in Colonial America," 141, and in Blackburn's catalogue entry on the painting in Roderic H. Blackburn and Ruth Piwonka, *Remembrance of Patria: Dutch Arts and Culture in Colonial America 1609-1776* (Albany, NY: Publishing Center for Cultural Resources, for the Albany Institute of History and Art, forthcoming). *The van Bergen Farm* is discussed in the essay. Because of the fragility of *The van Bergen Farm*, a full-sized color reproduction—not the actual overmantel—was included in the current exhibition.

JOHN WILLIAM HILL

1812-1879

*Esopus Creek, Near Shokan, Ulster Co.
New York*

Watercolor on paper, 1858
12½ x 10 in.
Yale University Art Gallery; The Jerald D. Fessenden, B.A. 1960, Fund

Hunter and Dog

Oil on canvas, c. 1867
10 x 16 in.

Mr. and Mrs. Wilbur L. Ross, Jr.
Plate 97

Fawn's Leap, Catskill, New York

Oil on canvas, 1868
30 x 38 in.

Kennedy Galleries, Inc., New York
Plate 50

John William Hill was one of the best known and most influential of the mid nineteenth-century artists who called themselves American pre-Raphaelites and dedicated themselves to the pursuit of an art characterized by an extreme fidelity to observed natural detail. While most of the artists active in this movement were markedly young men, Hill did not adopt pre-Raphaelite principles until he was in his forties and had already achieved considerable success as a commercial artist.

Born in London in 1812, Hill was the fifth child and oldest surviving son of the aquatint engraver John Hill, who moved his family to the United States in 1816. In 1819, John William Hill began a seven-year apprenticeship with his father. According to family tradition, the young apprentice helped color his father's engravings for William Guy Wall's *Hudson River Portfolio*. Despite his training as an engraver, John William Hill quickly shifted the focus of his professional activities to drawing and painting. He first exhibited at the National Academy of Design in 1828. He was elected an Associate of the Academy in 1833 and continued to participate in its annual exhibitions until a few years before his death in 1879.

Most of John William Hill's early works were topographical watercolors in the style of English-trained artists such as Paul Sandby (plate 118) and William Guy Wall. During the 1830s, a number of his topographical views were engraved by his father, while others were published by the New York lithographer George Endicott. From 1836 until 1841, he was a topographer for the New York State Geological Survey. From 1850 to 1855, he

worked for the Smith Brothers, who published lithographs based on his views of numerous North American cities including Halifax, Bangor, Philadelphia, Charleston, New Orleans, St. Louis, and Cincinnati.[1]

According to Charles Herbert Moore, Hill's adoption of pre-Raphaelite principles was like a religious conversion and happened in 1855 when Hill first read John Ruskin's *Modern Painters*.[2] Although Moore's account may be a little exaggerated, by 1856 Hill left the Smith Brothers, and the pre-Raphaelite-sounding title of the *Study from Nature* he showed at the 1856 exhibition of the National Academy of Design suggests that he had already begun to work in a more meticulous style. His growing mastery of the style is apparent in the 1858 *Esopus Creek, Near Shokan, Ulster Co. New York*, in which Hill has abandoned the large strokes and broad washes of his earlier work and used the tiny strokes of pure color Ruskin advocated in his 1857 *The Elements of Drawing*. At the 1857 exhibition of the Pennsylvania Academy of the Fine Arts, Hill exhibited a watercolor view *On Esopus Creek* and a view of *Esopus Creek, Near Shokan, Ulster Co., N.Y.*, which was probably in oil. What seems to be the earliest printed recognition of Hill's adoption of pre-Raphaelite principles came in a review of the 1857 National Academy of Design exhibition, which praised his works as being "remarkable for good taste and careful execution" and singled out *A Sluggish Stream* as "a remarkably faithful study from nature."[3]

Plate 97. John William Hill, *Hunter and Dog*, c. 1867. Courtesy Mr. and Mrs. Wilbur L. Ross, Jr.

In mid-February 1863, a number of New Yorkers sympathetic to Ruskin's call for a more meticulous art organized themselves into an Association for the Advancement of Truth in Art and determined to publish a journal espousing their point of view. Hill did not attend the organizational meetings—nor is he known to have attended any later meetings—but in recognition of his age and long adherence to pre-Raphaelite principles he was nonetheless elected president. In so doing, the organizers may also have been trying to lure him away from his home in Nyack, New York; if so, however, the effort failed, and by March Hill had turned the presidency over to the journalist and art critic Clarence Cook. In November, members of the association urged Hill to assume the editorship of their journal—*The New Path*—but he declined this responsibility as well.[4]

Like the other American pre-Raphaelites, Hill devoted much of his energy to the production of still lifes and *plein air* studies. Hill was especially well known for his close-up studies of "weedy banks, and masses of garden flowers, wild flowers and grasses."[5] According to Ruskin's American publicists, it was only by doing these kinds of finely detailed studies that an artist could acquire the skills necessary to the production of more ambitious and larger works. Even sympathetic reviewers such as Clarence Cook admitted that these studies might be less than exciting but insisted that "just now we need studies and students more than high art, at least as the majority of artists understand that term, and shall never get a real 'high art' until we have had a long preparation of study." Therefore, Cook concluded, "we are willing to bear with the monotony for a few years."[6]

Although best known for his watercolor still lifes, Hill never stopped producing landscapes. Some of these were watercolors; others were oils. Surviving drawings and nineteenth-century exhibition records suggest that during the 1860s Hill traveled to Mount Desert Island in Maine and the White Mountains as well as to the nearby Catskills.[7] Though small in size, Hill's landscapes were sufficiently well known and aesthetically powerful that in his review of the 1867 Yale School of Fine Arts exhibition, Clarence Cook complained that "Mr. J. W. Hill sends a Fruit-Piece, which does justice to one side of his ability, but leaves the public uninformed on his success in landscape, in which, I think, he has no superior among American artists."[8]

Despite their spirited defense of detailed studies and the small landscapes being produced by the American pre-Raphaelites, sympathetic art critics looked forward to the creation of larger, oil landscapes that would combine finely drawn foregrounds with accurate middleground and background views. As early as 17 September 1863, the architect and critic Russell Sturgis had thus encouraged the pre-Raphaelite painter Thomas Charles Farrer to concentrate his energies on "a large picture" rather than on "drawings and studies which make no impression save on the initiated."[9] Less sympathetic observers were more caustic: "And who are the new-men, and what have they done, and what do they promise? They are reduced to a few fanatical young men with one idea—and that is, to spend a whole summer or a whole winter over a small canvas, producing a so-called painting from nature, which a photographer might have saved them all the labor of, and done it well—a feeble little cold colorless ghost of a picture, with about as much of the spirit of nature in it as there is heat in an icicle."[10] Or, as a slightly less angry reviewer wrote, "We fully appreciate the amount of care and hard work necessary to the production of one of these so-called pre-Raphaelite studies of nature, but they seem to fall short of high art, and to fail in giving that real satisfaction that we derive from a good picture. The attention is detracted from the effect of the whole by the lesser details that are of little or no real consequence...."[11]

In the mid-1860s, sympathetic art critics picked Farrer as the most promising painter of pre-Raphaelite landscapes working in America. Farrer seems to have tried to live up to his publicity, and in 1864 he began to work on larger canvases.[12] Although none of the reviewers sympathetic to the pre-Raphaelite project ever gave one of Farrer's larger paintings an altogether positive review, they usually found something good to say. In 1867, however, Farrer's two new landscapes were savaged by two of the reviewers most sympathetic to the pre-Raphaelite project. In the review that praised John William Hill as the equal of any landscape painter working in America, Clarence Cook noted that the exhibition included an unprecedented large selection of pre-Raphaelite works and wrote that almost "every drawing here, and every painting—we must perforce except several of Mr. Farrer's later pictures, *The Fawn's Leap* and *A Street in Northampton* for instance, to which we are sorry to see his name attached—is the result, sometimes successful, sometimes unsuccessful, of an independent experiment to accomplish some particular end."[13] Russell Sturgis, who had earlier encouraged Farrer to work on larger canvases, was equally scathing: let any one walk from Mr. Farrer's paintings of four and five "years ago, to the *Street Scene in Northampton* by moonlight, of a recent time, and the just completed *Fawn's Leap*, and he will probably wonder, as we do, what influences can be at work to cause such a change and such a breaking of promise to the hope. *The Fawn's Leap* is especially unfortunate; as mistaken a landscape as Mr. Farrer has ever painted, and as bad a painting of a waterfall and rocks as Mr. [John] Hill's [*The Falls of the Hudson*] is completely good."[14]

Fawn's Leap is one of the most prominent waterfalls in the central section of Kaaterskill Clove. It appears in numerous midcentury landscapes, including John Frederick Kensett's *The Fawn's Leap* (1859; plate 48) and, most famously, Asher B. Durand's *Kindred Spirits*

(1849; fig. 14). Durand's painting is—and would have been widely recognized as—a composite. Commissioned to paint a memorial painting of Thomas Cole to be given to the man—William Cullen Bryant—who had delivered Cole's funeral oration, Durand adapted the geography of Kaaterskill Clove so as to depict Cole showing both Kaaterskill Falls and Fawn's Leap to Bryant. Asher B. Durand was the president of the National Academy of Design from 1845 to 1861. For a pre-Raphaelite painter, the fact that the *Fawn's Leap* had been used by the long-time president of the National Academy of Design in a composite painting memorializing the painter universally recognized as the founder of the native school of landscape art would have made it a powerful symbol of the aesthetic values against which he was rebelling.

Farrer finished and first exhibited his *Fawn's Leap* in July 1867. Within a year, John William Hill painted two versions of the same scene. One is a watercolor; the other is an oil. Both are signed and dated 1868.[15] The subjects of the watercolor and the oil are almost identical, although the handling of the oil is much looser. The finished oil *Fawn's Leap, Catskill, New York* (plate 50) is far and away the largest known work by Hill done after his adoption of pre-Raphaelite principles.[16] Although there is no hard proof, the circumstantial evidence suggests that Hill painted his large view of Fawn's Leap in direct response to the lambasting Farrer's *Fawn's Leap* had received the previous summer. In attempting a large oil, Hill was finally accepting the group responsibilities he had declined in 1863. If none of the younger men could meet the calls for a successful larger painting, "old Mr. Hill" would.[17]

1. Biographical information on John William Hill's early life derives from the standard artist dictionaries, John Henry Hill, *John William Hill: An Artist's Memorial* (New York: n.p., 1888); Richard J. Koke, "John Hill, Master of Aquatint: 1770-1850," *New-York Historical Society Quarterly* 43 (1959): 62, 105-106; John Reps, *Views and Viewmakers of Urban America* (Columbia, MO: University of Missouri Press, 1984), 183-184; and Annette Blaugrund, "John William Hill," in Linda S. Ferber and William H. Gerdts, *The New Path: Ruskin and the American Pre-Raphaelites* (Brooklyn, NY: The Brooklyn Museum, 1985), 180.

2. Charles Herbert Moore, "An Artist's Memorial," in Hill, *John William Hill: An Artist's Memorial*, quoted in David H. Dickason, *The Daring Young Men: The Story of the American Pre-Raphaelites* (Bloomington, IN: Indiana University Press, 1953), 260.

3. *The Crayon* 4 (July 1857): 222.

4. Concerning the Association and *The New Path*, see Linda Ferber, "'Determined Realists': The American Pre-Raphaelites and the Association for the Advancement of Truth in Art," in Ferber and Gerdts, *The New Path*, 11-37. The fact that the association urged Hill to assume the editorship of *The New Path* is reported in Charles Herbert Moore's 30 November 1863 letter to Thomas Charles Farrer. This letter is in the Gordon Lester Ford Collection of the New York Public Library and on microfilm at the Archives of American Art. Elsewhere in this letter, Moore provided a clue as to the tone John William Hill took with his younger colleagues: "I've just got a letter from John Hill. He congratulates me upon being in the country, & thinks 'A young artist who has just commenced to work on the right

track, can employ his time to much better advantage, at any season of the year, in the country than in the city'—how are you '*Young artist who has just commenced to work on the right track!*'"

5. Moore, "An Artist's Memorial" quoted in William H. Gerdts, "Through a Glass Brightly: The American Pre-Raphaelites and Their Still Lifes and Nature Studies," in Ferber and Gerdts, *The New Path*, 57.

6. "The National Academy of Design," *New York Daily Tribune*, 14 June 1867, 2.

7. The watercolor *View on Catskill Creek* (1867; The Metropolitan Museum of Art) is signed and dated but is not inscribed with a location. The title comes from John William Hill's son—the pre-Raphaelite artist John Henry Hill—who donated the drawing to the Metropolitan Museum of Art in 1882. *Hunter and Dog* is neither signed nor dated but is probably from 1867 or 1868 and is probably a view of either Kaaterskill or Esopus Creek.

8. "Fine Arts in New-Haven," New York *Daily Tribune*, 14 August 1867, 2:1-2. The final catalogue of the Yale exhibition lists John William Hill watercolor landscapes of a *Mill Pond*, *Mount Carmel*, *Lake George*, and a *View Near Sing Sing*, while the preliminary catalogue lists none. Hill's landscapes probably arrived after Cook visited the exhibition.

9. The letter is in the Gordon Lester Ford Collection of the New York Public Library.

10. "The Editor's Easy Chair," *Harper's New Monthly Magazine* 32, March 1866, 523.

11. Oscuro, "The Fine Arts. The Exhibition at Yale College," *The New York Times*, 22 July 1867, 3:1-2.

12. Farrer's largest located canvas is a *View of Northampton from the Dome of the Hospital* (1865; Smith College Museum of Art). After seeing this canvas, Charles Herbert Moore wrote Farrer, "I must tell you that I am astonished that *you* could have done a thing so utterly coarse." Moore claimed that the dam in the middle of the painting reminded him of "the landscape subjects upon the glass fronts of Yankee clocks." Moore's letter is dated 25 April 1864 and is in the Gordon Lester Ford Collection.

13. "Fine Arts in New-Haven," 2:1-2.

14. "The Yale College Art Building and Exhibition," *The Nation* 5, 8 August 1867, 116.

15. The watercolor (13¾ x 17¾ in.) is in a private collection and is reproduced in Ferber and Gerdts, *The New Path*, 187. The oil is included in the current exhibition. Washburn Gallery, New York, owns a smaller unsigned and undated version of the same scene. It is reproduced in The Vatican Museums, *The Mirror of Creation: Fifty Years of American Nature Painting* (24 September-23 November 1980). In Ferber and Gerdts, *The New Path*, 187, May Brawley Hill suggests that the unfinished oil might be by John Henry Hill.

16. The finished oil *Fawn's Leap, Catskill, New York* is probably the painting Hill exhibited at the March 1868 exhibition of the Brooklyn Art Association. One of Hill's views of *Fawn's Leap* was shown at the 1872 exhibition of the National Academy of Design. The Inventory of American Paintings, Smithsonian Institution, lists two other large paintings by John W. Hill—a 30 x 38 inch view of *The Palisades* dated 1868, which was sold at Sotheby's in 1947, and a 30 x 38 inch view of a *Pool on the Lawrence Estate, Palisades, New York* dated 1868, which was sold at Sotheby Parke-Bernet Inc. in March 1968. The 1968 Sotheby Parke-Bernet Inc. catalogue *American & Canadian Paintings & Drawings* (14 March 1968) described it as a view of "two women in scarlet cloaks standing at the water's edge before a cascade and two rock ledges. Signed and dated 1868." Kennedy Galleries, Inc., bought *Fawn's Leap* (30 x 38 in.) in June 1968. The purchase order was made out for *Palisades, N.Y.*. Kennedy Galleries changed the title almost

immediately after the painting was acquired. The evidence suggests the Kennedy Galleries *Fawn's Leap* is the painting sold at Sotheby's in 1947 and 1968.

17. The quoted phrase is from [Clarence Cook], "The National Academy of Design," *New York Daily Tribune,* 14 June 1867, 2.

WINSLOW HOMER

1836-1910

Under the Falls, Catskill Mountains

Engraving, 1872
9⅛ x 13⅞ in.
Originally published in *Harper's Weekly,*
14 September 1872

Kennedy Galleries, Inc., New York
Plate 53

Winslow Homer was born in Boston and moved to nearby Cambridge when he was six. He exhibited talent in drawing from a young age. Homer's mother was herself an accomplished amateur artist and encouraged his interest. Homer's father bought him books of lithographs to study from, and when he was nineteen he was apprenticed to the Boston lithographer J.H. Bufford, where he was set to work making covers for sheet music. By the end of his two years at Bufford's, he had been commissioned to do the likenesses of all the members of the state senate. Homer hated it at Bufford's establishment, and he promised himself that he would never work on a regular basis for anyone again. He opened a studio as a free-lance artist in 1857. His first work was done for *Ballou's Pictorial,* where he made many drawings from photographs for portrait engravings. In 1858, he began receiving regular commissions from the new and very popular New York magazine *Harper's Weekly.* This relationship with *Harper's* would turn out to be long and prosperous for Homer. Homer went to stay in New York for a short time in 1859 and finally moved there in 1861. He supposedly entered night painting classes at the National Academy, although there is no evidence to support this speculation.[1] Later in 1861, he was commissioned by the Harper Brothers to go to Washington to draw Lincoln's inauguration and then to tour the battlefields in Virginia. His first drawings of the Civil War were mostly camp scenes and humorous incidents. He returned home late in 1862 and began painting war subjects in preparation for the National Academy show of 1863. He continued to show war paintings in 1864, was elected an Associate of the Academy in 1865, and was elected a full Academician in 1866 when the oil painting *Prisoners from the Front* received rave reviews. In 1867, his *Prisoners from the Front* was to be shown at the Paris

International Exposition, at Brussels and at Antwerp, so he felt he had a compelling reason to travel to Europe. He held a sale of his work to raise money and left for Paris. Homer's time in Paris had a deep influence on his later work, both in terms of his choice of subjects and the development of his style. Homer was exposed to the work of Corot and Millet, to the young Impressionists Manet, Monet, and Degas, and to the current fad of collecting things Japanese. The simple line and color of Japanese prints influenced Homer's work throughout the later phases of his career.

Upon his return to New York, Homer engaged in a flurry of work for magazines, probably trying to rebalance his finances after his trip. He drew designs for engravings in *Harper's Weekly, Appleton's Journal, Galaxy, Our Young Folks, Hearth and Home, Every Saturday, Scribner's Monthly,* and other publications. Most of Homer's pictures after his return were of light-hearted pursuits attractive to a public exhausted by the Civil War. Those who could afford it turned to tourism for fun and entertainment, and the seventies were boom years for the tourism industry. Tourists went to the places that had been popularized before the war—the Catskills, the White Mountains, the Adirondacks, the beaches. Homer followed to draw the tourists. He went to the White Mountains in 1868, the Jersey shore and the White Mountains in 1869, the Jersey shore and the Adirondacks in 1870. By 1873, however, he sharply decreased his output of illustrations to concentrate on watercolor work.

Homer first went to the vicinity of the Catskills in 1871, when he visited Lawson Valentine and his family at their rented summer home in Walden, near Hurley.[2] He probably did not stay in their house. Gordon Hendricks suggests that he stayed at A.H. Sutton's Bridge Hotel, a brand-new and highly recommended hotel in Hurley on the bank of Esopus Creek. Just a few blocks from the hotel were the Hurley country store and the school that figured in the well-known paintings *The Country School* (1871; St. Louis Art Museum), *Crossing the Pasture* (c. 1871; Amon Carter Museum), *The Mill* (*The Morning Bell*) (c. 1871-1872; Yale University Art Gallery), *The Country Store* (1872; Hirshhorn Museum), and *Snap the Whip* (1872; Butler Institute of American Art). *The Four Leaf Clover* (1873; Detroit Institute of Arts) was done in Walden itself. During this first visit to the Catskill area, Homer made the side trip to Kaaterskill Falls that resulted in the engraving that appeared in the 14 September 1872 issue of *Harper's Weekly, Under the Falls, Catskill Mountains.*[3]

Homer's view invites comparison with other views from under the falls: Cole's *Kaaterskill Falls* of 1826 (fig. 6), William Guy Wall's *Cauterskill Falls on the Catskill Mountains, Taken from under the Cavern* of 1826-27 (fig. 10), and Gherlando Marsiglia's *Catskill Falls* of circa 1831 (plate 17). These three views, created within five years of each other but more than forty years before Homer's engraving, illustrate how greatly attitudes about nature had changed in four decades. The cavern behind the falls seemed to fascinate the earlier painters as a yawning gash in the irregular and tremendous cliff. The Cole, the earliest of the four, shows no tourists in the scene, although the Catskill Mountain House was already well established. An Indian is on the ledge, a part of the savage sublimity Cole wanted to represent. Cole uses the landscape to evince a feeling of wildness, with his stormy sky, the uneven pines lining the edge of the hillsides, the mist raised by the pounding water, and the bits of trees fallen from the heights above and lying broken and twisted on the rocks in the foreground. The only element that offers refuge from the violence of the scene is the roof of the cavern that forms a rather regular awning overhead. Wall introduced tourists, but their presence seems only to emphasize the sublimity of the scene. One of them ventures into the cavern, which has taken on more sweeping proportions than in the Cole, while three other tourists express their fear for his safety. The cavern is dark and forbidding, a frightening but thrilling place to be. The Marsiglia engraving exaggerates the form of the cavern until it becomes like a whirlpool, spiraling around the falls, the vista, and the two tiny tourists below.

Forty years later, Homer's tourists hardly cower in fear. There are now many tourists in the cavern, and the two most prominent figures are unaccompanied women. One couple has even dared to scramble down the slope and is now working to get back up as the water is released from above. Homer, in fact, showed very little of the actual falls and instead concentrated on the people enjoying them.

Homer returned to Walden in 1874. In 1876, the Valentines moved their summer home nearly fifty miles south of Walden when they purchased Houghton Farm. Homer went to Houghton Farm in the late summer and fall of 1876, 1877, and 1878. While he stayed in the guest lodge at the Farm, he made annual voyages to the town of Leeds.[4] After 1878, Homer's visits to upstate New York seem to have been restricted to the Adirondacks. Homer moved to Prout's Neck, Maine, in 1882. He died in Prout's Neck in 1910.

MF

1. The best biography of Winslow Homer is Gordon Hendricks, *The Life and Work of Winslow Homer* (New York: Abrams, 1979). Also see Helen A. Cooper, *Winslow Homer Watercolors* (New Haven, CT: Yale University Press, 1986).

2. Lawson Valentine was a succesful varnish manufacturer in New York. When Homer's brother Charles Savage Homer, Jr., left his job as a chemist at Lawrence, Massachusetts, he went to work for Valentine. There he invented Valspar, a very durable varnish still used for wooden masts.

3. During this period, Homer most often drew his designs in pencil and then painted in wash directly on the wood block. He provided firm outlines and simple blocks of light and shadow, which made it easy for the engraver to transform his work accurately. In an effort to bolster his reputation as a painter, however, Homer occasionally had the engravers copy one of his existing paintings for a design. *Under the Falls* seems to be one of these, as it was published accompanied by the phrase, "From a painting by Winslow Homer." The painting has not been located. On *Under the Falls*, see Philip Beam, *Winslow Homer's Magazine Engravings* (New York: Harper & Row, 1979), 36, 216.

4. Evidence of his 1876 visit is provided by the oil painting *Twilight at Leeds, N.Y.* (1876; Museum of Fine Arts, Boston), which is signed and dated. It was first exhibited under the title *Landscape* at the National Academy exhibition in 1877. A reproduction of it is #244 in Hendricks's checklist. A letter by the Catskill area artist Benjamin Bellows Grant Stone to his wife Mary dated 25 September 1877 indicates that Homer was planning to go to Leeds that autumn. The letter is in the Greene County Historical Society. A sketch in the Cooper-Hewitt Museum is inscribed "Leeds, Oct 10th/1878."

DANIEL HUNTINGTON

1816-1906

William Cullen Bryant

Oil on canvas, 1866
40 x 32⅛ in.

The Brooklyn Museum; Gift of A. Augustus Healy, Carll H. De Silver, E. G. Blackford, C. W. Seamans, H. J. Morse, R. B. Woodward, James R. Howe, W. B. Davenport, F. S. Jones, A. Abraham, and C. A. Schieren, 01.1507
Plate 98

One of the most versatile painters working in mid nineteenth century New York, Daniel Huntington painted historical and religious scenes, genre scenes, still lifes, and landscapes as well as the portraits for which he is now best known. Born in New York City, Huntington studied at a preparatory academy in New Haven before entering Yale College. Expelled after a year at Yale, he enrolled at Hamilton College in upstate New York, where he met the portait painter Charles Loring Elliott (plate 87). Huntington took lessons from Elliott before returning to New York City in 1835. Once back in New York City, he studied with Samuel F. B. Morse and Henry Inman before opening his own studio in 1836. Huntington made his first trip to Europe in 1839 and was elected a member of the National Academy of Design upon his return to New York City in 1840. During the early years of his career, Huntington specialized in landscapes and religious allegories, but he quickly found that portraits were more lucrative; by about 1860, he had largely stopped working in other genres. Huntington lived in Europe from 1842 to 1845 and from 1851 to 1858. He returned to Europe for a last visit in 1882. He was president of the National Academy of Design from 1862 to 1870 and again from 1877 to 1890. He was vice-president of The Metropolitan Museum of Art for thirty-three years and president of the prestigious Century Club from 1879 to 1895. He died in New York City in 1906.[1]

In 1866, William Cullen Bryant (1794-1878) was at the height of his influence as editor and half owner of the New York *Evening Post*. As a teenager, Bryant had written "Thanatopsis," "To a Waterfowl," and "Forest Hymn," which were widely recognized as some of the first important nature poems written in the United States. He wrote less poetry after becoming editor of the *Evening Post* in 1826, but he quickly became one of the most active promoters of the appreciation of nature and the virtues of landscape painting. Friendly with both Thomas Cole and Asher B. Durand, Bryant served on the boards of the Sketch Club, the American Art Union, and the Century Club. In 1830, he wrote the landscape descriptions that accompanied Durand's engravings in *The American Landscape*.[2] In 1839 and 1840, he published accounts of his trips with Cole to Kaaterskill and Plattekill Cloves. And in 1848, he gave Cole's funeral oration at the National Academy of Design. Late in life, Bryant wrote the introduction for and edited the two volumes of the hugely successful *Picturesque America*.[3]

In 1866, Bryant and Huntington had known each other for more than twenty years. In the early 1840s, one of Bryant's closest friends was Huntington's brother-in-law, the landscape and portrait painter Cornelius Ver Bryck (1813-1844).[4] Huntington seems to have been a regular visitor at Bryant's country house on Long Island. In 1844, when the Philadelphia publishers Carey & Hart proposed doing an illustrated version of Bryant's poems and suggested that Huntington be hired to do the illustrations, Bryant happily concurred: "I could not suggest a better artist than Huntington for the designs...."[5] In 1845, Bryant visited Huntington in Paris. In 1850, Bryant helped organize a promotional exhibition of Huntington's paintings. In the fall of 1864, Huntington organized an elaborate celebration at the Century Club to honor Bryant on the occasion of his seventieth birthday. At the celebration, Huntington presented Bryant a portfolio containing nearly fifty sketches by the most prominent members of the National Academy of Design and said: "Of the vast multitudes who with ever-growing delight bend over your pages, there are none whose hearts glow with deeper joy and pride than those of the artists..., who, for many years, by mountain and stream, and in the stillness of the studio, have been cheered by your vivid pictures of American scenery and inspired by your songs of human freedom."[6]

Huntington's portrait of Bryant seems to carry both a private and a public meaning. His decision to paint Bryant in an autumnal setting and carrying a book of poems open to "La Primavera," evokes not only the poet's advancing years but also his well-documented depression following the death of his wife in July 1865.[7] The fact that the book is only partially opened to expose

Plate 98. Daniel Huntington, *William Cullen Bryant*, 1866. Courtesy The Brooklyn Museum.

the title of the poem suggests that this reference is somewhat cloaked, an internal meaning that Bryant would understand. Bryant never titled one of his own poems either "La Primavera" or "The Spring." In his youth, however, one month after taking over as editor of the *Evening Post*, Bryant had published a translation called "Spring-time" after an untitled ode by the Spanish lyric poet Estevan Manuel Villegas (1596-1669).[8] The last stanza of Bryant's translation is particularly appropriate to his sadness at the time Huntington painted his portrait:

Thou, who alone art fair,
And whom alone I love, art far away.
Unless thy smile be there,
It makes me sad to see the earth so gay;
I care not if the train
Of leaves, and flowers, and zephyrs go again.

Huntington had evidently chosen this poem for its biographical resonance. But at the same time, by positioning the writer leaning on a rock, Huntington invited Bryant to seek support from nature, the very source of consolation and inspiration Bryant had celebrated in his early poetry.

As a public portrait, Huntington's decision to paint Bryant in a landscape setting carrying a volume of poems evokes Bryant's universally recognized position as the great American nature poet. In a public portrait, the depiction of the otherwise obscure poem "La Primavera" seems to hint at Bryant's historical position as the fountainhead or "spring" of American landscape poetry and painting. Huntington's painting is thus a portrait of the source of American landscape poetry in the "fall" of his life.[9]

MF

1. Biographical information derives from artist dictionaries, E. Anna Lewis, "Art and Artists of America," *Graham's Magazine* 45 (August 1854): 141-144; Tuckerman, *Book of the Artists*, 321-332; D. O. C. Townley, "Daniel Huntington, Ex-President NAD," *Scribner's Monthly* 2, May 1871, 44-49.

2. William Cullen Bryant, ed., *The American Landscape* (New York: Elam Bliss, 1830).

3. Bryant's account of the trip he and Cole took to the Plattekill Clove is in the *Evening Post* for Friday, 24 July 1840. His account of the trip he and Cole took to the Kaaterskill Clove appeared in the *Evening Post* the previous summer.

4. William Cullen Bryant II and George Voss, eds., *Letters of William Cullen Bryant*, vol. 2 (New York: Fordham University Press, 1977), 261. Like Huntington, Ver Bryck had studied with Samuel F. B. Morse and was a close friend of Thomas Cole. Ver Bryck exhibited a portrait of Bryant at the National Academy of Design in 1841.

5. Bryant and Voss, eds., *Letters of William Cullen Bryant*, vol. 2, 273. Carey & Hart eventually settled on Leutze for the task of illustrating the volume. Although Bryant respected Leutze's work, he was disappointed with some of the results. In a letter of 31 August 1846 (vol. 2, 468), Bryant wrote, "The 'Greek Boy' it seems to me, is extremely faulty in drawing. One of the legs is so strangely drawn that I cannot bring myself to believe the artist left it so in his design, ... Can nothing be done to remedy the defect? Covering it up with a *bush*? or something of that sort?" The picture was not changed, and it appears in *Poems by William Cullen Bryant, with illustrations by E. Leutze* (Philadelphia: Carey & Hart, 1847), facing 200.

6. Parke Godwin, *A Biography of William Cullen Bryant* (New York: D. Appleton & Co., 1883), 220.

7. Bryant was also depressed by the illness of his youngest daughter. Bryant's depression is noted both in Godwin's biography (250) and in the Bryant entry in the *Dictionary of American Biography*.

8. Bryant's translation was first published in the *United States Literary Gazette*, July 1826, and was reprinted in the various collections of his poems. Villegas began publishing poetry at the age of fourteen. He stopped writing at the age of twenty-one in order to devote all his attentions to the practice of law. His only collection of poems was titled *Amatorias* and was published in 1620. Concerning Villegas, see Henry W. Longfellow, *Poets and Poetry of Europe* (Philadelphia: Carey & Hart, 1845), 706, and George Ticknor, *History of Spanish Literature*, vol. 2 (New York: Harper and Brothers, 1849), 541-544. Concerning Bryant's knowledge of Villegas, see Stanley T. Williams, *La Huella Española en la Literatura Norte Americana* (Madrid: Biblioteca Romanica Hispanica, n.d.), 156-192, 410-426.

9. This seems to be the interpretation of the setting advanced by Tuckerman in *Book of the Artists*, 325. According to Tuckerman, Huntington's portrait of Bryant "differs from previous 'counterfeit presentments' of the poet, in giving him a more familiar air; the attitude is natural and the costume simple; a background of autumnal foliage is very appropriate, and the expression of the noble head is genial, such as Bryant's friends will gladly recognize."

GEORGE INNESS

1825-1894

Catskill Scene

Pencil on paper heightened with white, 1869
10 x 16 in.

George Walter Vincent Smith Art Museum, Springfield, Massachusetts

Leeds, N.Y. Looking towards the Catskills

Engraving by Robert Hinshelwood, 1869
8¾ x 13¾ in.

Mr. and Mrs. R. M. Decker
Plate 99

Greene County, New York

Oil on canvas, 1878
25½ x 38½ in.

Orlando Museum of Art; Gift of Martin Garcia Andersen Foundation in memory of Martin Andersen, and the Acquisition Trust
Plate 100

Red Oaks

Oil on canvas, c. 1893
14½ x 22 in.

New Jersey State Museum, Trenton; Gift of James L. Johnson and Purchase, FA1972.54
Plate 101

George Inness was born on a farm near Newburgh, New York. He was raised in New York City and in Newark, New Jersey. In 1841, he studied with the itinerant artist John Jesse Baker, and from 1841 to 1843 he apprenticed with the New York engravers Sherman & Smith. After leaving Sherman & Smith, Inness spent a short time, probably in 1843, studying with the painter Régis François Gignoux. The first recorded exhibition of Inness's work was in the spring of 1844, when two of his paintings were shown at the annual exhibition of the National Academy of Design. He exhibited at the National Academy of Design and the American Art Union annually from 1844 to 1850.

Inness married Elizabeth Hart in late 1850, and in December 1850 or early 1851 Inness and his wife sailed from New York for Italy. Their first child was born in Florence in 1851. Inness and his family returned to New York in May 1852. He was elected an associate member

Plate 99. George Inness, *Leeds, N.Y. Looking towards the Catskills,* 1869. Courtesy Mr. and Mrs. R. M. Decker.

of the National Academy of Design in 1853. In late 1853 or early 1854, Inness and his family returned to Europe; they settled in Paris, where they remained until the fall of 1854, when they returned to New York. In 1860 Inness moved his family to Medfield, Massachusetts, where they remained until late 1863 or early 1864. They then moved to Eagleswood, New Jersey. Inness and his family lived in New Jersey until 1867, when they moved to Brooklyn. He was elected a full member of the National Academy of Design in 1868. In the spring of 1870, Inness and his family returned to Europe, where they remained until early 1875.[1]

Inness exhibited Catskill subjects throughout his career. The first of these were *Landscape, View in Ulster County, New York* and *Scene near Marbletown, New York,* which he sold to the American Art Union in 1847. In 1853, he exhibited a view of a *Nook in Catskill Clove* at the National Academy of Design. None of these early works are currently located.

Although Inness worked in the Catskill area intermittently throughout his career, he was most active in the area in the years between his 1864 move to Eagleswood and his 1870 departure for Europe. Unlike most earlier landscape painters who worked in the Catskills, Inness ignored the sites associated with both the Mountain

House and Kaaterskill Clove. Except for early works such as the 1853 *Nook in Catskill Clove,* all the paintings Inness did of the Catskills were done in the valley below the mountain top, and most seem to depict views in the area surrounding the village of Leeds. Leeds is located on Catskill Creek northwest of the village of Catskill. In the mid-1860s and 1870s, the boarding houses in Leeds became popular resorts for a number of New York artists. Other artists who boarded in Leeds during these years included Winslow Homer and James Renwick Brevoort.

Both the catalogue to the Inness Memorial Exhibition held in December 1894 and the catalogue to the Inness Executor's Sale held in February 1895 list five 1864 oil studies done in the neighborhood of Leeds.[2] The first large paintings Inness worked up from these sketches were probably the *Landscape near Leeds, New York* (Ireland #318, currently unlocated) and the *Mountain Landscape—The Painter at Work* or *Leeds in the Catskills, with the Artist Sketching,* now in the collection of the Berkshire Museum, Pittsfield, Massachusetts (Ireland #317). The Inness Executor's Sale contained two oil sketches of Leeds dated 1865 (Ireland #335 and #344) and two more dated 1866 (Ireland #378 and #379). That Inness spent at least part of the summer of 1866 in the Catskills is also suggested by an unsigned article in *The*

Plate 100. George Inness, *Greene County, New York*, 1878. Courtesy Orlando Museum of Art.

Round Table.[3] *Summer in the Catskills* (Art Institute of Chicago, Ireland #389) is dated 1867. On 1 July 1868, Inness wrote Thomas B. Carroll that his family was at Leeds and he was planning on joining them the next week. In a later letter, Inness wrote Carroll that he planned on staying in Leeds until September, when the children would have to begin school.[4] *Overlook Mountain in the Catskills* (with the Jordan-Volpe Gallery, New York, in 1987) is dated 1868 and was probably done at this time.[5] That Inness returned to Leeds the following summer is suggested by the pencil drawing *Catskill*

Scene, dated 1869, in the collection of the G. W. V. Smith Museum.[6] The engraving by Robert Hinshelwood after Inness's painting *Leeds, N. Y. Looking towards the Catskills* (plate 99) was published by the *Ladies' Repository* in 1869. By the time he departed for Europe the following spring, Inness had completed the large *Catskill Mountains*, now in the collections of the Art Institute of Chicago (Ireland #510), as well as the smaller *Landscape, Hudson Valley*, now in the Cincinnati Art Museum (Ireland #503), and *Toward Evening, The Catskills*, now in the Lyman Allyn Museum, New London, Connecticut (Ireland #508). All three of these paintings are dated 1870 and are of the area near Leeds.

When they returned from Europe in 1875, Inness and his family settled in New York. In 1878 they moved to Montclair, New Jersey, where they lived until the artist's death in 1894. After 1875, Inness spent most of his summers in Durham, Connecticut, in Milton-on-Hudson, New York, or on Nantucket. He nonetheless made occasional visits to the Catskills. *Greene County, New York* (plate 100) is one of at least three Greene county scenes Inness painted in 1878.[7] Inness seems to have returned to the village of Leeds in 1883.[8] His last

Plate 101. George Inness, *Red Oaks*, c. 1893. Courtesy New Jersey State Museum.

major painting of the Catskills was *Morning—Catskill Valley (The Red Oaks)*, which he exhibited at the National Academy of Design in the spring of 1894. *Morning—Catskill Valley (The Red Oaks)* is now in the Preston Morton Collection of the Santa Barbara Museum of Art. The oil sketch *Red Oaks* (plate 101) is neither signed nor dated, but it is a late work and seems to be related to *Morning—Catskill Valley.*[9] George Inness died in Bridge-of-Allan, Scotland, on 3 August 1894.

1. The best sources of biographical information are George Inness, Jr., *The Life, Art, and Letters of George Inness* (New York: The Century Co., 1917); LeRoy Ireland, *The Works of George Inness, An Illustrated Catalogue Raisonné* (Austin: University of Texas Press, 1965); Nicolai Cikovsky, Jr., *The Life and Work of George Inness* (New York: Garland Publishing, 1977); Nicolai Cikovsky, Jr., *George Inness* (New York: Praeger Publishers, 1971); Nicolai Cikovsky, Jr. and Michael Quick, *George Inness* (Los Angeles: Los Angeles County Museum of Art, 1985).

2. In his catalogue raisonné, Ireland assigns these sketches numbers 291, 305, 306, 307, and 308. Ireland could not locate numbers 304, 305, and 306 but reproduces numbers 291 and 307. Whenever possible, I will use Ireland's numbers to identify Inness's paintings.

3. *The Round Table* 3 (14 July 1866): 438.

4. Inness's letters to Carroll are in the New-York Historical Society and are described in Cikovsky, *Life and Work of George Inness*, 50, 132.

5. This painting is not listed in Ireland. It was reproduced in *Antiques* 131 (June 1987): 1142.

6. An oil painting *Near Leeds* dated 1869 (not in Ireland) was with David Findlay, Jr., Inc., New York, in 1987.

7. The others are *Sunburst, Greene County, N.Y.* (Ireland #861) and *Landscape, Greene County* (Ireland #862). Neither of these paintings are currently located. *Greene County, New York*, is not listed in Ireland.

8. *Leeds, New York* (Ireland #1058) is signed and dated 1883.

9. *Morning—Catskill Valley (The Red Oaks)* is listed in Ireland (#1504) and is reproduced in color in Cikovsky and Quick, *George Inness*, 201.

JOHN WESLEY JARVIS

1780-1840

James Fenimore Cooper

Oil on canvas, c. 1820
36⅛ x 25 in.

Yale University Art Gallery; Gift of Edward Stephen Harkness, B.A. 1897, M.A. 1925

John Wesley Jarvis was born in England and brought to Philadelphia as an infant. Until he was five, he was raised by his uncle John Wesley. As a child, Jarvis haunted the studios of several Philadelphia painters and developed an interest in printmaking. At sixteen, he was apprenticed to the engraver Edward Savage, whom he later described as "the most ignorant beast . . . ever imposed upon the public," who "could neither draw nor engrave."[1] Jarvis later claimed that he had been taught to draw by one of the other apprentices in Savage's shop. Jarvis acccompanied Savage when he moved to New York in 1801 but soon left him and entered into a partnership with the miniature painter Joseph Wood. In the early years of this partnership, Jarvis continued to work as an engraver, but by 1807 he had given up engraving. Wood and Jarvis advertised miniatures on ivory, silhouettes on glass, and profiles in gold leaf as well as oil portraits on canvas. It was during this period of his career that Jarvis painted the well-known portrait of Washington Irving (1809) now in the drawing room at Sunnyside in Tarrytown, New York.

Jarvis dissolved his partnership with Wood in 1810. In 1814, he took on Henry Inman as an apprentice, an association that lasted until about 1822. When business was good, Jarvis and Inman could handle as many as six sitters a day. Jarvis would paint the sitter's likeness, and Inman would fill in the background and clothing. Together they could complete up to six portraits a week. Jarvis's romantic portrait of James Fenimore Cooper was done during this period of his career, although the particular circumstances surrounding its creation are not known. Jarvis exhibited the portrait at the 1828 exhibition of the National Academy of Design. The reviewer for *The Mirror*, probably William Dunlap, described it as "a faithful likeness and an excellent painting."[2]

Jarvis suffered a stroke and lost most of his physical and mental faculties during an 1834 trip to New Orleans. He died six years later at his sister's home in New York.

MF

1. Dunlap, *History of the Rise and Progress*, quoted in Theodore Bolton and George Groce, Jr., "John Wesley Jarvis: An Account of his Life and the First Catalogue of his Work," *Art Quarterly* 1 (Autumn 1938): 299-300. The standard biography is Harold E. Dickson, *John Wesley Jarvis: American Painter 1780-1840* (New York: The New-York Historical Society, 1949).

2. Bolton and Groce , "John Wesley Jarvis," 299.

Plate 102. C. Kelsey, *Catskill, Greene Co., N.Y. South-West View*, 1854. Courtesy Kennedy Galleries, Inc.

C. KELSEY

Active 1850-1854

Catskill, Greene Co., N.Y. South-West View

Lithograph printed by R.H. Pease, Albany, New York, 1854
12¼ x 30¼ in.

Kennedy Galleries, Inc., New York
Plate 102

According to Groce and Wallace, C. Kelsey was a portrait painter active in about 1850. This identification was based on information supplied by James Thomas Flexner, who then owned a portrait Kelsey had signed and dated. This is the only view by Kelsey catalogued by John Reps in his *Views and Viewmakers of Urban America*. Other impressions survive in the Mariners Museum (Newport News, Virginia) and the Albany Institute of History and Art.

JOHN F. KENSETT

1816-1872

Catskill Mountain Scenery

Engraving by H. Beckwith, 1851
Specimen plate
9½ x 7¾ in.
Originally published in the *Bulletin of the American Art-Union* (October 1851)
Reprinted in Henry Beckwith, ed., *The Home Book of the Picturesque* (1852)

New York State Library, Special Collections
Plate 103

Reminiscences of the Catskill Mountains

Oil on canvas, 1853
22½ x 18¼ in.

Private Collection
Plate 104

Sunset over the Catskills

Oil on canvas, 1855
18 x 24 in.

Private Collection
Plate 105

Hudson River Scene

Oil on canvas, 1857
32 x 48 in.

The Metropolitan Museum of Art; Gift of Mr. H. D.
Babcock, in memory of S. D. Babcock, 1907

The Fawn's Leap

Oil on canvas, 1859
29½ x 24½ in. (oval)

Mead Art Museum, Amherst College; Gift of Herbert W.
Plimpton: The Hollis W. Plimpton '15 Memorial
Collection
Plate 48

View on the Hudson

Oil on canvas, 1865
28 x 45 in.

The Baltimore Museum of Art; Gift of Mrs. Paul
H. Miller
Plate 106

John Frederick Kensett was one of the best known and
most financially successful of the mid nineteeth-century
American painters of landscape. Born in Cheshire,
Connecticut, he was the second son of the English-born
engraver Thomas Kensett. Kensett trained as an engraver
with his father and uncle in New Haven, Connecticut,
and with Peter Maverick in New York City. He seems to
have been a competent engraver and found steady
employment at the craft throughout the 1830s.

Plate 103. John F. Kensett, *Catskill Mountain Scenery*, 1851.
Courtesy New York State Library.

Despite his success as an engraver, Kensett aspired to
be a landscape painter. In June 1840, he sailed from New
York for Europe. He traveled in the company of Asher B.
Durand and John Casilear (both ex-engravers in the
process of making names for themselves as painters of
landscape) and Thomas P. Rossiter. Kensett stayed in
Europe for a little more than seven years. During the
early years of this prolonged residence overseas, Kensett
continued to work as an engraver while he studied
painting. It is unclear precisely when Kensett finally
stopped working as an engraver, but it seems to have
been within two or three years of his arrival in Europe.

Kensett's earliest known oil landscapes are European
scenes painted while he was still in Europe. Many of
these were sent to New York for exhibition. Kensett first
sold paintings to the American Art Union in 1843. In
1845, four of his European landscapes were accepted for
exhibition at the National Academy of Design. By the
time of his November 1847 return to New York, Kensett
was widely recognized as one of the most promising of
the younger American painters. He was elected associate
of the National Academy in 1849 and was made a full
member the following year.[1]

Prior to his return from Europe, Kensett did not
exhibit and does not seem to have produced *plein air* oil
studies. Like earlier American landscape painters, he
spent his summer sketching trips doing pencil drawings
which were then worked up into finished studio paintings. Immediately upon his return from Europe, Kensett
began a series of oil studies of the most important mountain environments in the northeastern United States. He
spent the sketching season of 1848 in the Adirondacks
near Lake George, the sketching season of 1849 in the
Catskills, and the sketching season of 1850 in the White
Mountains. Kensett made his 1848 and 1849 trips in the
company of Casilear. On both of these trips, he and
Casilear were joined for at least a month by Durand.[2]

Kensett's longest visit to the Catskills was in 1849,
when he and Casilear stayed there for more than four
months. Although Kensett probably returned to the
Catskills in 1851 and again in the mid-1850s—and may
have returned for short visits at other times—most of his
later paintings of the area were probably based on oil
studies, pencil drawings, and memories from 1849. On
20 May 1849, Kensett wrote his uncle, John R. Kensett,
that he and John Casilear were about to leave New York
for the Catskills, where they planned on spending the
summer sketching. By the middle of June, Kensett and
Casilear had settled in the Tannersville boarding house
run by John Rusk. On July 15, Kensett wrote his
brother-in-law, Noah Kellog, that he and Casilear had
found the area around Tannersville such a "rich spot" for
scenery that they had decided to stay there through the
end of the season: "We find the ravine abundantly rich in
material—sufficient at any rate to keep us busily occupied
for a couple of months—the Kaaterskill a small stream

flows thro' it & forms a combination of two or three falls of exceeding beauty & our first trial has been at the upper fall on a canvas 25 x 30—two others we propose making the same size—& each will not take less than 10 or 12 days—so that over a month will be occupied on them. Supposing we do have that time of uninterrupted fine weather." On 23 September, Kensett wrote his sister, Sarah Kensett Kellogg, that

> the season thus far (& it is about at its close) has been very favorable to us of the palette & brush tho' in the early part of it excessively hot. It is now giving way to the somewhat searching winds & hoar frosts of autumn —& we shall soon be driven by them from the mountains to the plains having concluded to tarry a couple of weeks at Catskill prior to our return to the city. The Summer has only been tolerable productive to us tho' we have laboured hard in the cause, still I think I have some of my best studies [numbered] among the efforts of the season[.] one consoling result at any rate—the region here abouts is rich in cascades, waterfalls, rocks, trees, etc. & within convenient distance of our temporary mountain abode—no slight recommendation— besides, we can leave our [implements] under the shelter of rocks without the fear of their being disturbed.—thus saving on the fatigue of carrying heavy boxes to & fro

Kensett and Casilear seem to have stayed in Tannersville at least until the end of September, after which time they spent at least a week in the village of Catskill. During September, Asher B. Durand and the German artist John Vollmering were also boarding at Rusk's. For at least some of the time while they were at Rusk's, Kensett and Casilear were accompanied by David Johnson, who seems to have been studying with Casilear.[3]

Kensett and Casilear were not the first American painters to heed the Ruskinian call for a closer study of nature and the production of *plein air* oil studies. Durand, who is generally supposed to have been the first, had begun to exhibit such studies in 1845. But Kensett's studies—if not Casilear's—were quickly singled out for special praise. By 1850, for example, the art reviewer for the prominent journal *The Literary World* linked Kensett with Durand as the two most important painters of landscape working in America and described their oil studies as virtually indistinguishable:

> As a painter of trees and rocks we know of no one superior to KENSETT. The characteristic of his style and finish are in many respects very similar to those of the President of the Academy [Durand]. Indeed, there are two studies of rock (Nos. 226 and 233), the former by Durand and the latter by Kensett, which one would suppose, even after a close inspection, to have been the work of but a single hand. This No. 233 [by Kensett], and two other studies [by Kensett] . . . , are remarkably true to nature, and felicitous in effect. There is a care

in the management of the minutest details, and a faithfulness in the execution, which have their reward in a striking success. No one can fail to notice how far superior are the leaves and branches of the trees in these studies, the grey broken masses of rocks with their rifts and seams, and their patches of moss, and the clear running streams, to the blotches of green, grey, and white, which pass in so many landscapes for trees, rocks, and water.[4]

Although the catalogue to the 1850 National Academy of Design exhibition did not identify the geographical subject of Kensett's three studies, they were done in Kaaterskill Clove during the four months Kensett spent there in the summer and early fall of 1849. Although we might have suspected this from the fact that Kensett had spent all of the 1849 sketching season in the Catskills, it is firmly established by a 24 September 1850 letter from Jasper Cropsey to his wife Maria. Writing from Rusk's boarding house on the evening after his first day in Kaaterskill Clove, Cropsey explained that it was on Kaaterskill Creek that "Mr Kensett made those beautiful studies which were in the exhibition, that one which you admired so much, today I have seen its original."[5]

As became his usual habit, Kensett sold some of his 1849 studies but kept many of them in order to use them in the creation of large studio compositions. Two of the studies were sold to the American Art Union in the late fall of 1849, and at least one more was sold to the Art Union in the late fall of 1850.[6] The three studies shown at the National Academy of Design were not offered for sale. The whereabouts of the 1849 Catskill studies is unknown.

The major painting Kensett prepared for the spring 1850 National Academy of Design exhibition was a large (54 x 36 inches) studio composition titled *Catskill Mountain Scenery*.[7] Although this painting is unlocated, two related works are known. The *Waterfall in the Woods with Indians* (fig. 16), now in the collections of the Amon Carter Museum, is almost certainly a studio composition, produced after Kensett's *plein air* studies and before the large composition he showed at the National Academy. The *Catskill Mountain Scenery* (plate 118) engraved by H. Beckwith and first published in the *Bulletin of the American Art Union* (October 1851) is probably based on the missing painting.[8]

The topographical subject of both *Waterfall in the Woods with Indians* and the engraved *Catskill Mountain Scenery* is the Kaaterskill Clove and the distinctive double leap of Kaaterskill Falls, but neither image is a topographically accurate representation of that site. In both images, Kensett extended the length of the vista up the creek, changed the shape of the Falls, dropped the observation platform from the top of the Falls, and added the background hills. Indeed, except for the shape of the waterfall, all three images seem to owe as much to the geography of Haines Falls as they do to the geography of

Plate 104. John F. Kensett, *Reminiscences of the Catskill Mountains*, 1853. Private collection.

Kaaterskill Falls. Unlike Kaaterskill Falls, Haines Falls does have a mountain rising behind it. The three known nineteenth-century descriptions of the oil *Catskill Mountain Scenery* suggest that it too was unfaithful to geographical fact. Two of them describe the hills behind the falls. The third, from Jasper Cropsey's 24 September letter to his wife, complained that Kensett's painting was too pretty: "that prettyness which Mr K. gave it [Kaaterskill Falls] is scarcely in the original. It is wild and grand and has almost a soul, so much has the Creator displayed his handy work in it."[9]

As in his 1852-1854 paintings of Niagara Falls, Kensett has indeed robbed the Falls of their sublimity.[10] In both the engraving and the *Waterfall in the Woods with Indians*, the potential sublimity of the distant falls is pictorially *contained* by being set at a distance and within the space defined by the sweep of the foreground details, the *repoussir* trees, and the (imaginary) mountain in the distance. This is especially true of *Waterfall in the Woods with Indians*, where the rocks in the left foreground and the carefully painted, sun-dappled forest interior to the right pull the viewer's attention away from the broadly painted falls in the rear. Even when we try to fix our attention on the falls, the organization of Kensett's images makes it almost inevitable that we look not at the falls but at the Indians looking at the falls. The Indians gaze at the falls, and, by implication, experience its majesty. We gaze at the Indians gazing.

Of course, Kensett's representation of the Indians is no more accurate than his representation of the Clove. Kensett's Indians are neither Munsees nor Mahicans—the tribes that might have visited the area. Rather, they belong to the tribe written about by Chateaubriand and Cooper and painted by Cole. They are uncivilized but not dangerous. They are not of European descent, but—unlike many supposedly civilized nineteenth-century Americans who were of European descent—they have a well-developed taste for wild scenery. Kensett has painted his Indians as a species of enlightened tourist. Indeed, despite their dress, Kensett's figures probably derive as much from the figure of Thomas Cole in Durand's Kaaterskill painting of the previous year—*Kindred Spirits* (fig. 14)—as they do from the Indians in Cole's early landscapes. Like Durand's Cole, Kensett's Indians simultaneously appreciate the scenery and show the viewer "how to" appreciate it. As in the slightly later *Along the Hudson* (1852; National Museum of American Art) and *Fawn's Leap* (plate 48), the Indians in Kensett's Kaaterskill images direct our attention to the distant waterfall, cut us off from too close an encounter with the power of the waterfall, and suggest the possibility that we might learn to establish an *aesthetic* relationship with the object that would be intimate enough to be moving but distant enough to be altogether safe.[11]

During the summer and fall of 1851, Kensett's friend George W. Curtis made a leisurely tour of the most important summer resorts in the northeastern United States.[12] Curtis began his tour by taking a steamboat from New York to the Catskill Mountain House. From the Mountain House, he traveled to Trenton Falls on the Mohawk River, Niagara Falls, Saratoga, Lake George, Nahant, and Newport. Curtis reported his travels in a series of letters published in the New York *Tribune*. The following winter, these letters were published as *Lotus-Eating: A Summer Book*, with illustrations by Kensett. As Kensett prepared illustrations for all the letters, it seems likely that he accompanied Curtis on the entire tour.[13]

Reminiscences of the Catskill Mountains (plate 104) is a view looking east over the Hudson Valley and River from the main Catskill escarpment. The Taconic Mountains are clearly visible in the distance. The view is probably from South Mountain and may derive from drawings Kensett did while on his 1851 trip with George W. Curtis. The subject bears no relation to the James Smillie engraving of Kensett's *A Reminiscence of the Catskill Mountains* published in the *Ladies' Repository* in 1859.[14]

The mid-1850s was a period of artistic experimentation for Kensett. In the 1840s and early 1850s, most of his major paintings were panoramic views of hilly or mountainous landscapes. *Waterfall in the Woods with Indians* is typical of these early works. Although many of them included bodies of water, Kensett was almost always most interested in the close observation of rocks and trees. By the mid-1850s, however, Kensett had become increasingly interested in water, a preoccupation that led him in two directions. On the one hand, he began to paint the movement of water over rocks, as shown in a series of large, close-up views of Bash-Bish Falls in South Egremont, Massachusetts, and Fawn's Leap in Kaaterskill Clove. These paintings are closely related to the *plein air* studies Kensett had been doing in the previous decade. But where he had earlier felt a need to work his studies up into landscape panoramas, he was now willing to use them as models for what we might call waterfall portraits. At about the same time that he became interested in the movement of water over rocks, he also became interested in the play of light on large bodies of still or only slightly moving water. This preoccupation resulted in the paintings of the Hudson River, Lake George, the beach at Newport, and Long Island Sound which Kensett worked on until his death and for which he is now best known.

Sunset over the Catskills (plate 105) seems to be a view of the Catskills from east of the Hudson River. The vibrant reds of the sunset recall the luminous sunsets of contemporary paintings by Frederic Church. They are unusual for Kensett, who was sometimes criticized for relying so heavily on browns, greys, and greens.[15] Kensett does not seem to have shown *Sunset over the Catskills* at any of the major New York exhibitions.[16]

Plate 105. John F. Kensett, *Sunset over the Catskills*, 1855. Private collection.

The waterfall *Fawn's Leap* is located in Kaaterskill Clove about a mile east of George Brockett's boarding house. It served as the source for the lower waterfall in Durand's *Kindred Spirits* (fig. 14) and was later painted by Charles Herbert Moore (plate 49), Thomas Charles Farrer, and John W. Hill (plate 50). Kensett completed at least two views of the Fawn's Leap. The other is currently unlocated. None of the nineteenth-century exhibition catalogues list a painting of Fawn's Leap by Kensett.[17]

View on the Hudson (plate 106) depicts the west bank of the river in the area of West Point. A Hudson River Railroad train is clearly visible on the far (eastern) side of the river. The beautiful handling of the afternoon light crisping the foreground trees and rocks and glowing on the apparently still river is characteristic of Kensett's mature work.[18]

1. John Paul Driscoll and John K. Howat, *John Frederick Kensett: An American Master* (New York and London: W. W. Norton & Co., 1985), 40-46; Nathalie Spassky et al., *American Paintings in the Metropolitan Museum of Art, Volume II. A Catalogue of Works by Artists Born Between 1816 and 1845* (New York: Princeton University Press, 1985), 31-32.

2. Kensett's travels can be reconstructed from the dated pencil drawings in John Paul Driscoll, *John F. Kensett Drawings* (University Park, PA: The Pennsylavania State University Museum of Art, 1978) and from Kensett's letters in the Edwin D. Morgan Collection and the James R. Kellogg Collection. The Morgan Collection is in the New York State Library in Albany and on microfilm at the Archives of American Art. The Kellogg Collection is on microfilm at the Archives of American Art. According to Tuckerman, *Book of the Artists*, 511, "Upon his return to his native land," Kensett "commenced a series of careful studies of our mountain, lake, forest, and coast landscape; and in his delineation of rocks, trees, and water, attained a wide and permanent celebrity."

3. Kensett's letter to his uncle is in the John Frederick Kensett Papers, Archives of American Art, microfilm reel #1533. Kensett's letters to his brother-in-law and sister are in the John Frederick Kensett Papers, Archives of American Art, microfilm reel #N68-84. Three of Kensett's October 1849 pencil drawings of Catskill trees and scenery are reproduced in Driscoll, *John Frederick Kensett Drawings*, 56-57. Concerning Durand and Vollmering, see Durand's 28 September 1849 letter to his son, John Durand. This letter is to be found in the Asher B. Durand Papers at the New York Public Library and on microfilm at the Archives of American Art. In 1978, Hirschl & Adler Galleries had an oil painting by David Johnson, which was inscribed on the back of the canvas: "Haines Fall. Kauterskill Clove. David Johnson. 1849.— My first Study from Nature—made in company with J. F. Kensett. & J. W. Casilear." Johnson's painting is reproduced in John I. H. Baur,

"'...the exact brushwork of Mr. David Johnson,' An American Landscape Painter, 1827-1908," *American Art Journal* 12 (1980): 33. The painting is now in a private collection in the Midwest.

4. "The National Academy," *The Literary World*, 6 (27 April 1850): 424.

5. For the complete letter, see the entry for Jasper Cropsey.

6. The 1849 *Bulletin of the American Art-Union* contained two Catskill titles: "392. *Scene on the Cauterskill.* 13 x 14. A study of rocks, water and foliage, with a rustic bridge in the middle distance" and "396. *Scene among the Catskills* 12½ x 14. A study of rocks and foliage, with a distant view of the mountains." Kensett sold eight paintings to the AAU in 1850 but only identified one as a Catskill scene: "42. *Old Mill on the Kauterskill.* 17 x 12½. On the right is the old wooden mill, while the dam is seen in the centre of the picture, and a bit of still water in front." This was probably a view of Scribner's mill, which was located between the outlet of the lower lake and Kaaterskill Falls. Given their titles, descriptions, and the fact that they were painted on the uncharacteristically large canvas Kensett told his brother-in-law he was using for his July 1849 studies, *The Ravine* (AAU; 1850, #71) and *The Mountain Stream* (AAU; 1850, #83), both 25 by 30 inches, were probably also Kaaterskill views from 1849.

7. Kensett did not succeed in selling *Catskill Mountain Scenery* at the NAD. He sold it the following fall to the American Art Union. Its dimensions are given in the catalogue to the fall 1850 AAU exhibition. In AAU catalogues, horizontal dimensions usually precede vertical.

8. The engraving was reprinted in Beckwith, ed., *The Home Book of the Picturesque* (1852). According to Kensett's list of paintings sold (Archives of American Art microfilm reel N68-85), Kensett sold publisher George Putnam a *Catskill Scene* for $100 in 1853. According to this same list, Kensett had charged the Art Union $40 for each of the three Catskill studies (each of which was approximately 13 x 14 inches in size) and $350 for the large *Catskill Mountain Scenery* (54 x 36). Assuming that Kensett's prices reflected the size of his canvas, it seems likely that the $100 painting he sold Putnam would have been about the size of the 17 x 24-inch painting owned by the Amon Carter Museum. Given the circumstances, it is impossible to resist making the suggestion that the painting now owned by the Amon Carter Museum is the painting bought by George Putnam as *Catskill Scene* and that Putnam bought the painting as a way of celebrating the success of *The Home Book of the Picturesque.*

9. Jasper Cropsey to Mary Cropsey, 24 September 1850, Newington-Cropsey Foundation. The reviewer for *The Literary World* liked *Catskill Mountain Scenery* as much as he liked the studies, but he too noticed the changes Kensett had worked on the Kaaterskill geography. Where he praised the studies for being "remarkably true to nature," he praised the large composition for what he called its "truth of feeling." *Catskill Mountain Scenery* is the largest of Kensett's works "in the present exhibition. It is deserving of very high praise. The foreground is made up of heavy rocks, and the bed of the Cauterskill; the stream itself forms the centre of the picture, the eye follows it back to the falls and the background of hills, while on either hand is the thick forest; on the left of the picture it lies in sunshine, and on the right is shade. The whole picture has a freshness, and a clear atmosphere pervading it, which make it a delightful work. Its *truth of feeling* speaks for itself, and will be recognized with pleasure by many a lover of Nature." "The National Academy," *The Literary World* 6 (27 April 1850): 424 (emphasis added). Unlike the reviewer for *The Literary World* and Cropsey, the author of the catalogue to the 1850 American Art Union Exhibition described the painting in the vocabulary of the sublime: "On a broad, grey, moss-covered rock, in the foreground, are a party of Indians. Beyond, overshadowed by trees, opens a wild gorge, through which a torrent passes, with frequent waterfalls that here and there catch the light. In the extreme distance are blue hills."

10. The best comparisons are with the c. 1851 *Niagara Falls* in the Mead Art Museum of Amherst College and the c. 1853-1854 *Niagara Falls* in The White House Collection. Both are reproduced in Driscoll and Howat, *John Frederick Kensett*, 86-89.

Plate 106. John F. Kensett, *View on the Hudson,* 1865. Courtesy The Baltimore Museum of Art.

11. Although twentieth-century scholars have tended to praise Kensett for his verisimilitude, nineteenth-century reviewers often noticed—and accepted—the fact that he did not pursue topographical accuracy. The verisimilitude Kensett sought was primarily a matter of particular details: lichens, rocks, trees, etc. In *Book of the Artists*, (511-512), Henry Tuckerman thus noticed that it was on account of "the literal minuteness" with which Kensett painted natural details that he enjoyed "an exceptional reputation among the extreme advocates of the Pre-Raphaelite school, who praise him while ignoring the claims of other American landscape-artists. But this fidelity to detail is but a single element of his success. His best pictures exhibit a rare purity of feeling, an accuracy and delicacy, and especially a harmonious treatment, perfectly adapted to the subject.... Kensett does not merely imitate, or emphasize, or reflect nature—he interprets her—which we take to be the legitimate and holy task of the scenic limner."

12. George W. Curtis was a long-time editor of *Harper's New Monthly Magazine.* Kensett had first met him and his brother James in Rome in 1847. According to Howat, "Kensett's World," in Driscoll and Howat, *John Frederick Kensett*, 34, "George Curtis' friendship with Kensett became close, lasting until Kensett's death." Curtis recalled the early days of their friendship in a memorial piece published in the "Editor's Easy Chair," *Harper's New Monthly Magazine* 46, March 1873, 610-612.

13. In his letter from "Catskill Falls," Curtis wrote, "With his delicately sensitive artistic eye, Swansdowne glanced among the trees, and from time to time, announced 'a Kensett,' as a broad bit of mossed rock, or a shapely stretch of trees with the mountain outline beyond, recalled the poetic accuracy and characteristic subjects of that artist." George W. Curtis, *Lotus-Eating: A Summer Book* (New York: Dix, Edwards, 1856), 55. Curtis made up playful pseudonyms for all his traveling companions. It is possible that this was an inside joke and that Swansdowne was his name for Kensett.

14. *The Ladies' Repository* 19 (1859), opposite 577.

15. For example, the reviewer for *The Literary World* 10 (8 May 1852): 332, had complained, "Why will not Mr. Kensett give us some sunlight! His pictures are never sultry, never glowing with the light that is the great feature of nature, and even in that which we have instanced, though the sky is luminous, and the distance sunny enough, the whole middle distance and foreground are murky and heavy."

16. *Sunset over the Catskills* is a twentieth-century title. During the later nineteenth century, this painting was exhibited at the Boston Art Club (1875) and the Museum of Fine Arts, Boston, as *Landscape Sunset.* It was owned by Charles C. Perkins.

17. In a manuscript list of paintings he sold (Archives of American Art microfilm, #N68-85), Kensett noted that in 1857 he sold a painting of *Fawn's Leap* for $250 (no purchaser listed) and that in 1859 he sold Mr. Hoxall (?) a painting of *Fawn's Leap, Cattskill Clove* for $250. One of these may have been the *Fawn's Leap* (25 x 36 inches) that brought $275 at the Leeds & Co. auction held on 16-17 March 1859. The results of this auction are described in *The Crayon* 6 (April 1859): 126.

18. On the provenance of this painting, see Sona K. Johnston, *American Paintings 1750-1900 from the Collection of the Baltimore Museum of Art* (Baltimore: The Baltimore Museum of Art, 1983), 98-100. The provenance is clear since 1868, when the painting was exhibited by J. Stricker Jenkins at the annual exhibition of the Maryland Historical Society. It may be the painting exhibited as *Hudson River* at the National Academy of Design in 1865. *Hudson River* was exhibited without a listed owner. The only review I have found was published in the *New York Times* 7 June 1865 and is decidedly mixed: "We prefer the *Ullswater* in the corridor . . . to the *Hudson River*, number 366. The foreground of the latter is decidedly weak. The water between is admirable."

ERNEST LOTICHIUS

Active 1841-1873

Falls of the Kaaterskill

Oil on canvas, 1857
30 x 24½ in.

Private Collection
Plate 107

A painter of landscapes and hunting scenes, Ernest Lotichius was active in Düsseldorf and Munich about 1841. He immigrated to the United States before 1857. Nine of his paintings were included in the January 1857 exhibition of the Cosmopolitan Art Association in Sandusky, Ohio. These included a *Scene near Fort Hall, Oregon*, the *Source of the Missouri*, and a *View near Newburgh*. Lotichius exhibited two more of his paintings at the December 1858 exhibition of the Sandusky Association. He first exhibited at the National Academy of Design in 1858, when he showed paintings of *A Pointer and Setter Pointing Quails* and the *Catskill Mountains near Palenville*. He listed his address as 347 Broadway. The last recorded nineteenth-century exhibition of one of his works was at the Zanesville (Ohio) Industrial Exposition in 1873. In the catalogue of that exhibition, Lotichius is listed as living in New York.[1]

Falls of the Kaaterskill is signed and dated "Ernest Lotichius New York 1857." The blurring of the flowing water evokes the passage of time and suggests the influence of contemporary photographs of waterfalls. But the muted colors and creeping mists are evocative not so much of the contemporary aesthetic of photography as they are of the older aesthetic associated with what S. T. Coleridge called the Germanic or Gothic Sublime. Like many other nineteenth-century artists, Lotichius exaggerated the height of the falls by concealing the horizontal distance separating the two upper leaps and by introducing two exaggeratedly small figures. Surprisingly, Lotichius undercut the intimations of danger evoked by the high falls, small figures, and smashed trees by painting the observation platform at the top of the falls. It is as if he wanted to remind his audience that although aficionados of the sublime might enjoy being frightened by the grand scenes of nature, such fears are enjoyable only when the viewer knows that the danger is mainly in his or her own mind.

1. In addition to artist dictionaries and nineteenth-century exhibition records, see John Paul Driscoll, *All That is Glorious Around Us: Paintings from the Hudson River School on Loan from a Friend of the Museum of Art* (University Park, PA: The Pennsylvania State University Museum of Art, 1981), 94-95.

Plate 107. Ernest Lotichius, *Falls of the Kaaterskill*, 1857. Private collection.

GHERLANDO MARSIGLIA

1792-1850

Catskill Falls

Lithograph printed by Anthony Imbert, c. 1828
9 x 11⅜ in.

The New-York Historical Society
Plate 17

An Italian-born painter of portraits, history paintings, landscapes, and copies after old masters, Marsiglia is supposed to have arrived in New York City by 1817. The first recorded exhibition of one of his works was at the American Academy of Fine Arts in New York in 1824. His name does not appear in the New York City directories until 1825, at which time he is listed as a history and portrait painter. Marsiglia was a founding member of the New York Drawing Association (organized in 1825) and was one of the founders of the National Academy of Design (1826). From 1826 to 1828, he exhibited at both the American Academy and the National Academy. He continued exhibiting at the National Academy of Design annually until 1842. Marsiglia also exhibited at the Pennsylvania Academy of the Fine Arts (1828), the Boston Athenaeum (1829), the Stuyvesant Institute (1838), and the Apollo Association in New York (1838-1841). As he does not seem to have had much financial success as a painter of original works, it is not surprising that he is known to have worked both as a book illustrator and as an art dealer selling paintings imported from Europe. He died in New York in 1850.[1]

Marsiglia's lithograph *Catskill Falls* (plate 17) is inscribed, "Drawn on stone by G. Marsiglia from his own original painting." Between 1828 and 1831, Marsiglia exhibited at least four Catskill landscapes: *View of the Upper Falls of Catskill Mountain* (1828) at the American Academy; and *Mountain-House, in the Catskill Mountains* (1828), *Fall of Catskill* (1829), and *Cavern and Water Fall, at the Katskill Mountain* (1831) at the National Academy. Although the title of the 1831 *Cavern and Water Fall, at the Katskill Mountain* most precisely describes the subject of Marsiglia's lithograph, the lithograph probably dates from the late 1820s, and, if any of the three Catskill paintings he exhibited in the late 1820s is the "original" to which Marsiglia referred, it is probably the *View of the Upper Falls of Catskill Mountain* exhibited at the American Academy in 1828.

Marsiglia no doubt drew his lithograph "from his own original painting" as he says he did, but the composition of his painting was scarcely original, if by "original" we mean inventive. By "original" Marsiglia probably meant something like "original copy"—the phrase would have seemed less oxymoronic in the late 1820s than it does now—because in the still small New York art world of the late 1820s, it was common knowledge that the organization of Marsiglia's image was borrowed from the well-received view of *Cauterskill Falls on the Catskill Mountains, Taken from under the Cavern* that William Guy Wall had exhibited at the National Academy in the spring of 1827 (fig. 10), and that the organization of Wall's image had been borrowed from the painting of Kaaterskill Falls from the cavern that Thomas Cole had exhibited in the window of Colman's Picture Gallery (October 1825) and at the American Academy (in December 1825 and again in the spring of 1826). Cole's 1825 painting is unlocated, but the 1826 copy he made for his patron Daniel Wadsworth survives (fig. 6). The compositional similarity of all three works is too obvious for comment, although it should be noted that Marsiglia's lithograph derives most directly from Wall's painting. Marsiglia even used two of Wall's four well-to-do tourists.

The relationship between Marsiglia's, Wall's, and Cole's paintings points to the *View of the Upper Falls of Catskill Mountain* as Marsiglia's original only because the progression from Cole (1825-1826) to Wall (1827) to Marsiglia suggests an 1828 date for both Marsiglia's painting and lithograph. Of the two paintings Marsiglia exhibited that year, the lithograph is surely not "drawn from" his *Mountain-House, in the Catskill Mountains*. Another piece of evidence for this identification is that although Cole titled the painting he sent Wadsworth *The Falls of Kaaterskill*, he had exhibited his original view from the cavern as *Catterskill Upper Fall, Catskill Mountains*.[2] Marsiglia described his view not as the view from the cavern—as would have been most topographically accurate, as Wall had done, and as later guidebooks and engravings would do—but as a view of the upper falls. He did this because it is what Cole had done.

1. Information in this paragraph derives from Groce and Wallace, a paragraph biography in the Stuyvesant Institute catalogue reprinted in the *Index to American Art Exhibition Catalogues*, and the entry on Marsiglia in Koke, *American Landscape and Genre Paintings*.

2. Further confirmation of this date is found in John Carbonell, "Anthony Imbert: New York's Pioneer Lithographer," in Tatham, ed., *Prints and Printmakers of New York State*, 20-21. Carbonell does not have any new biographical information about Marsiglia to contribute, nor does he seem to know about the paintings by Cole and Wall, but he reproduces Marsiglia's lithograph and, on the basis of his knowledge of Imbert's career, dates it c. 1828. The relationship between Cole's two paintings of the view from the cavern and Wall's is most fully explored in John Howatt, "A Picturesque Site in the Catskills," 16-29. My information concerning the title and exhibition history of Cole's original version of the view derives from this source. Cole's title for his second version is to be found in McNulty, ed., *Correspondence of Thomas Cole and Daniel Wadsworth*, 1. The painting is now titled *Kaaterskill Falls*.

JERVIS McENTEE

1828-1891

Sketches of Home Scenery

Oil on paper, c. 1857
14^{11}/$_{16}$ x 11^{15}/$_{16}$ in.

Yale University Art Gallery; Gift of
Mr. and Mrs. Samuel Schwartz
Plate 42

Kaatskill Mountain House

Oil on paper, c. 1857
10^{13}/$_{16}$ x 14^{1}/$_{4}$ in.

Yale University Art Gallery; Gift of
Mr. and Mrs. Samuel Schwartz
Plate 108

A Cliff in the Kaatskills

Oil on canvas, c. 1866
36 x 30 in.

The Brooklyn Museum; Gift of the Roebling Society in
honor of Carl Selden, 84.81
Plate 39

Autumnal Landscape

Oil on canvas, c. 1860-1870
10 x 17^{1}/$_{2}$ in.

Private Collection
Plate 109

Jervis McEntee was the first son of the engineer James McEntee, who lived in Rondout, New York, a Hudson town in the southern Catskills. James McEntee's mentor was the chief engineer for the Erie Canal and the Delaware & Hudson Canal, John Jervis. When James's first son was born, the name Jervis was a natural choice. James McEntee was well known in his community for his political Republicanism and moral correctness.[1]

In 1848, McEntee applied to Asher Durand to be taken on as a student.[2] Nothing came of this request, but in 1850-1851 McEntee studied with Frederic Church. McEntee began exhibiting at the National Academy immediately upon commencing his studies. He was married in 1854 to Gertrude Sawyer, the daughter of a Rondout minister. In the mid-1850s, McEntee worked in the flour and feed business, an endeavor that convinced him to commit himself fully to a career as a painter. He

Plate 108. Jervis McEntee, *Kaatskill Mountain House*, c. 1857. Courtesy Yale University Art Gallery.

opened a studio in the Tenth Street Building in 1858, went to Europe with the painter Sanford Gifford in 1859, and was elected a full Academician in 1861.

From the beginning of his career, McEntee was intimate with many of the most prominent American painters. By the 1860s, his close friends included Church, Sanford Gifford, Worthington Whittredge, John Kensett, and Eastman Johnson. Whittredge wrote that McEntee "was one of my most intimate friends. Summer after summer we were together in the Catskills. His home had always been near them and he knew every nook and corner of them and every stepping-stone across their brooks."[3] Throughout his life, McEntee considered Rondout his home. He lived there from early spring until late fall and went reluctantly to New York City for a winter of studio work and socializing.

McEntee's work developed from early representations of easily recognizable views in the 1850s to, by the 1870s, mood pieces of unidentifiable forest interiors. One early view is the *Croton Dam* in the collections of the New-York Historical Society. It is painted in the traditional manner of presenting public views, with standing figures gesturing toward the recognizable subject. The Yale *Sketches of Home Scenery* (plate 42) and *Kaatskill Mountain House* (plate 108) are from this public category of McEntee's work. They may have been intended for a volume of travel engravings like William Henry Bartlett's *American Scenery*. At any rate, they were the source for the two engravings of the Catskills in T. Addison Richards's *Appleton's Illustrated Hand-Book of American Travel*, published in 1857.[4]

A Cliff in the Catskills (plate 39) is a transitional work. The painting represents a cliff called Indian Face or Dominie's Nose, both names bearing particular historical importance to the Catskill area. During the Revolutionary War, a certain Dominie Schuneman, or the "Dutch Dominie," was instrumental in working for the

Plate 109. Jervis McEntee, *Autumnal Landscape*, c. 1860-1870. Private collection.

cause of independence. At the same time, some of the last Indians in the area helped the Tories in their infamous burning of Esopus. Both the Indians and the Dominie were featured in a work of historical fiction called *The Dutch Dominie of the Catskills*, written by Rev. David Murdoch and published in 1861. Given McEntee's familiarity with the Catskills, it seems likely that he would have read Murdoch's book. Although the painting is of a recognizable site, McEntee was most interested in the texture of the rocks and the play of light and shadow on its surface. It is therefore not surprising that, if McEntee ever exhibited this work, he did so without giving it a geographically specific title.

The *Autumnal Landscape* (plate 109) is also a view that would have been recognizable to others who knew the site. It seems to be of Hunter Mountain and is strikingly similar to paintings done by Gifford in 1865 and Whittredge in 1866 (plates 92 and 51). It is imaginable that the three friends went to the area, perhaps staying at Mrs. Parker's farm, and painted Hunter Mountain together. The three views of the mountain seem to be made from almost exactly the same point, varying only yards in one direction or another. *Autumnal Landscape* is a mood painting, demonstrating McEntee's affinity for autumn scenes and the pensive attitude they imply. After his wife's death in 1878, McEntee's work became much more dramatically melancholy. Some of his peers considered the added emotion an improvement over his earlier autumn scenes, but McEntee's late work never received

the critical praise his earlier paintings had.[5] He died in February 1891 in Rondout after a three-month battle with Bright's disease.

MF

1. For genealogical information on James McEntee and his family, see Nathaniel Bartlett Sylvester, *History of Ulster County, New York* (Philadelphia: Everts & Peck, 1880).

2. McEntee's letter is in the Asher B. Durand papers at the New York Public Library and on microfilm at the Archives of American Art (roll N20).

3. John Baur, ed., "The Autobiography of Worthington Whittredge," 60.

4. The images appear on pages 144 and 146 of the *Hand-Book*.

5. For praise McEntee received from his peers during this period, see his manuscript diary, 14 February 1879 and 1 March 1879. A microfilm copy is in the Archives of American Art (roll #0180).

WILLIAM RICKARBY MILLER

1818-1893

Catskill Clove
Watercolor on paper, 1856
19⅞ x 14¾ in.

The Metropolitan Museum of Art; Gift of Mrs.
A. M. Miller, 1893
Plate 43

Waterfall in Palingsville [*sic*]

Pencil and watercolor on mill board, 1856
10 x 14 in.

The George F. McMurray Collection, Trinity College,
Hartford, Connecticut
Plate 110

The watercolorist and commercial artist William
Rickarby Miller was born in Staindrop, County Durham,
England. He immigrated to the United States in the fall of
1844 or the winter of 1845. He first settled in Buffalo,
New York, but moved to New York City by 1847 and
lived there until his death. Before emigrating, Miller
received training in the use of watercolors from his father.
Almost immediately upon moving to New York, he began
to sell watercolors to the American Art Union. He
continued to sell watercolors to the Art Union until it
ceased operation in 1852. Miller's commercial work dates
from after the closing of the Art Union. In 1853, G. P.
Putnam & Co. hired him to do the illustrations for the
book *Homes of American Authors*, engravings after his
designs were published in both *Gleason's Pictorial
Drawing-Room Companion* and Frank Leslie's *Illustrated
News*, and he began exhibiting at the National Academy
of Design. Interestingly, the first drawing he exhibited at
the National Academy was listed as being owned by John
W. Hill. Miller continued to sell designs to magazines
through the latter part of the 1860s. He continued to
exhibit at the National Academy through the mid-1870s.[1]

Plate 110. William Rickarby Miller, *Waterfall in Palingsville*
[*sic*], 1856. Courtesy Trinity College.

Miller occasionally painted in oil. In the later 1870s and 1880s, he produced a large number of pen-and-ink sketches. But through the end of the 1860s, he most often worked in watercolor. Miller's first visit to the area of the Mountain House seems to have been in August 1856. Although there are numerous Catskill drawings by Miller inscribed with later dates, I know of none with an earlier date.[2] Judging from the surviving 1856 drawings, Miller probably boarded in Palenville. Both *Catskill Clove* (plate 43) and *Waterfall in Palingsville* (plate 110) seem to have been drawn on site. Miller's carefully drawn and vibrantly colored works were completed in two stages. He would begin by using colored pencil to build up a detailed line drawing of his subject. He would then finish the drawing by applying a sequence of watercolor washes. As in *Catskill Clove* and *Waterfall in Palingsville*, pale greens and blue-greens usually predominate, although these are relieved by patches of clear blues in the sky and occasional touches of yellow, orange, and red in the foreground.[3]

1. Grace Miller Carlock, "William Rickarby Miller," *The New-York Historical Society Quarterly* 31 (1947): 199-209; Donald Shelly, "Addendum: William R. Miller," *The New-York Historical Society Quarterly* 31 (1947): 210-211; Koke, *American Landscape and Genre Paintings*, 342.

2. In 1982, Kennedy Galleries had an 1856 oil painting by Miller of *Moonlight, The Lock, High Falls, N.Y.* High Falls is on Rondout Creek in Ulster County. A watercolor *Catskill Clove, N.Y.* in the New-York Historical Society is inscribed "Catskill Clove, No. 4 [or 9]" and is dated "Aug 1856." The pencil drawing *In the Catskill Clove* in the Karolik Collection of the Museum of Fine Arts, Boston (not in the published catalogue) probably dates from this time.

3. Miller did not have any works in the spring 1857 National Academy of Design exhibition. He had eight works, including *Study for a Picture—Catskill Clove* and *Water-Fall, Catskill Clove*, in the spring 1858 exhibition. The reviewer in *The Crayon* 5 (June 1858): 178, noted that Miller's works were among a "number of water-color drawings [which] deserve special study" and described them as "literal drawings."

CAPTAIN JOHN MONTRESOR

1736-1788?

A Map of the Province of New York, with Part of Pensilvania, and New England

Hand-colored engraving by P. Andrews, 1775
28¼ x 36¼ in.

Sterling Memorial Library, Yale University Map Collection
Plate 4

The military engineer and cartographer Captain (later Major) John Montresor was the son of the military engineer James Montresor (1702-1776). Born in Gibraltar, John Montresor was in North America by 1755, when he was wounded in General Braddock's unsuccessful campaign to capture Fort Duquesne (now Pittsburgh). All five of the maps Montresor is known to have drawn were first published between 1766 and 1777, and all identify him as a Captain. The earliest of these was *A Plan of the City of New York* (1766; reissued 1775). In addition to his maps of New York City and Province, Montresor mapped Nova Scotia (1768), Bunker Hill (1775), and Boston (1777). A 1778 reissue of Montresor's 1777 map of Boston identifies him as "His Majestie's Chief Engineer in America."[1]

Montresor's *Map of the Province of New York* was printed in four separate sheets. The copy borrowed for the current exhibition contains the two sheets showing the northern half of the province. The coloring was added by hand.

Montresor's *Map of the Province of New York* was one of a large number of highly detailed maps of the American colonies produced in the politically tense years surrounding the beginning of the American Revolution. In addition to Montresor's, the most important maps of the Hudson River Valley were Captain Holland's *The Provinces of New York and New Jersey with Parts of Pensylvania* (first issued in 1775) and Claude Joseph Sauthier's *A Topographical Map of Hudson's River . . . from Sandy Hook . . . to Fort Edward* (first issued in 1776). All three maps accurately illustrate the fact that up until the end of the eighteenth century, European settlement was largely confined to the area east of the Catskills. The lack of detail in the illustration both of the Catskills and of the Delaware and Susquehanna Valleys is an accurate reflection of the state of geographical knowledge at the time. Except for a few trappers and hunters, Hudson Valley settlers did not venture deeply into the mountains and were therefore unable to give the cartographers much information. What information the cartographers did acquire was often misleadingly used. For example, Sauthier's map shows a path through Kaaterskill Clove. But because Sauthier fails to distinguish different kinds of paths, it is easy to mistake the existing Indian trail for a European-style road. The maps by Montresor, Sauthier, and Holland were not superseded by newer or more accurate maps until after the turn of the century.[2]

1. Ronald Vere Tooley, *Tooley's Dictionary of Mapmakers* (Tring, Hertfordshire, England: Map Collector Publications Limited, 1979), 446; Ronald Vere Tooley, *The Mapping of America* (London: Holland Press Cartographica 2, 1980), 43-44, 74, 76-77, 213. Useful background information can be found in Seymour Schwartz and Ralph Ehrenberg, *The Mapping of America* (New York: Harry N. Abrams, Inc., 1980).

2. For bibliographic information on the Holland and Sauthier maps see Tooley, *The Mapping of America*, and James C. Wheat and Christian Brun, *Maps and Charts Published in America Before 1800: A Bibliography*, rev. ed. (London: Holland Press Cartographica 3, 1978).

CHARLES HERBERT MOORE

1840-1930

Mountain View

Oil on canvas, 1860
34¼ x 49½ in.

Indiana University Art Museum, Bloomington, Indiana
Plate 49

Winter Landscape, Valley of the Catskills

Oil on canvas, 1866
7 x 10 in.

The Art Museum, Princeton University
Plate 111

Leeds Bridge

Oil on canvas, 1868
11⅛ x 16⅛ in.

The Art Museum, Princeton University; Gift of Frank
Jewett Mather, Jr.
Plate 112

The Catskill Mountains

Oil on canvas, 1872
8½ x 17 in.

Harvard University Art Museums (Fogg Art Museum);
Purchased from the Louise E. Bettens Fund
Plate 113

The pre-Raphaelite painter and educator Charles
Herbert Moore was born in New York City in 1840.
Moore first exhibited at the National Academy of Design
in 1858. By 1859, he had rented space in the prestigious
Tenth Street Studio building, his name had begun to turn
up in the columns of *The Crayon*, and he had sold a

Plate 111. Charles Herbert Moore, *Winter Landscape, Valley of
the Catskills*, 1866. Courtesy The Art Museum, Princeton
University.

painting of a scene *In Berkshire County* (The New-York Historical Society) to the New York collector Robert L. Stuart.[1] By the spring of 1862, he had been elected an Associate of the National Academy of Design and had sold at least four paintings of various Hudson Valley scenes to the well-known collector the Reverend Elias Lyman Magoon.[2]

Moore's first recorded trip to the Catskills was in June 1859. In May 1860, he exhibited a view of a scene *In the Catskills* at the National Academy of Design. According to the reviewer in *The Crayon*, "Of the landscapes by younger members of the profession, Moore shows rapid progress *In the Catskills*. The bluff on the right is beautifully painted, also the logs and the roots in the foreground. There is a fine poetic feeling in the picture."[3] *In the Catskills* was the only painting Moore exhibited at the National Academy of Design in 1860. On 18 August 1860, John William Hill wrote Thomas Charles Farrer that "Charley" Moore was "at his parents and seemed to feel pretty dull. could not sell his big picture, *poor fellow.*"[4] The big painting Moore could not sell in August is likely to have been the painting he had sent to the National Academy in May. *Mountain View* (plate 49) is by far the largest known painting by Moore. Given the similarity between *Mountain View* and the description of *In the Catskills* from *The Crayon*, it is probable that the two are the same work.

By the winter of 1861, Moore had given up his New York studio and moved to the town of Catskill, where he rented a studio from Thomas Cole's son Theodore.[5] On 26 May 1861, he wrote Reverend Magoon to tell him that the painting *Evening over the Catskills* was finished and ready to be delivered. Elsewhere in this letter, Moore gave Magoon an extended description of that evening's sunset as seen from Jefferson Hill:

> I went to the place where we walked in the evening, this evening, and oh! if you could only see it under such a sky, I never saw anything more *glorious*. The mountains were of the pure blue that you love so dearly with rays of rosy light bursting through the cloves and kindling the highest points into living light, the delicate forms of the forest trees at the base of the mountain relieved against the pure *cool air* of their flanks, nearer the broad valley lay stretched in tranquil repose in cool shadow, with light catching the most prominent tree forms, and lighting the foliage into that *ineffable* glory of warm olive green. The creek winding up to the mountain was a perfect mirror of the sky, except where that little rapid far up among the pines broke the quiet surface with its sweet music.[6]

Moore married Mary Jane Tomlinson of Schenectady, New York, in July 1865. The following spring, the Moores moved into a cottage about half a mile north of town and seem to have remained year-round residents of Catskill until the fall of 1871, when Charles received an appointment as Instructor of Freehand Drawing at the Lawrence Scientific School of Harvard University. Moore spent the rest of his professional career at Harvard, where he was appointed Assistant Professor of Design (1891), Professor of Design (1896), and director of the newly opened William Hayes Fogg Art Museum (1896). Moore retired from Harvard in 1909 and died in Hartfield, England, in 1930.[7]

Moore's decision to move to Catskill seems to have been motivated by a desire to study nature more closely. He is known to have read Ruskin as early as the summer of 1859. Although his paintings of the late 1850s and early 1860s show an attention to foreground detail that contemporary reviewers might have described as Ruskinian, they are not nearly as meticulously observed as the works he produced in the later 1860s and early 1870s. In February 1863, Moore was one of a small group of persons interested in art and architecture who organized the Association for the Advancement of Truth in Art. In the summer of 1863, he began to spend increasingly long hours out of doors doing minutely detailed studies of specific natural details. Some of these were in pencil; others were in oil.[8] Whereas Moore had earlier used relatively broad brush strokes in his oil paintings, he now tried to hide his work by using tiny strokes of pure colors that would not be noticed by someone viewing the canvas. Because he was working so much more carefully, he began to use much smaller canvases. One of his major works of this period, the *Winter Landscape, Valley of the Catskills* of 1866 (plate 111), is only seven by ten inches. Something of the pains Moore took is suggested by his 10 July 1864 letter to his close friend Thomas Charles Farrer, where he notes that his "work has . . . progressed very slowly . . . I cover about as much canvass as I could cover with the end of my thumb in a forenoon of three hours work."[9] Moore's goal was to make his brush strokes unnoticeable so that the viewer might forget the intermediary presence of the artist and experience the represented scene as if for him or herself. Moore did not mean for his canvas to be an object of aesthetic satisfaction. He meant it to be a window the viewer might see *through.*

Moore's first completed landscape in his more meticulous style was a presently unlocated *Study in the Catskill Valley,* which he showed at the National Academy of Design in 1865. The *Study in the Catskill Valley* seems to have been of the view from Jefferson Hill that Moore described in his 1861 letter to Magoon. Russell Sturgis, a founding member of the Association for the Advancement of Truth in Art and the art reviewer for *The Nation,* singled it out for special notice:

> There is one picture, we have said, to which the painter gave his whole strength. It is Mr. Charles H. Moore's "Study in the Catskill Valley," No. 60. It is a representation on a very small scale of a very wide range of country. The spectator stands on a slightly

Plate 112. Charles Herbert Moore, *Leeds Bridge*, 1868. Courtesy The Art Museum, Princeton University.

rising ground, and looks across perhaps ten miles of low-lying country to the Catskill Mountains beyond. There is, in this small picture, the material for a very large one; it is so minutely painted throughout that it *is*, in amount of incident, a very large one. . . . The merit of this picture is in its almost perfect truth of drawing, and in the love of nature so evident in it, and the evident purpose to get perfect truth. . . . [T]he middle distance . . . is admirably rendered in a narrow belt of canvass, which, as one looks too close, is merely mottled with color, but resolves itself into broad tracts of land as the eye is withdrawn. This middle distance is the best part of the picture, and hardly to be surpassed.[10]

In the years 1865 to 1867, Moore finished one major winter study in oil every winter—*Winter Study in the Catskills* (first shown at Artists' Fund Society exhibition in the fall of 1865); *High Peak and Round Top (Catskill) in Winter* (first shown at the Artists' Fund Society exhibition in the fall of 1866); and *October Snow Squall—Catskill Mountain* (first shown at the National Academy exhibition in the spring of 1867). The winter landscape

now owned by Princeton University and included in the present exhibition is the painting Moore exhibited as *High Peak and Round Top (Catskill) in Winter*. Moore gave a lengthy description of the painting in a February 1866 letter to the Harvard professor Charles Eliot Norton:

My principle [*sic*] winter work is a view of the mountains and the valley in snow. . . . The peculiar structure of these hills is very marked in Winter, & their sculpture brought out in most ineffably subtle light and shade . . . The color of the shaded parts in clear mornings is purest blue & in the lights the soft redish [*sic*] purple of the bare trees coming up through the snow is most lovely. . . . In the middleground I have part of the village—ugly white houses &c—but I do not think they are altogether ugly associated as they are with the rest of the subject and drawn in various perspective and light and shade—It is quite wonderful how the 'play of the light of heaven,' makes many ugly things interesting. In the foreground are some naked willows, & the color of these in the sunlight is very beautiful, & especially so in contrast with the prevailing blue of the subject. This picture is quite small (7 x 10 inches). I could not make it larger without risk of being unable to finish it while the snow lasts.[11]

In an 8 April 1866 letter to Norton, Moore wrote, "I have just finished my little winter study & should be pleased if you would see it."[12] Moore's painting seems to be of the view through one of the windows in the studio he was renting from Theodore Cole. The *High Peak and Round Top (Catskill) in Winter* was the only landscape Moore sent to the Artists' Fund Society exhibition in 1866.[13] In his review of the exhibition, Clarence Cook wrote of the painting, "Nor must we forget Charles Moore's lovely 'Catskill,' whose truth to nature and beauty of color have at last conquered opposition and compelled admiration. This little picture shares with Mr. Whistler the honor of making it worth while to go into the South Room."[14]

In the summer of 1867, Moore sent nine oil paintings and three drawings to the First Annual Exhibition of the Yale School of Fine Arts. Never before had Moore sent so many works to one exhibition. Among the paintings he sent to Yale were the *High Peak and Round Top (Catskill) in Winter* and the *October Snow Squall—Catskill Mountains*.[15] Interestingly, one of the drawings, a *Pencil Portrait*, was owned by Charles L. Beach, the proprietor of the Catskill Mountain House.

Moore's painting of *Leeds Bridge* (plate 112) is dated 1868. Located on Catskill Creek a few miles northwest of the town of Catskill, Leeds Bridge was built late in the eighteenth century and rebuilt early in the twentieth. It is still standing. Other nineteenth-century artists to draw the bridge include William Sidney Mount, Jervis McEntee, Homer Dodge Martin, James Renwick Brevoort, and George Inness.[16] Moore had been interested in the bridge for a number of years before he painted it in oil. In a 23 March 1864 letter to Farrer, Moore wrote that as soon as the weather got warm he was going to spend his mornings working on his *Study in the Catskill Valley* and that in the afternoons he was going to "go out to Leeds & do the bridge in watercolor on a large bristol board."[17] It is unclear whether Moore did this watercolor, because, on 8 April 1866, he wrote Charles Eliot Norton, "There is a fine old stone bridge which I think I must draw. It is something like this [sketch of a five arched bridge] the main arch spanning the channel. It is quite what Mr. Ruskin calls the 'ideal of a bridge.' "[18] Moore's 1868 oil was painted for his patron Samuel Wilde. Moore forwarded the finished painting to Wilde in March 1869 together with a letter in which he explained that he had chosen the subject because he thought the "bridge in the middleground . . . the most interesting thing of the kind in the country."[19]

High Peak and Round Top (Catskill) in Winter was the third and *Leeds Bridge* the last of at least six meticulously painted oil landscapes Moore completed between the spring of 1865 and March of 1869. The other four of these six canvases are currently unlocated. During these years, Moore also worked on still lifes and nature studies in both pencil and oil, but it was primarily on the basis of these six landscapes that he came to be considered the member of the Association for the Advancement of Truth in Art most likely to become a truly great painter.

By the end of 1868, however, the Association had ceased to function as a cohesive group, the Association's journal had long since lapsed into silence, and the winds of aesthetic change were blowing from Barbizon. Perhaps as importantly, it had taken Moore from 1863 to 1869 to complete a handful of quite small paintings. Sometime in late 1868 or early 1869, Moore seems to have realized that although art may be long, life is short. From 1868 until his move to Harvard in 1871, Moore seems to have devoted most of his energies either to watercolors or to a projected volume of engravings "illustrating the Hudson River [from] its source to the sea[.]"[20] Closely related to his 1868 oil painting, Moore's 1869 drawing of *Leeds Bridge* (New York State Museum, Albany) was apparently intended for this volume. Moore painted occasional oils after 1868. But, like the 1872 oil of the *Catskill Mountains* (plate 113), these later oils are more painterly than the tightly controlled canvases he had done previously. In the *Catskill Mountains* of 1872, Moore does not try to conceal his presence by hiding his brushwork. The scene is still carefully observed, but the painter either no longer desires to eliminate his presence from his work—no longer desires to become like Emerson's famous transparent eyeball—or has realized that such self-effacement is impossible.

Like the young Emerson, the founders of the Association for the Advancement of Truth in Art were apostles of 'the new' who taught that every person could, and that every successful artist had to, escape the blinders of inherited ways of seeing and representing and learn to see for themselves—without mediation. By the time he left Catskill for Harvard, Moore seems to have realized that there is no such thing as an unmediated vision of things as they intrinsically are. All perception is colored by learned habits of seeing and interpreting. Moore's new willingness to let his viewer see the traces of his brush strokes implies an acceptance of the inevitability of influence and the inescapability of the past.

1. *The Crayon* noticed Moore in volume 6 (May 1859): 153 and (December 1859): 379; volume 7 (February 1860): 57 and (May 1860): 140; and volume 8 (June 1861): 133.

2. On Magoon's collection, see Ella Foshay and Sally Mills, *All Seasons and Every Light: Nineteenth Century American Landscapes from the Collection of Elias Lyman Magoon* (Poughkeepsie, NY: Vassar College Art Gallery, 1983). Matthew Vassar bought Magoon's collection, including four paintings by Moore, in 1864. All four are now in the collection of the Vassar College Art Gallery.

3. *The Crayon* 7 (May 1860): 140.

4. Hill's letter is in the Gordon Lester Ford Collection at the New York Public Library and on microfilm at the Archives of American Art.

Plate 113. Charles Herbert Moore, *The Catskill Mountains,* 1872. Courtesy Harvard University Art Museums.

5. In his account book entry for 12 May 1866, Theodore Cole noted the receipt of $135.58 from "C. H. Moore for studio rent Cash in full Note & Interest[.]" Theodore Cole's account book is owned by the Thomas Cole Foundation, Catskill, New York.

6. Moore's letter is in Magoon's collection of *Artistic Autographs* (volume 4, opposite page 97), which is in Special Collections, Vassar College Library, Poughkeepsie, New York.

7. Biographical information derives from Frank Jewett Mather, Jr., *Charles Herbert Moore: Landscape Painter* (Princeton, NJ: Princeton University Press, 1957) and the essays in Ferber and Gerdts, *The New Path.*

8. On the chronology of these changes, see Moore's 17 November 1864 letter to John Frederick Kensett in Kenneth Myers and Margaret Favretti, " 'In Most *Extreme Need* ': Correspondence of C.H. Moore with J. F. Kensett," *Archives of American Art Journal* 26, 1 (1986): 16.

9. Moore's letter is in the Gordon Lester Ford Collection in the New York Public Library and on microfilm at the Archives of American Art.

10. "The Fortieth Annual Exhibition of the National Academy of Design [Second Notice]," *The Nation* 1, 13 July 1865, 57. Sturgis is identified as the reviewer in Gerdts, "Through a Glass Brightly," 63.

11. Quoted in Mather, *Charles Herbert Moore,* 24. The original is in the manuscript collection of the New York State Library in Albany.

12. Quoted in ibid., 27. The original is also in the New York State Library.

13. The only other work he sent was titled *Pine Tree at Catskill* and was probably a pencil drawing.

14. *New-York Daily Tribune,* 20 December 1866, 4:5. Cook is identified as the reviewer in Gerdts, "Through a Glass Brightly," 63.

15. I am assuming that the *October Snow Squall—Catskill Mountains* shown at the National Academy is the same painting as *Snow Squalls In October* shown at Yale.

16. According to Vedder's usually reliable *Official History of Greene County, New York,* 50-51, the oldest parts of the bridge are the two eastern arches, which are supposed to have been built around 1765. It is believed that when the bridge was first completed, the other arches were made of wood, that the wooden arches burned in 1785, and that the western stone arches were built by August 1792. Mount's oil sketch is dated 20 October 1843 and is in the Thyssen-Bornemisza Collection. McEntee's pencil drawing is inscribed *Leeds, Kaaterskill Creek* and is dated 16 October 1858. It was at Hirschl & Adler Galleries in 1976 and is now in a private collection in New York City. Martin's pencil drawing is inscribed "Leeds, Green Co. Aug. 4 1859" and is in the collections of The Art Museum, Princeton University. Brevoort's unlocated *Old Bridge at Leeds* was exhibited at the National Academy of Design in the spring of 1862. Inness's oil sketch *Leeds, New York* is in a private collection. It is reproduced in Ireland, *The Works of George Inness,* 77.

17. Gordon Lester Ford Collection, New York Public Library.

18. Quoted in Mather, *Charles Herbert Moore,* 27.

19. Moore's letter was kept with the painting and is now attached to the back of the frame. Samuel Wilde already owned Moore's *Fruit* (probably an oil). He would later buy Moore's watercolor *Dog-Tooth Violet.* He also owned paintings by Farrer and the pre-Raphaelite Henry Roderick Newman. Joseph Wilde owned Moore's *Apples* (shown at the National Academy in 1867) and *Hudson River above Catskill* (shown at Yale in 1867).

20. The quoted phrase comes from a long description of the project inscribed on the back of a pen-and-ink drawing of *The Valley of the Catskill from Jefferson Hill* (1869) in the collections of The Art Museum, Princeton University. The entire inscription is quoted in Mather, *Charles Herbert Moore,* 34.

THOMAS NAST

1840-1902

Sketches among the Catskill Mountains

Engraving, 1866
13⅝ x 20¾ in.

Originally published in *Harper's Weekly*, 21 July 1866
Mr. and Mrs. R. M. Decker
Plate 22

The cartoonist Thomas Nast was born in Landau, Germany, and was brought to New York City when he was six years old. As a boy, he studied first with Theodore Kaufman and later at the National Academy of Design with Alfred Fredericks and the portrait painter Thomas Seir Cummings. Nast was hired by Frank Leslie and began to work on Leslie's *Illustrated Newspaper* when he was just fifteen years old. In 1859, he quit Leslie's to cover assignments for the *New York Illustrated News*. Nast returned to Leslie's when the *News* faltered in 1860-1861, but in 1862 he left to become a full-time staff artist at *Harper's Weekly*, for which he had begun work in 1859. Nast's satires proved enormously effective and popular, and he was given the freedom to choose his own assignments. Nast stayed with *Harper's* until its editorial policy became more restrictive in 1885-1886. In 1892, he established his own journal, but *Nast's Weekly* failed in 1893, leaving him in a precarious financial situation. In 1902, Theodore Roosevelt appointed him United States Consul in Guayaquil, Ecuador, where he died of yellow fever.[1]

Best known for his political caricatures and as the creator of the Republican elephant, the Democratic donkey, the dollar sign, and Uncle Sam, Nast also produced more lighthearted satires. Drawn the summer after the demobilization at the end of the Civil War, *Sketches among the Catskill Mountains* is a gentle caricature of the tourist activities most closely associated with the Catskill Mountain House. The largest images in the sheet are done straight—without satiric bite—and are landscape views of the best-known sites in the area of the Mountain House. The satire resides in the smaller images. Some poke fun at the Mountain House by noting the steepness of the *The Last Mile or So* of the Mountain House road and the regularity with which the escarpment is shrouded *In the Clouds*. But most of the satiric images focus on the tourists, who are uniformly well heeled but ill prepared for a walk *In the Woods* or for *The Bear at the Laurel House*.

MF

1. Albert Bigelow Paine, *Th. Nast: His Period and His Pictures* (New York: Macmillan, 1904). See also Koke, *American Landscape and Genre Paintings*, vol. 2, 3-4, and *Dictionary of American Biography*.

GILBERT STUART NEWTON

1794-1835

Portrait of Washington Irving

Oil on canvas, 1830
19½ x 15½ in.

Historic Hudson Valley, Tarrytown, New York
Plate 114

The portrait and genre painter Gilbert Stuart Newton was born in Halifax, Nova Scotia. His parents had moved to Nova Scotia in 1776 when the British army evacuated Boston. His maternal grandfather was the Boston snuff manufacturer Gilbert Stuart, and his maternal uncle was the Boston portrait painter Gilbert Stuart. Newton's father died about 1803, and his mother moved the family back to Boston, where Newton later studied—and fought—with his uncle. In 1817, he moved to Europe, where he continued his studies in Florence, Paris, and London. Newton was elected an associate of the Royal Academy in 1829 and an Academician in 1832.

Plate 114. Gilbert Stuart Newton, *Portrait of Washington Irving*, 1830. Courtesy Historic Hudson Valley.

His health began to fail soon after his election to the Academy, and he died at Chelsea, England, on 5 August 1835.

Shortly after moving to Europe, Newton developed close and long-lasting friendships with Washington Irving and Irving's friend, the American-born portrait painter Charles R. Leslie. (Leslie's 1820 portrait of Irving is in the collections of the New York Public Library.) In a November 1819 letter, Irving wrote of Newton,

He is not so experienced in his art as Leslie, but has uncommon requisites for it. There is a native elegance about everything he does; a delicate taste, a playful fancy, and an extraordinary facility at achieving, without apparent labor or study, what other painters, with the labor and study of years, cannot attain. His eye for color is almost unrivalled, and produces beautiful effects, which have surprised experienced painters, who have been aiming at coloring all their lives. The only danger is, that his uncommon natural advantages may make him remiss in cultivating the more mechanical parts of his art; and he may thus fall short of that preëminent stand in his profession which is completely within his reach, though he cannot fail at all events to become a highly distinguished painter. He is yet but a student in his art...[1]

Newton painted two portraits of Irving. The larger was painted in London in May 1820 while Irving was making arrangements for the first English edition of *The Sketch Book*. The portrait included in the current exhibition was painted in London in 1830. Of this portrait Irving wrote, "It is the most accurate likeness that has ever been taken of me."[2]

1. Irving, *Life and Letters of Washington Irving*, vol. 1, 407.

2. Ibid., vol. 2, 460. In addition to Irving's biography of his uncle, see Dunlap, *History of the Rise and Progress*, vol. 2, 300-306; Andrew B. Myers, "Washington Irving and Gilbert Stuart Newton: A *New York Mirror* Contribution Identified," *Bulletin of the New York Public Library* 76 (1972): 237-241; Joseph T. Butler, *Sleepy Hollow Restorations: A Cross-Section of the Collection* (Tarrytown, NY: Sleepy Hollow Press, 1978), 195; and the biographical entries on Newton in the *Dictionary of National Biography* and *Appleton's Cyclopedia of American Biography*.

A. P.

Active c. 1797

Sketch of the Town of Kaats-Kill, Hudson's River

Engraving by Benjamin Tanner, c. 1797
3⅞ x 6¼ in.

Vedder Memorial Library, Greene County Historical Society, Coxsackie, New York
Plate 115

Nothing is known about the artist who signed himself or herself "A.P."

The earliest known published view of Catskill, the *Sketch of the Town of Kaats-Kill, Hudson's River*, was the frontispiece of *The New York Magazine, or Literary Repository* for September 1797. The view is from the south side of Catskill Creek looking north. The background landscape is stylized and does not correspond to the actual geography—if the view is from the south side of Catskill Creek, the artist has put the mountains to the east, rather than to the west, of the town. As in Alexander Robertson's pen-and-ink drawing of the previous year, the number of buildings attests the flood of New Englanders who settled in the area in the years after the Revolution. The large building to the left of the engraving is probably the Catskill Academy, which is also visible in *Sketch of a Sunken Hill Opposite Town of Katts Kill* (plate 55).

When the *Sketch* was printed in the *The New York Magazine*, a descriptive text explained that "the plate annexed represents a view of Kaats' Kill, in the state of New-York, on the west side of Hudson's River, about 130 miles north of the city of New-York. This village contains nearly one hundred houses and stores, and is in a thriving condition. It has the advantage of a considerable extent of back country, which is rapidly settling by an industrious set of people. Vessels of 80 or 90 tons approach it from the Hudson through a creek.—The mountains in this vicinity, known by the name of the Katts' Kill Mountains, make a majestic appearance, and, it is said, furnish many things for the gratification of the curious."

Plate 115. A.P., *Sketch of the Towns of Kaats-kill, Hudson's River*, c. 1797. Courtesy Greene County Historical Society.

WALTER LAUNT PALMER

1854-1932

Catskill Clove

Pastel on paperboard, 1880
25⅜ x 19½ in.

Albany Institute of History and Art; Bequest of
Evelyn Newman
Plate 116

Road to Olana

Watercolor on paper, 1888
13¼ x 17¼ in.

Albany Institute of History and Art;
Bequest of Evelyn Newman Estate
Plate 117

Walter Launt Palmer was born in Albany, New York,
son of the well-known sculptor Erastus Dow Palmer. At
his father's studio he met many of the leading artists of
the day. Legend has it that Charles Loring Elliott (plate
87) gave him his first box of paints, and when in 1870
Palmer wanted to learn drawing and oil painting he was
sent to his father's close friend Frederic Church.[1] In
1872, Church wrote the elder Palmer that Walter was the
best of his four students. Palmer first exhibited in 1872 at
the National Academy. From 1873 to 1877, Palmer was in
Europe. His father's connections enabled him to meet
other artists and facilitated his acceptance into a Paris
atelier. Upon his return home in 1877, Palmer and
Church opened a studio together in New York City.
During the late 1870s, Palmer specialized in painting
fashionable home interiors, although he found this work
a strain on his eyes. In an effort to vary his projects and
save his eyesight, Palmer began to specialize in landscapes
and developed facility with several different media,
including pastel, watercolor, and oil. The landscape
Catskill Clove (plate 116) is a beautifully textured pastel
drawn in 1880 and never exhibited. In 1881, Palmer
returned to Europe, sketching in Venice. Beginning in
1882, he regularly exhibited Venice scenes.[2]

In the mid-1880s, Palmer returned to an earlier interest
in painting winter scenes.[3] In the 1884-1885 American
Water Color Society show, he exhibited *Winter Morning*,
which elicited an intriguing response from Clarence Cook.

... Palmer comes to the front this year as a painter of
winter landscape, and ... seems a little too much
pleased with his discovery that, under certain conditions, the shadows on snow may be blue. Some years
ago, when our budding school of pre-raphaelites

Plate 116. Walter Launt Palmer, *Catskill Clove*, 1880. Courtesy
Albany Institute of History and Art.

announced the same discovery ... the air was thick with
disputed natural phenomena ... the pre-raphs were
right, and so is Mr. Palmer. ... To return to Mr.
Palmer: his drawings show a delicate feeling, independent study, and love of nature; the visitor comes again
and again to his pictures and remembers them when
the exhibition is over.[4]

Palmer was probably introduced to this method of
painting shadows on snow when he first began his studies
with Frederic Church. Church had begun using a white
ground for his oils and sketches in 1870 and had experi-
mented with winter landscapes during the time Palmer
was with him. There are at least half a dozen winter
sketches from Olana made between 1870 and 1872—
studies by Church with plenty of blue shadows. These
sketches were never exhibited but likely were seen
by Palmer.[5]

In 1887, Palmer found added inspiration for his winter
painting. As he recorded in his diary for that year, "Went
to visit the Tolls, near Schenectady for two days or so and

Plate 117. Walter Launt Palmer, *Road to Olana*, 1888. Courtesy Albany Institute of History and Art.

studied and photographed Winter effects. This proved to be one of the most fortunate events professionally that ever happened to me, as I immediately commenced painting Winter pictures from which I have made my greatest successes. . . . "[6] The following spring, one of Palmer's new winter paintings, *January*, won the Hallgarten Prize at the National Academy. A *New York Daily Graphic* interview mentioned that Palmer's winter scenes were "painted entirely from memory, aided by slight notes, photographs, etc; the painter never having made a winter sketch from nature in his life."[7]

In his 1888 *Road to Olana* (plate 117), however, Palmer painted a scene he probably knew well. Frederic Church had remained close to Palmer throughout the 1880s—Palmer always introduced the women he was courting to Church, who would then report his opinion of the lady to Erastus Dow Palmer. Church's relationship to nature had become even more intimate as his arthritis forced him to stop painting. Instead of traveling and painting large landscapes, Church landscaped Olana: "I have made about one and three-quarters miles of road this season, opening entirely new and beautiful views—I can make more and better landscapes in this way than by tampering with canvas and paint in the studio."[8] It was this new road that Palmer chose for the subject of his delicate watercolor. Instead of representing one of the great vistas, however, Palmer presented an intimate portrait of an intensely private landscape.

MF

1. The relationship between Erastus Dow Palmer and Frederic Church was long and is well documented. Letters from the 1860s and 1870s indicate that Church sought Palmer's advice and opinion frequently in the design and construction of Olana. In 1870, the year Walter Launt Palmer went to study with Church, the responsibility as consultant to Church for the design of the villa had just been turned over to Calvert Vaux. For detail on Church and Olana, see Huntington, *The Landscapes of Frederic Edwin Church*, 114-127.

2. For biography and a catalogue raisonné, see Maybelle Mann, *Walter Launt Palmer: Poetic Reality* (Exton, PA: Schiffer Publishing Ltd., 1984).

3. Palmer had exhibited *Winter Sundown* at the National Academy in 1875 but did not show another winter view at the National Academy until 1887.

4. Clarence Cook quoted in Mann, *Walter Launt Palmer*, 45.

5. One of Church's winter sketches is reproduced in color as Plate V in Huntington, *Landscapes of Frederic Edwin Church*.

6. Undated 1887 entry in Walter Launt Palmer Diary, quoted in Mann, *Walter Launt Palmer*, 45.

7. *New York Daily Graphic*, 2 July 1887; quoted in Mann, *Walter Launt Palmer*, 46.

8. Frederic Church to Erastus Dow Palmer, 18 October 1884, manuscript in the Albany Institute of History and Art.

THOMAS POWNALL

1722-1805

A View in Hudson's River of Pakepsey & the Catts-kill Mountains. From Sopos Island in Hudson's River.

Engraving by Paul Sandby, 1761
17 x 22⅝ in.

New York State Library, Albany
Plate 118

The colonial administrator Thomas Pownall was born in Lincolnshire, England. He received a bachelor's degree from Trinity College, Cambridge, in 1743 and shortly after entered the office of the Board of Trade. He first traveled to British North America in 1753 as secretary to the new governor of New York and quickly became friendly with a wide range of influential politicians, including the governor of Massachusetts, William Shirley, and Benjamin Franklin. Pownall was appointed lieutenant governor of New Jersey in May 1755, and, after breaking with Shirley, succeeded him as governor of Massachusetts in August 1757. He served in this capacity until the end of 1759, when he was appointed to the less important but more lucrative post of governor of South Carolina. In June 1760, Pownall returned to London, where he declined his appointment as governor of South Carolina. He never returned to North America.

In the years following his return to London, Pownall solidified his position as an expert on colonial affairs by publishing a series of books based on his North American experiences. Probably the most influential of these was his treatise on *The Administration of the Colonies*, in which he argued that the colonies ought to be reorganized into one administrative unit and that they ought to be repre-

Plate 118. Thomas Pownall, *A View in Hudson's River of Pakepsey & the Catts-kill Mountains. From Sopos Island in Hudson's River,* 1761. Courtesy New York State Library.

sented in Parliament. *The Administration of the Colonies* was published in 1764 and reprinted in 1765, 1766, 1768, 1774, and 1777.

The first book Pownall published after his return to London was a volume of engravings adapted from sketches he had done while in America. Pownall's drawings were first worked up into finished paintings by the well-known watercolorist and engraver Paul Sandby (1725-1809) and then engraved either by Sandby himself or by one of his associates. *Six Remarkable Views in the Provinces of New-York, New-Jersey, and Pennsylvania, in North America* was published in London in 1761. Sandby reprinted the six engravings in the 1768 and subsequent editions of his widely distributed *Scenographia Americana. A View in Hudson's River of Pakepsey & the Catts-kill Mountains. From Sopos Island in Hudson's River* (plate 118) is by far the earliest known mechanically reproduced image of the Catskills. The next earliest known mechanically reproduced view is the little woodcut *Sketch of the Town of Kaats-Kill, Hudson's River* (plate 115) published in September 1797. Like the woodcut, Sandby's engraving after Pownall is not topographically accurate, but, unlike the woodcut, it effectively suggests the expansiveness of the American wilderness just west of the Hudson River. The left foreground

trees dwarf the boats just as the background clouds dwarf the signs of settlement on the distant shore. In the vast natural panorama sketched by Pownall and worked up by Sandby, man is still a visitor—not yet a conqueror.

Six years after the publication of *Six Remarkable Views* and two years after the first publication of *The Administration of the Colonies*, Pownall was elected to Parliament, where he argued for the legitimacy of colonial grievances even as he opposed colonial independence. He served in Parliament from 1767 until he retired from public life in 1780. Thomas Pownall died at Bath in 1805.[1]

1. On Pownall, see the entries in the *Dictionary of National Biography* and the *Dictionary of American Biography.* More detailed information on his years in America, but not on the genesis of the *Six Remarkable Views*, can be found in John A. Schutz, *Thomas Pownall, British Defender of American Liberty: A Study of Anglo-American Relations in the Eighteenth Century* (Glendale, CA: A. H. Clark Co., 1951). On Sandby, see the entry in the *Dictionary of National Biography*; Adolph Paul Oppé, "The Memoirs of Paul Sandby by His Son," *Burlington Magazine* 88 (June 1946): 143-147; and Bruce Robertson, *The Art of Paul Sandby* (New Haven, CT: Yale Center for British Art, 1985). On the *Six Remarkable Views*, see Nygren, ed., *Views and Visions*, 84-87, 283-284, 288.

THOMAS ADDISON RICHARDS

1820-1900

Meditations in the Catskills

Oil on canvas, 1851
50 x 39¾ in.

J. B. Speed Art Museum, Louisville, Kentucky
Plate 1

Palenville

Engraving by Leslie Hooper, 1854
In T. Addison Richards, "The Catskills," *Harper's New Monthly Magazine,* July 1854

Abernethy Library, Middlebury College, Middlebury, Vermont
Plate 44

Thomas Addison Richards was a painter, a commercial illustrator, and the author of popular travel narratives and tourist guidebooks. The son of a Baptist minister, Richards was born in London, England. In 1831, his father moved the family to the United States; they settled in Hudson, New York. The Richardses remained in Hudson until 1838, when they moved to Penfield, Georgia. Sanford R. Gifford (1823-1880) also grew up in Hudson, New York, and it seems likely that the two future artists met as boys.

Instead of joining his parents in Penfield, Richards moved to Augusta, Georgia, where he established himself as an art teacher. During the six years he remained in the South, Richards made drawings of southern cityscapes and landscapes. Richards moved to New York City in October 1844 and immediately registered for classes at the National Academy of Design. In 1845, he sold three paintings of southern scenes to the American Art Union. The following year, he sold two more paintings to the American Art Union, including the view *On Claverack Creek, Near Hudson, New York,* now in the collections of the Brooklyn Museum. Richards first exhibited at the National Academy of Design in 1846. He was elected an Associate of the Academy in 1849 and became a full member in 1852. He was corresponding secretary of the Academy from 1852 until 1892.

Richards published poems, essays, stories, and travel narratives while still living in Georgia. Many of these appeared in journals edited by his brother, William Carey Richards, who in 1848 began publishing the *Southern Literary Gazette.* T. Addison Richards began sending him a regular column titled "All About: With Pen and Pencil." As with his later magazine pieces, Richards supplied both the text and drawings, which were engraved as illustrations. Between 1853 and 1864, Richards contributed fifteen of these illustrated travel narratives to *Harper's New Monthly Magazine.* His article "The Catskills" appeared in the July 1854 issue of *Harper's* and included fourteen engravings. In 1855, Richards published the first edition of his popular *The Romance of American Scenery.* Two years later, he wrote the text and drew many of the illustrations for the first edition of *Appleton's Illustrated Hand-Book of American Travel.* Regularly revised, *Appleton's* remained one of the most popular tourist guides for the next twenty years.[1]

Richards seems to have worked in the Catskills pretty much annually from 1846 until 1852 or 1853. On his 1848 visit, he was accompanied by Sanford Gifford. On most, or all, of these forays, Richards boarded in Palenville. The subject of *Meditations in the Catskills* (plate 1) may be a scene in Plattekill Clove, but it is probably a scene in Kaaterskill Clove. It was exhibited at the National Academy of Design in the spring of 1851 and sold to the American Art Union in the fall of 1852.

1. T. Addison Richards, *The Romance of American Scenery* (New York: N. A. Leavitt & Allen, 1855); Richards, *Appleton's Illustrated Hand-Book.* In addition to the standard artist dictionaries, see Louis T. Griffith, "T. Addison Richards: Georgia Scenes by a Nineteenth Century Artist and Tourist," Georgia Museum of Art *Bulletin* (Fall 1974): 9-16, and Mary Levin Koch, "The Romance of American Landscape: The Art of Thomas Addison Richards," Georgia Museum of Art *Bulletin* 8 (1983): 1-36.

WILLIAM RIDGWAY

1787-1864

Village of Catskill

Cream-colored transfer-printed earthenware gravy tureen
Staffordshire, England, after 1844
7¾ x 4 in.

The Margaret Woodbury Strong Museum,
Rochester, New York

The transfer-printed earthenware manufacturer William Ridgway was born in Hanley, Staffordshire, in 1787. Ridgway owned and managed the Bell Bank Works in Hanley from 1830 to 1854. In 1843, he produced a complete dinner service based on the engravings after William Henry Bartlett in Nathaniel Parker Willis's popular *American Scenery* (1838-1842). The service was so successful that he produced another complete dinner service based on Bartlett's American views in 1844. The gravy tureen with the *Village of Catskill* is from the second service, which was called Catskill Moss. Pieces in this set are marked with a printed scroll bearing the words "Catskill Moss," the name of the view, and the initials "C.C." (cream color). Ridgway died in 1864.[1]

1. Larsen, *American Historical Views on Staffordshire China*, 3d ed., 96-97, 108. On the history and technology of transfer-printed earthenware, see the entry for Enoch Wood.

ALEXANDER ROBERTSON

1772-1841

Clermont the Seat of Mrs. Livingston

Pen and ink on paper, 14 September 1796
8⅝ x 11⅜ in.

McKinney Library, Albany Institute of History and Art
Plate 119

Clermont the Seat of R. R. Livingston Esqr.

Pen and ink on paper, c. 6-14 September 1796
8⅝ x 11⅜ in.

McKinney Library, Albany Institute of History and Art
Plate 120

Catskill

Pen and ink on paper, in sketchbook, 24 September 1796
8⅝ x 11⅜ in.

McKinney Library, Albany Institute of History and Art
Plate 5

Near Esopus

Pen and ink on paper, 25 September 1796
8½ x 11½ in.

Kennedy Galleries, Inc., New York

Like his older brother Archibald Robertson (1765-1835), the painter and painting instructor Alexander Robertson was born in Scotland, attended King's College in Aberdeen, and completed his training at the Royal Academy in London. In the early 1790s, a group of New Yorkers, including Chancellor Robert R. Livingston, encouraged Archibald Robertson to move his drawing academy from Aberdeen to Manhattan, where he founded the Columbian Academy of Painting in 1791. Alexander joined him the following year. One of the first successful art schools in the United States, the Academy offered instruction "in drawing and painting in water colours, chalks, &c., on paper, tiffany, silks, &c.; history devices, heads, figures, landscapes, flowers...architecture and perspective, &c."[1] The Robertsons operated the Columbian Academy at least through the end of the War of 1812, although after 1802 most instruction was offered by Alexander. Prominent among the persons who are known to have studied with the brothers are Washington Irving and John Vanderlyn. The Robertsons reached out to an even larger audience in 1803 when Archibald

Plate 119. Alexander Robertson, *Clermont the seat of Mrs. Livingston,* 14 September 1796. Courtesy Albany Institute of History and Art.

Robertson published his *Elements of Graphic Art.* Heavily influenced by William Gilpin's writings on the "picturesque," the *Elements* was one of the first drawing books published in the United States.

Both brothers were active in the management of and frequent exhibitors at the American Academy of Fine Arts. At the 1826 exhibition, Alexander showed a *View of Pine Orchard House, Catskill Mountain.*[2] Both as practitioners and as teachers, the Robertsons played an important role in the transmission of English styles of portraiture and topographical drawing to the United States. Archibald Robertson died in 1835. Alexander Robertson died in New York City in 1841.[3]

Built by a younger son of the first lord of Livingston Manor, the first building known as Clermont was erected about 1730. It was located on the east bank of the Hudson River opposite the Catskills. Clermont was burned by the British in October 1777 and rebuilt by Margaret Beekman Livingston (1724-1800) between 1779 and 1782 (plate 119). The oldest son of Margaret Beekman Livingston was Robert R., known as Chan-

cellor, Livingston (1746-1813). The best-known member of the Livingston family, Chancellor Livingston was a member of the Continental Congress, helped draft the Declaration of Independence, administered the oath of office when George Washington first assumed the Presidency of the United States, negotiated the Louisiana Purchase with France, and gave Robert Fulton the financial backing necessary to construct his steamboat. Although Chancellor Livingston had inherited title to Clermont in 1775, he allowed his mother to retain possession and built himself a French classical mansion nearby. He called this house Clermont (plate 120) to distinguish it from his mother's house, the name of which was pronounced in the English style and usually spelled Claremont (plate 119).[4]

Chancellor Livingston was a founder and first president of the American Academy of Fine Arts. Livingston family tradition has it that his daughters Elizabeth Stevens (1780-1829) and Margaret Maria (1782-1818) studied at the Columbian Academy with the Robertsons.[5]

Plate 120. Alexander Robertson, *Clermont the seat of R. R. Livingston Esqr.*, c. 6-14 September 1796. Courtesy Albany Institute of History and Art.

All four of the pen-and-ink drawings included in the exhibition date from a month-long trip up the Hudson River that Alexander Robertson took in late August and September 1796. The evidence of the surviving drawings suggests that he spent at least a week at Clermont as a guest of Chancellor Livingston. Robertson left New York in late August. By 29 August, he had passed West Point and was sketching in the area of Storm King. He spent a few days in Poughkeepsie and arrived at Clermont by 6 September. Robertson stayed at Clermont until 15 September, when he took a boat bound for Albany. Spending a day there, he took another boat west up the Mohawk River to Schenectady. He spent a few days on the Mohawk and then quickly retraced his way east to the Hudson. He was in Troy on 19 September. From Troy he made his way slowly south towards Clermont. Robertson seems to have spent the night of 24 September at Clermont. The last dated drawing is the 25 September view *Near Esopus.*[6]

Together with the early eighteenth-century *van Bergen Farm* (plate 3) and Paul Sandby's stylized engraving of Thomas Pownall's mid eighteenth-century *A View in Hudson's River of Pakepsey & the Catts-kill Mountains* (plate 118), the backgrounds of Robertson's views of the Livingston houses at Clermont are the earliest surviving representations of the Catskills. Together with the 1797 engraving after A.P. (plate 115), his 24 September 1796 view of Catskill as seen from a boat in the river is by far the earliest known view of the town (plate 5).[7] Robertson's 25 September view *Near Esopus* is a precisely rendered view of the kind of Hudson River sloop he would have been traveling on and that would have carried most Hudson River passenger traffic prior to the development of the steamboat.

1. Rita Suswein Gottesman, *The Arts and Crafts of New York, 1777-1799* (New York: The New-York Historical Society, 1954), 17.

2. The following year Alexander showed a painting listed as *Pine Orchard House, Catskill Mountain.* It is probable that these two listings refer to the same painting.

3. Emily Robertson, ed., *Letters and Papers of Andrew Robertson, A. M.* (London: Eyre and Spottiswoode, 1895); John E. Stillwell, "Archibald Robertson, Miniaturist," *New-York Historical Society Quarterly Bulletin* 13 (1929): 1-33; James Callow, *Kindred Spirits: Knickerbocker Writers and American Artists, 1807-1855* (Chapel Hill, NC: University of North Carolina Press, 1967), 39; Kennedy Galleries, Inc., "A. & A. Robertson, Limners," in *American Drawings, Pastels, and Watercolors* (New York: Kennedy Galleries, Inc.,1967); Theodore Stebbins,Jr., *American Master Drawings and Watercolors* (New York: Harper & Row, 1976), 52-54; and Koke, *American Landscape and Genre Paintings*, vol. 3, 98-99. See also the entry on Alexander Robertson in the *Dictionary of American Biography.*

4. On the Livingston family, see the relevant entries in the *Dictionary of American Biography;* George Dangerfield, *Chancellor Robert Livingston of New York 1746-1813* (New York: Harcourt, Brace and Co., 1960); and Ruth Piwonka, *A Portrait of Livingston Manor 1686-1850* (np: The Friends of Clermont, 1986). On the two houses, see Piwonka, *Portrait of Livingston Manor,* 58-59, 68-69; and H.D. Eberlein and C.V.D. Hubbard, *Historic Houses of the Hudson Valley* (New York: Architectural Book Publishing Co., Inc., 1942), 94-105.

5. Piwonka, *Portrait of Livingston Manor,* 59.

6. Robertson recorded his trip in two or possibly more sketchbooks. Both of the known sketchbooks were at one time owned by Lewis P. Clover, Jr., a noted supplier of artists' materials and a publisher of prints. Among the prints he published were the well-known American views after William James Bennett. One of the Robertson sketchbooks was acquired and broken up by Kennedy Galleries. This sketchbook is reproduced in Kennedy Galleries, Inc., "A. & A. Robertson, Limners." The other sketchbook, containing most of the drawings from the second half of Robertson's tour, is in the McKinney Library of the Albany Institute. The cover is inscribed, "Sketches from nature made by Alexander Robertson, 1796-1797. Presented to the Maryland Historical Society—1845 by Lewis P. Clover Jr. 6th March 1845." How the sketchbook got from Baltimore to Albany is not known.

7. The next earliest topographically accurate view of Catskill is probably William Henry Bartlett's c. 1836 *Village of Catskill.*

GEORGE HENRY SMILLIE

1840-1921

Man in the Mountains

Oil on canvas, 1866
25¾ x 47½ in.

Mrs. Judith Filenbaum
Plate 121

Son of the engraver James Smillie (1807-1885) and younger brother of the engraver and painter James David Smillie, George Henry Smillie was born and educated in New York City. He received his first art lessons from his father and studied with James MacDougal Hart for a brief time in 1861. He began exhibiting oil paintings a year or two before his brother did, and his example

Plate 121. George Henry Smillie, *Man in the Mountains*, 1866. Courtesy Mrs. Judith Filenbaum.

probably influenced his brother's decision to give up the security of his work as an engraver. George Smillie first exhibited at the National Academy of Design in 1862 and at the Brooklyn Art Associaton in 1863. He was elected an associate of the National Academy of Design in 1864 but was not elected a full member until 1882. He was elected recording secretary from 1892 to 1902. Like his brother, George Henry Smillie was an early member and subsequently an officer of the American Water Color Society. He died in Bronxville, New York, in 1921.[1]

George Henry and James David Smillie shared studio space for much of their careers, and surviving exhibition records suggest that in the late 1860s and early 1870s they usually made their summer sketching tours together. The brothers seem to have traveled to the Catskills in 1864, the White Mountains in 1867, the Adirondacks in 1868 and 1870, and Yosemite in 1871. George Henry Smillie exhibited *Under the Kauterskill Fall* at the National Academy of Design in the spring of 1865, *View in the Catskills* at the Brooklyn Art Association in December 1865, *View From Sunrise Rock, Catskill Mountains* at the Utica Mechanics' Association in 1865, *Catskill Mountains* at the Boston Athenaeum in 1867, and *Reminiscence of Catskill Mountains* at the Utica Art Association in 1868.[2]

1. In addition to the sources listed in the entry for James David Smillie, see the entry for George Henry Smillie in the *Dictionary of American Biography;* Peter Birmingham, *American Art in the Barbizon Mood* (Washington, D.C.: Smithsonian Institution Press, 1975), 166; and Maureen C. O'Brien and Patricia C. F. Mandel, *The American Painter-Etcher Movement* (Southampton, NY: The Parrish Art Museum, 1984), 46.

2. A *Sunset Rock, Catskill Mountains* (1865, oil on canvas, 10½ x 18 in.) was sold at Sotheby Parke-Bernet Inc. in 1976. A painting titled *Reminiscences of the Catskills* was at The Old Print Shop, New York City, in 1947. A *View of Margaretville, in the Catskills, New York* (1867, oil on canvas, 24 x 36 in.) was sold at Sotheby Parke-Bernet Inc. in 1946.

JAMES DAVID SMILLIE

1833-1909

Kaaterskill Clove

Oil on canvas, January 1865
20¼ x 14⅜ in.

National Museum of American Art,
Smithsonian Institution
Plate 122

The eldest son of the prominent New York engraver
James Smillie (1807-1885) and the brother of the painter
George Henry Smillie (plate 136), James David Smillie
was raised in New York City and educated at private
academies and the University of the City of New York
(now New York University). James Smillie trained his
son as a bank note engraver. According to his brother
George, by the early 1860s James David Smillie's work
was "in great demand among the banknote people," and
he was earning six thousand dollars a year from his craft.[1]

Smillie traveled to Europe in 1862. Shortly after his
return to the United States, he began to paint landscapes
in oil, although he continued to supplement his income
by working as an engraver. He first exhibited one of his
oils either at the Brooklyn Art Association in December
1863 or at the National Academy of Design the following
spring. In 1864, Smillie exhibited not only at the
National Academy of Design and the Brooklyn Art Association but also at the Boston Athenaeum, the Artist
Fund Society (New York), the Metropolitan (New York)
Sanitary Fair to raise funds for the Union wounded, and
the Yonkers (New York) Sanitary Fair.

Although he was never as financially successful as a
painter as he had been as an engraver, Smillie quickly
won public recognition as an artist. In 1865, he was
elected an Associate of the National Academy of Design.
In 1866, he helped found the American Water Color
Society, of which he was subsequently treasurer (1866-
1871) and president (1871-1877). In 1876, he was elected
a full member of the National Academy of Design and
was later elected treasurer of the NAD. In the later 1870s
and 1880s, he was active in the promotion of etching as a
fine art. He helped found the New York Etching Club in
1877 and became its president in 1879. James David
Smillie died in New York City in 1909.

Smillie's first known trip to the Catskills was in August
1860, when he made a pencil drawing inscribed
"Meadow, Lexington, New York" (private collection).
Smillie almost undoubtedly returned to the Catskills with
his brother George in 1864, as both painters exhibited
Catskill landscapes in the spring of 1865.

The history of Smillie's painting *Kaaterskill Clove*
(plate 122) is fully described in his meticulous diary.[2] The

Plate 122. James David Smillie, *Kaaterskill Clove,* January
1865. Courtesy National Museum of American Art, Smithsonian Institution.

diary makes clear that Smillie's title for the painting was
From the Top of West Brook—Catskill Clove. He began
work on the painting in early January 1865. On 16
January 1865, he wrote, "Painted 5th day on 'From the
Top of West Brook—Catskill Clove'—14 x 20 repainted all
the sky, distance & middle distance." He worked on
"West Brook" on 17, 19, 21, and 23 January. By the
25th, the painting was largely finished, and Smillie began
work on a painting of Haines Falls which he intended
for the spring exhibition of the National Academy of
Design.[3] On 6 February, he added the figures to *From the
Top of West Brook—Catskill Clove;* on the 13th he finished
them. All told, Smillie spent ten and a half days on the
painting. On 20 February, he sold it to the auctioneer
H. H. Leeds for one hundred dollars. On 24 February,
Leeds sold it at auction for two hundred and forty dollars. Smillie was pleased with the price. On 25 February,
he noted that the price "is very flattering to me & much
talked about in our building."

*Kaaterskill Clove (From the Top of West Brook—Catskill
Clove)* is probably a view from the top of Haines Falls.
The image recalls Asher B. Durand's composition
Kindred Spirits (fig. 14), but Smillie's painting is even

more closely related to Durand's later and larger composition *A Reminiscence of Catskill Clove* (1859; The Walters Art Gallery, Baltimore, Maryland). The similarities between Durand's paintings of the Clove and Smillie's reflect the conservatism of the younger artist's work. Concerning a much later watercolor, Smillie wrote in his diary that it was "nice...And yet—it is 'conventional'— in color—in treatment—in composition—and I can't help it—I can't get the wheels of my cart out of the ruts."[4] Smillie might just as well have been writing about *Kaaterskill Clove (From the Top of West Brook—Catskill Clove)*. Despite the heaviness with which Smillie laid on his paint, it is an attractive composition. But the compositional formula dates from the 1850s. By 1865, not only had the pre-Raphaelites forsaken the grand views and fixed their attention on particular rocks and trees, but even such mainstream painters as Durand and Kensett had long since moved off the mountain tops and begun to paint more closely observed studies of particular forest interiors. In the context of earlier paintings of the Clove, the most original element in Smillie's painting is undoubtedly the tourist grouping on the rock. For reasons that remain obscure, surprisingly few paintings of the Clove included groups of tourists. But by 1865, even Smillie's tourists would have looked conventional. Similar figures filled the foregrounds of the popular stereographs of Kaaterskill Clove distributed by E. & H. T. Anthony Co. from the early 1860s on (plates 33, 34, and 131).

1. George Henry Smillie, "A Correction," *The New York Times*, 10 October 1909, 5 (magazine): 12. The author of this letter to the editor is identified in Rona Schneider, "The Career of James David Smillie (1833-1909) as Revealed in his Diaries," *American Art Journal* 16 (1984): 32n. See also the entry for Smillie in the *Dictionary of American Biography*; Rona Schneider, "James David Smillie: The Etchings (1877-1909)," *Imprint* 6 (Autumn 1981): 2-13; and Brucia Witthoft, "The James D. Smillie Diaries, 1865-1880: Artist Friends," *The Archives of American Art Journal* 25 (1985): 24-26.

2. Smillie's manuscript diary is on microfilm at the Archives of American Art (reel #2849).

3. This would be the currently unlocated *Upper Fall-Haines' Ravine, Catskill Mountains* which Smillie showed at the National Academy in May 1865.

4. The diary entry is for 29 December 1886 and is quoted in Schneider, "The Career of James David Smillie," 25.

JOHN RUBENS SMITH

1775-1849

Catskill Mountain House. A Celebrated Summer Hotel

Engraving, 1830
22 x 28 in.

The New York Public Library, Astor, Lenox, and Tilden Foundations; Miriam and Ira D. Wallach Division of Arts, Prints and Photographs
Plate 10

The son of the mezzotint engraver John Raphael Smith and the grandson of the landscapist Thomas Smith of Derby, John Rubens Smith was born in London and trained in his father's studio and at the Royal Academy. By 1799, he was teaching his own drawing classes at the Academy. Smith worked both as an engraver and in watercolor and was a regular exhibitor at the Royal Academy from 1796 to 1811.

Smith toured the United States in 1802 before emigrating in 1806. He arrived with letters of introduction from Benjamin West to Gilbert Stuart and Washington Allston and thus settled in Boston, where he opened a drawing school. Although Smith later moved to New York, back to Boston, and then to Philadelphia, he maintained a drawing school almost to the time of his death. Among his many students were Thomas Seir Cummings, Emanuel Leutze, and Sanford Gifford. Smith influenced even greater numbers of young artists through his drawing books. These included *The Juvenile Drawing Book* (1822), *A Compendium of Picturesque Anatomy* (1827), the *Key to the Art of Drawing the Human Figure* (1831), *Chromatology* (1839), and *The Elementary Drawing Book* (1841).[1]

From about 1816 to 1827, Smith lived in Brooklyn and ran his school in New York. In 1820, he was hired to do the aquatint engravings after William Guy Wall's drawings for the *Hudson River Portfolio*. Smith worked on four plates for the *Portfolio*, including the view of *Troy from Mount Ida* (plate 6), before being replaced by John Hill.[2] Smith moved back to Boston in 1827 and to Philadelphia in 1829. All of his known views of the Catskills seem to have been done after his move to Philadelphia.

Smith's engraving of the Catskill Mountain House is inscribed, "Drawn Engraved & Pub.d by J. R. Smith Philad.a June 21, 1830." The complete title is *Catskill Mountain House. A Celebrated Summer Hotel about 12 miles S. W. of the Village of Catskill Greene Co. N. York. Stands on a rock near 3000 feet above the level of the Hudson River.* Smith's representation of South Mountain, the Mountain House, the escarpment below the Mountain House, and especially the two trees leaning from the right recalls Felix Duponchel's 1826 lithograph (plate 19) and suggests that Smith's engraving may derive from it rather than from a visit to the site.[3] Whatever the immediate source of Smith's image, it is the unacknowledged source for the lithograph *Catskill Mountain House* drawn by C. Parsons and published by Endicott & Co. in the mid-1840s.[4]

In the years following the publication of his engraving of the Mountain House, Smith exhibited views of the Catskills at the Boston Athenaeum (1831), the Apollo Association in New York (1839), The Philadelphia Art Association (1840), the Artist Fund Society of Philadelphia (1841), the National Academy of Design in New York (1844), and the Brooklyn Institute (1845). Most of the works he exhibited were probably watercolors, although the *Catskill Mountain House* he showed at the Boston Athenaeum in 1831 may have been the 1830 aquatint. John Rubens Smith died in New York in 1849.

1. The most important source of information on Smith is Edward S. Smith, "John Rubens Smith: An Anglo-American Artist," *Connoisseur* 85, May 1930, 300-307. But see also "Reminiscences of John R. Smith," *The Crayon* 2 (7 November 1855): 287; Marian S. Carson, "*The Duncan Phyfe Shops* by John Rubens Smith, Artist and Drawing Master," *The American Art Journal* 11 (1979): 69-78; and Trudi Y. Ludwig, "John Rubens Smith," in Nygren, ed., *Views and Visions*, 291-293. Gifford studied with Smith in 1845. He mentions this fact in his autobiographical 6 November 1874 letter to O. B. Frothingham. This letter is cited in Weiss, *Sanford Robinson Gifford (1823-1880)*, 14. The original is on microfilm in the Sanford Gifford Papers at the Archives of American Art.

2. Koke, "John Hill, Master of Aquatint," 87-88.

3. The New York Public Library collection contains two impressions of Smith's engraving. One is incomplete and has had no color added except the blue in the sky. The other is finished and is signed in ink "Presented to Isaac J. Greenwood by the author in 1831." Beneath this inscription another hand has written, in pencil, "Father's instructor in drawing." A second copy of the finished engraving is in the Karolik Collection at the Museum of Fine Arts, Boston.

4. The lithograph by Parsons is reproduced in Van Zandt, *Catskill Mountain House, 56.*

BENJAMIN BELLOWS GRANT STONE

1829-1906

Caterskill Falls

Colored lithograph by C. Parsons, 1856
19½ x 12¾ in.

Published by Endicott & Co.
Mr. and Mrs. R. M. Decker
Plate 123

The son of a prosperous Watertown (now Belmont), Massachusetts, farmer, B. B. G. Stone was apprenticed to a maker and repairer of nautical instruments in Boston. He began to take art lessons from the Boston painter Benjamin Champney in March 1851. During the summer of 1851, he made a sketching trip to the White Mountains in the company of Champney, John W. Casilear, David Johnson, and John Williamson. Later that summer he made his first trip to the area of the Mountain House.[1] In early 1853 Stone moved to New York, where he took lessons from Jasper Cropsey. He first exhibited at the National Academy of Design in the spring of 1853. Stone spent most of the summer and early fall of 1853 in the Catskills. His diaries and surviving drawings reveal that he spent much of this time in Kaaterskill Clove, that this was the first time he had ever visited the Clove, and that other New York artists working in the Clove that summer included Cropsey, Casilear, and David Johnson.[2] Stone returned to the area in 1854 and 1855 and moved there by 1856, when he is known to have been renting Thomas Cole's studio. In the spring of 1857, Stone married Mary Allen DuBois, a local woman, whom he had met in early 1855.

As a young man, Stone aspired to be a painter of landscapes in oil, but by the middle of the 1850s he had discovered that he had little aptitude for the medium and had redirected his efforts towards the production of pencil and charcoal drawings.[3] In December 1856, *The Crayon* noted, "Mr. B.G. Stone exhibited the early part of last month, at Messrs. Goupil & Co.'s gallery, a series of lead-pencil drawings, consisting of views in the Catskills and White Mountains. They are more elaborate productions of this class of drawing than is usually seen, and are very creditable performances."[4] A reviewer in the New York *Express* wrote that they are "of really remarkable character. They are quite large, and in style, handling, and effect quite original. . . . [They are] executed with a minuteness and finish and closeness to the actual forms of nature rivalling a photograph . . . [N]otwithstanding his minuteness, however, Mr. Stone maintains a fine freedom and boldness in his forms."[5]

This exhibition of Stone's drawings was no doubt intended to drum up attention for the lithograph after Stone's drawing of *Caterskill Falls* (plate 123), which had been published in October 1856 by Endicott & Co. and was being distributed by Goupil & Co. Probably the most attractive large engraving of the Falls ever published, *Caterskill Falls* was favorably reviewed and sold well. By May 1857, Goupil's was planning a large series of lithograph views based on Stone's drawings of "West Point ... the Hudson, Catskill Mountains, Trenton Falls, Bashbish Falls in Berkshire County Massachusetts, White Mountains, New York City, and a full set of as many views as possible of Lake George."[6] Stone worked on this project for the rest of the decade, although by 1860 he seems to have set out to learn how to do his own lithography.[7]

After the outbreak of hostilities in April 1861, Stone enlisted in the First Massachusetts Heavy Artillery. He served until the end of the war, by which time he had risen to the rank of Colonel. Stone afterwards returned to Catskill, but, like many landscape artists, he found that public taste had shifted and that sales came hard. For a while he seems to have contemplated trying to complete the series of paintings entitled *The Cross and The World*, which Thomas Cole had been working on at the time of his death and which had remained with the Cole family. Nothing ever came of this idea. Engravings after Stone's drawings did appear in *Harper's New Monthly Magazine*, *Lippincott's Magazine*, and Walton Van Loan's *Catskill Mountain Guide* during the 1870s. But from the late 1860s on, Stone seems to have made most of his income by selling what he advertised as "Accurate views of Catskill Mountain Scenery" to tourists. The artist called himself "Stone of Catskill," and his studio seems to have been a regular stop on the itinerary of late nineteenth-century visitors to the area. In 1894, engravings after Stone's designs were published in Roland De Lisser, *Picturesque Catskills: Greene County* (1894).[8] Benjamin Bellows Grant Stone died in Catskill on 11 August 1906.

Plate 123. Benjamin Bellows Grant Stone, *Caterskill Falls*, 1856. Courtesy Mr. and Mrs. R. M. Decker.

1. Biographical information comes from artist dictionaries and Campbell, "Benjamin Bellows Grant Stone," 22-42.

2. Campbell, "Benjamin Bellows Grant Stone," 26. Stone's surviving personal papers are in the Greene County Historical Society, Coxsackie, New York.

3. Stone seems to have communicated his decision to give up oil painting in an early 1856 letter to his former teacher Benjamin Champney. On 11 February 1856, Champney wrote Stone, "I have no doubt you make very beautiful drawings for I know you are capable of it. As for coloring I am not able to judge of that. I do not know that you exhibited any particular deficiency in that when you were with me." Quoted in Campbell, "Benjamin Bellows Grant Stone," 29.

4. *The Crayon* 3 (December 1856): 375.

5. Quoted in Campbell, "Benjamin Bellows Grant Stone," 28.

6. The quote is from a 12 May 1857 letter from "B.C." (who seems to have been the director of Goupil & Co.) to Stone. The letter is transcribed in Campbell, "Benjamin Bellows Grant Stone," 30. Elsewhere in the letter B.C. informed Stone "that your views of Caterskill Falls have met with marked success and we received quite a number of complimentary notices. The sales have amounted to about 400 copies, another lot of 200 has just been finished." One of the complimentary notices appeared in *The Crayon* 3 (October 1856): 313: *The Caterskill Falls* "is a highly creditable production in the department of Lithographic Art.... The view is the best we know of, and the scene is faithfully rendered."

7. The Greene County Historical Society has Goupil & Co. lithographs after Stone's drawings of *Old Casements*, *Fort Putnam*, *West Point* and *West Point from Fort Putnam*. A Goupil & Co. lithograph after Stone's drawing of the *Summit of Mount Washington: 6380 Feet above the Level of the Sea* is reproduced in University Art Galleries, University of New Hampshire, *The White Mountains: Place and Perceptions* (Hanover, NH: University Press of New England, 1980), 23. There is a lithograph proof by Stone in the Greene County Historical Society inscribed, "First attempt at lithography at Bufford's, Boston, 1860." Van Zandt, *Catskill Mountain House*, 181, reproduces an impression of what seems to be Stone's own lithographic drawing of the *Catskill Mountain House* (1860; 13½ x 19 in.), published by J. H. Bufford's Lithographers of Boston.

8. Roland De Lisser, *Picturesque Catskills: Greene County* (Northampton, MA: Picturesque Publishing Co., 1894).

PAVEL PETROVICH SVININ

1788-1839

Deck Life, Probably on the "Paragon," one of Fulton's Steamboats, with Fort Putnam and West Point in the Background

Watercolor on paper, c. 1811
9⅞ x 14⁵/₁₆ in.

The Metropolitan Museum of Art; Rogers Fund, 1942
Plate 7

The Sailing Packet "Mohawk" of Albany Passing the Palisades

Watercolor on paper, c. 1811
9¹³/₁₆ x 15⁵/₁₆ in.

The Metropolitan Museum of Art; Rogers Fund, 1942
Plate 124

Born in Russia in 1788, Svinin was educated at a school for the nobility in Moscow and studied drawing at the Academy of Fine Arts in St. Petersburg. He was elected a member of this academy in 1811. He received an appointment to the Foreign Office in 1811 and was sent first to the Mediterranean as an aide to the commander of the Russian fleet and then to Philadelphia as secretary to the Russian Consul General. Svinin lived in Philadelphia until his June 1813 return to Europe. In 1812, he exhibited watercolors of Russian scenes at the Pennsylvania Academy of the Fine Arts. A number of his drawings of Russian scenes and people were engraved by William Kneass and David Edwin and published in *The Port Folio.* In 1813, the Philadelphia printer Thomas Dobson published Svinin's *Sketches of Moscow and St. Petersburg.*

Like many other well-to-do European visitors to the new nation, Svinin spent much of his time traveling. During his nineteen months in the United States, he traveled not only in Pennsylvania, but also through Virginia, New York, and most of the New England states. In 1814, Svinin published a series of articles on the United States in the Russian journal, *Son of the Fatherland.* The following year, he reworked these materials in his *Picturesque Voyage in North America.* This volume included engravings after six of his watercolor views of American scenes. In 1818, Svinin founded a patriotic magazine, and the focus of his writings shifted to Russian ethnography and history. He died in St. Petersburg in 1839.[1]

The fifty-two watercolors attributed to Svinin were bought by the Metropolitan Museum in 1942. At least fourteen of them are based on published engravings. Svinin's identified sources include Isaac Weld, the Marquis de Chastellux, Henry Gilpin's *Northern Traveller,*

and the Philadelphia periodical *The Port Folio.* His views of the Hudson River packet *Mohawk* and an early Hudson River steamboat seem to be based on personal observation.

Prior to the launching of their first steamboat, Chancellor Livingston and Robert Fulton had secured a monopoly on all Hudson River steam transportation from the New York State legislature. This monopoly was maintained by the North River Steamboat Company until 1824, when it was declared unconstitutional by the United States Supreme Court in the landmark decision *Gibbons v. Ogden.* Although Svinin's drawing of an early steamboat is not inscribed, it is a view of one of the early Livingston-Fulton steamboats. Svinin is known to have observed a trial run of the steamboat *Paragon,* and this drawing is thought to be of that boat.

The third steamboat built by Livingston and Fulton, the *Paragon* began regular service between New York and Albany on 21 November 1811. Faster than the *Clermont* and the *Car of Neptune,* she remained on the New York-Albany run until 1818, when she was shifted to the New York-Poughkeepsie run. The *Paragon* fouled a log and sank in 1820.[2]

Svinin's watercolor is one of the most detailed drawings of an early Livingston-Fulton steamboat known, but it gives a misleading picture of the size of these early boats. In Svinin's drawing, the relative size of the figures has been exaggerated, which makes the side paddle seem smaller than it was, makes the steamboat seem shorter than it was, and makes it seem to ride lower in the water than it did. Svinin's prose description of the *Paragon* is more accurate: the boat, he wrote,

is 170 feet long and twenty-eight feet wide. The interior is divided into two sections: one for women, the other for men. The first consists of two large cabins, one for sleeping, with sixteen berths and eight sofas, the other a dining-saloon, furnished with twenty berths and ten sofas. In addition, there is in this section a water-closet and a pantry. The men's section is also divided into two large cabins, with 104 berths along the walls, each accommodated with a soft clean bed, with shelves for clothes, curtains and everything necessary for making one's toilet. In the fore-part of the boat there is a fine cabin for the captain, offices for the engineer, and servants' quarters. The kitchen is very remarkable both for its cleanliness and its location: all the cooking and frying is done with the aid of steam, and every day food for 150 persons is prepared with great ease. The order and cleanliness are astonishing! Gleaming silver and bronze, shining mirrors and mahogany are everywhere, and the most fastidious person of the most refined taste can find here everything to his liking: the best wines, all manner of dainties, and even ice-cream in the hot season.

Plate 124. Pavel Petrovich Svinin, *The Sailing Packet "Mohawk" of Albany Passing the Palisades*, c. 1811. Courtesy The Metropolitan Museum of Art.

A tent is usually pitched on the upper deck, and everywhere there are comfortable seats which lure the passenger thither. Regarding the diversity of garments, the variety of physiognomies, the oddity of tastes, I often regretted that I did not possess the brush of a Hogarth or the pen of a Sterne! What an opportunity for a Lavater! It is a perfect masquerade, where everybody is at home, where everybody is master for his money. Here you see a happy pair of lovers, near them a politician absorbed in the newspapers; there people play chess; in another place a Federalist is arguing hotly with a Democrat, to the sound of a flute or guitar played by a neighbor; in a corner there is a greedy money-chaser annoyed by the children whose clamor distracts him from his accounts; finally dogs and cats add to the fascination, so that you do not know where you are. It is not a house, but a whole floating town![3]

1. Abraham Yarmolinsky, ed., *Picturesque United States of America, 1811, 1812, 1813: being a Memoir on Paul Svinin, Russian Diplomatic Officer, Artist and Author* (New York: W. E. Rudge, 1930); D. Fedotoff White, "A Russian Sketches Philadelphia, 1811-1812," *Pennsylvania Magazine of History and Biography* 75 (1951): 3-24; Abbott Gleason, "Pavel Svin'in: Russian," in Marc Pachter and Frances Wein, eds., *Abroad in America: Visitors to the New Nation* (Reading, MA: Addison-Wesley Publishing Company, 1976), 12-21; Bruce Robertson, "Pavel Petrovich Svinin," in Nygren, ed., *Views and Visions*, 297.

2. Heyl, *Early American Steamboats*, vol. 2, 191.

3. Quoted by Yarmolinsky, ed., *Picturesque United States*, 9-10.

WILLIAM GUY WALL

1792-after 1863

Troy from Mount Ida

Colored aquatint engraved by John Rubens Smith
and John Hill, 1821-1822
14¼ x 21⅜ in.

Originally published in *The Hudson River Portfolio*
(1821-1825)

The Hudson River Museum of Westchester; Gift of
Miss Susan D. Bliss, 1966
Plate 6

View near Hudson

Colored aquatint engraved by John Hill, 1822
14³/₁₆ x 21 in.

Originally published in *The Hudson River Portfolio*
(1821-1825)

The Hudson River Museum of Westchester; Gift of
Miss Susan D. Bliss, 1966
Plate 125

View from Fishkill Looking to West Point

Colored aquatint engraved by John Hill, 1825
14⅜ x 21⁹/₁₆ in.

Originally published in *The Hudson River Portfolio*
(1821-1825)

The Hudson River Museum of Westchester; Gift of
Miss Susan D. Bliss, 1966

Best known for the twenty engravings after his work
published in the *Hudson River Portfolio* (1821-1825),
William Guy Wall was one of a number of British topographical artists working in the United States in the early
decades of the nineteenth century. Born in Dublin, Wall
seems to have received formal training in the use of
watercolor in either Ireland or England. He entered the
United States in New York on 1 September 1818 and
almost immediately began exhibiting watercolors at the
American Academy of Fine Arts. He lived in New York
continuously from 1818 until 1828 and was actively
involved in the organization of the National Academy of
Design in 1825.

Wall's work on the *Hudson River Portfolio* dates from
the summer of 1820, when he made an extended
sketching tour of the river. The evidence of the completed

Portfolio suggests that Wall spent much of his time on the
upper reaches of the river. Despite the developing vogue
for wild scenery—and although the upper Hudson was
then only sparsely settled—Wall's drawings always show
evidence of European settlement and almost always
emphasize ways in which European settlers manipulated
their environment. Even when he drew potentially
sublime waterfalls, Wall almost always showed their
power harnessed by human ingenuity and a mill.

Like his choice of subject, Wall's technique was conservative. The surviving original drawings are all horizontally composed, and most include foreground elements
that both establish scale and direct the viewer's attention
to the topographical subject filling the middleground.
They contain few bright patches of color or vigorous
brush strokes that might detract attention from the topographical subject. Although William Dunlap later wrote
that Wall's "practice of late is to color all his drawings
from nature on the spot," the surviving Hudson River
watercolors seem to be studio works completed after
Wall's return to New York.[1]

Like most eighteenth- and nineteenth-century books of
engravings, the *Hudson River Portfolio* was serially issued
in short sections, or "numbers." According to the
prospectus printed on the inside cover of the first number
(1821), the complete *Portfolio* was to be issued in six
numbers, each of which was to contain four aquatints and
accompanying text. The prose was written by John Agg.
Perhaps because of the great expense of the project, only
five numbers containing twenty aquatints were actually
issued. The four aquatints of the first number were
begun by John Rubens Smith (plate 10); his work proved
unsatisfactory, however, and he was replaced by the
London-born engraver John Hill (1770-1850). Hill
reworked the four plates begun by Smith and did all the
work on the other sixteen plates. *Troy from Mount Ida*
(plate 6) was published in the first (1821-1822) number.
View near Hudson (plate 125) was published in the second
(1822). *View from Fishkill Looking to West Point*
was published in the fifth (1825) and final number. Only
one to two hundred copies of each of the original
numbers seem to have been produced, but the prints
proved popular, and thousands of separate impressions
were sold in the late 1820s and early 1830s. A second
edition of the entire work was published in 1828.[2]

Like Wall's drawings, Agg's text expressed ambivalence about the wildness of the Hudson River landscape.
On the one hand, Agg was familiar with the vocabulary
of the beautiful, the sublime, and the picturesque and
knew that many sophisticated people found wild landscapes attractive. He was therefore able to adopt the stance
of the cosmopolite and deride, in his commentary on
View from Fishkill Looking to West Point, both the
husbandman who "pursues his daily labor, heedless of
the striking attractions with which the bounty of nature
has surrounded him" and the herdsman who "traverses

with thoughtless step paths in which painting and poetry would delight to sojourn." But even as he mocked the untutored who failed to appreciate the Hudson Valley landscape and proved his own sophistication by praising both the beauty and the sublimity of that landscape, Agg's writing revealed his own distaste for wildness: "Even in the vicinity of Hadley's Falls, the wearying tone of solitary wildness which marks the character of a country which has not yet become familiar with the stranger, man, is but imperfectly subdued; and he who delights to linger amidst the uncouth rudenesses of nature, will here find ample scope and abundant materials for enjoyment."[3] Like Wall and most other nineteenth-century Americans, Agg clearly preferred his wildness tamed. His warmest rhetoric was reserved for the sublimity not of nature but of human industry:

> there is a spirit of enterprise traversing this great State, out of which continual changes start forth to astonish and delight the traveller. Here has been literally illustrated the metaphorical language of Holy Writ: Here is a voice in the wilderness—here the crooked places have been made straight, and the rough places plain; the valleys exalted, and the mountains levelled: here, as

with the rod of Moses, the rock which has been stricken has poured forth waters in the desert; and where loneliness and sterility reigned, are now to be found the blessings of a fertile soil and an opulent population.[4]

In the years following the publication of the *Hudson River Portfolio*, Wall exhibited a number of oil paintings. These included an exceptionally well-received view of the *Cauterskill Falls on the Catskill Mountain, Taken from under the Cavern* (fig. 10), which was shown at the National Academy of Design in 1827. Wall's *Cauterskill Falls* was probably inspired by Thomas Cole's 1825 *Catterskill Upper Fall, Catskill Mountains* and was the immediate source for Gherlando Marsiglia's lithograph *Catskill Falls* (plate 17).[5] After 1828, Wall moved to Newport, Rhode Island, and then to New Haven, Connecticut, before returning to Dublin in 1836 or 1837. Wall returned to the United States in 1856, at which time he settled in the Hudson River town of Newburgh. Wall's second residence in the United States was less successful than his first, and, sometime after July 1862, he again returned to Ireland.[6]

Plate 125. William Guy Wall, *View near Hudson*, 1822. Courtesy The Hudson River Museum of Westchester.

1. Dunlap, *History of the Rise and Progress*, vol. 3, 103. All of the surviving original watercolors for the *Hudson River Portfolio* are in the collection of the New-York Historical Society. A few related drawings are in the Metropolitan Museum of Art and the Brooklyn Museum.

2. The two essential works on John Hill and the publishing history of the *Hudson River Portfolio* are both by Koke, "John Hill, Master of Aquatint," 51-117, and *A Checklist of the American Engravings of John Hill (1770-1850)* (New York: The New-York Historical Society, 1961).

3. Text for *Hadley's Falls* in *Hudson River Portfolio* (New York: Henry I. Megary, 1821-1825).

4. Text for *View from Fishkill Looking to West Point*, in *Hudson River Portfolio*.

5. On the relationship between Wall's painting and Cole's, see Howat, "A Picturesque Site in the Catskills," 17-29, 63-65. On the relationship between Wall's painting and Marsiglia's engraving, see the artist's entry on Marsiglia.

6. Biographical information derives from Donald A. Shelley, "William Guy Wall and His Watercolors for the Historic *Hudson River Portfolio*," *New-York Historical Society Quarterly* 31 (1947): 25-45, and Koke, "John Hill, Master of Aquatint." See also Nygren's entry on Wall in Nygren, ed., *Views and Visions*, 298-301.

JACOB C. WARD

1809-1891

Wolf in the Glen (Cattskill Falls)

Oil on canvas, 1833
28⅛ x 36⅜ in.

Wadsworth Atheneum, Hartford, Connecticut;
Gift of Mrs. Philip G. Stratton
Plate 18

Son of the painter Caleb Ward, Jacob C. Ward was born in Bloomfield, New Jersey. He exhibited at the National Academy of Design annually from 1829 until 1833 and intermittently thereafter. He was on the board of directors and exhibited at the American Academy of Fine Arts from 1833 to 1835. About 1836, Ward traveled west, getting at least as far as the Falls of St. Anthony, the site of modern Minneapolis-St. Paul. From 1845 to 1848, he was with his brother in South America, where they sketched scenery and made a living by selling daguerreotype portraits. In the 1852 National Academy of Design catalogue, the well-traveled Ward listed his address as London, England. After 1852, Ward's name disappears from the exhibition records. He seems to have spent the last forty years of his life in Bloomfield, where he died in 1891.[1]

The painting *Wolf in the Glen (Cattskill Falls)* is not signed. From the mid nineteenth century until recently, it was attributed to Thomas Cole.[2] This attribution was questioned by Professors Ellwood C. Parry III and Howard Merritt. On the basis of stylistic evidence, Professor Merritt suggested that the painting might be by Ward and that it might be the *Cattskill Falls* Ward showed at the American Academy of Fine Arts in 1833. *Cattskill Falls* is the only Catskill scene by Ward listed in the nineteenth-century exhibition records. Professor Merritt's suggested reattribution was subsequently confirmed by his discovery of a detailed description of Ward's *Cattskill Falls* in a review of the 1833 American Academy exhibition:

> A lovely picture—If there be any fault, it is the brilliant light in the sky, which interferes with the principal gleam upon the pitch of the falls. Mr. Ward should pay a little more attention to his animals—no details, however small, are beneath the notice of an artist; and the wolf at the edge of the basin is by no means so good as it might be.[3]

1. In addition to entries in biographical dictionaries, see Joseph F. Folsom, "Jacob C. Ward—One of the Old-time Landscape Painters," *Proceedings of the New Jersey Historical Society* 3 (1918): 83-93, and Elizabeth Mankin Kornhauser's entry on *Wolf in the Glen (Cattskill Falls)* in *Pre-1945 American Paintings in the Collection of the Wadsworth Atheneum* (forthcoming). I would like to thank Kornhauser for letting me use a draft of her yet-unpublished entry.

2. Benjamin Silliman Jr. of New Haven, Connecticut, bought the painting from Alfred Smith of Hartford (Daniel Wadsworth's lawyer) in 1844. The transaction is mentioned in Silliman's 28 February 1844 letter to Smith, which is now in the Wadsworth Atheneum Archive. Silliman seems to have bought the painting with the understanding that it was by Cole. He exhibited it as Cole's *Catskill Falls* at the 1858 Yale College exhibition. The "Cole" *Catskill Falls* is listed both in the exhibition catalogue and in a blurb on the exhibition in *The Crayon* 5 (September 1858): 268. The painting descended in the family of Benjamin Silliman, Jr. and was given to the Wadsworth Atheneum as a work by Cole in 1956. It was published as a Cole in *The Hudson River School: 19th Century American Landscapes in the Wadsworth Atheneum* (Hartford, CT: Wadsworth Atheneum, 1976), 14-15.

3. "American Academy of Fine Arts," *American Monthly Magazine* 1, July 1833, 330.

THOMAS WORTHINGTON WHITTREDGE

1820-1910

Portrait of an Artist with an Easel

Oil on paper, mounted on panel, 1861
11¼ x 8¼ in.

Irwin Goldstein, M.D.
Plate 54

Autumn, Hunter Mountain, Catskills

Oil on panel, 1866
14 x 16 in.

D. Wigmore Fine Art, Inc., New York
Plate 51

White Birches

Oil on canvas, c. 1868
34⅛ x 27⅛ in.

Yale University Art Gallery; Robert W. Carle, B.A.
1897, Fund
Plate 126

I Come from Haunts of Coot and Hern

Oil on canvas, n.d.
12⅛ x 20⅞ in.

The George F. McMurray Collection, Trinity College,
Hartford, Connecticut
Plate 52

Thomas Worthington Whittredge was born on his father's farm in Springfield, Ohio, in 1820. In 1837, he moved to Cincinnati, where he took up house and sign painting. In 1838 he began painting portraits. After 1843, he worked mainly on landscape paintings. After successfully exhibiting a painting at the National Academy in 1846, he began gathering subscriptions for landscapes from Cincinnati patrons to pay for his trip to Europe in 1849. He traveled in Belgium, Germany, and Paris and ended up at the Düsseldorf Academy. There he became friendly with Emanuel Leutze, Eastman Johnson, and other artists at the school and made frequent sketching trips with them. He boarded for a year at the home of Andreas Aschenbach, one of the leaders of the Düsseldorf school. After seven years at Düsseldorf, he left in 1856 to travel in Switzerland and Italy with Leutze, William Haseltine, John Irving, and Albert Bierstadt.

He settled in Rome for two years with Bierstadt and Sanford Gifford. In May 1859, he returned to the United States and rented a studio in the Tenth Street Building in New York City.[1]

Whittredge was a regular visitor to the Catskills in the 1860s and 1870s. He was accompanied on many of these trips by his friends Sanford Gifford and Jervis McEntee. All three seem to have been in the area during the summer of 1860. In December of that year, the *Crayon* noted that Whittredge and Gifford were working on "interesting studies from the Catskills," presumably gathered the summer before.[2] McEntee's Kaaterskill Clove pencil sketches dated 1860 are in the Corcoran Gallery of Art, the Albany Institute of History and Art, and the Yale University Art Gallery. In August 1861, the year Whittredge was made an Academician, the three friends were in the mountains again. The landscape painter James Suydam wrote John Kensett that "Gifford and Whittredge are up in the Catskills."[3] In fact, pencil drawings by both artists of a bear trap on North Mountain are dated 3 August 1861.[4] *Portrait of an Artist with an Easel* (1861; plate 58) seems to be a portrait of Jervis McEntee. This identification is circumstantial. The seated artist in this picture has a full red beard. Gifford did not wear a full beard. Whittredge did, but it was black. G.P.A. Healy's *Arch of Titus* (1871; Newark Museum; oil sketch in the Illinois State Museum) shows McEntee with a very red, full beard.[5]

The three friends continued to work together through the mid- and late 1860s. Whittredge's *Twilight on the Shawangunk* (1865; The Manoogian Collection) was exhibited at the National Academy in 1865, the same year that Gifford exhibited a currently unlocated painting titled *Shawangunk Mountains*. McEntee's *Woods of Asshokan* (1871; St. Johnsbury Atheneum) echoes Whittredge's *Woods of Ashokan* (1868; The Chrysler Museum). Gifford's *Twilight on Hunter Mountain* is very similar in tone and subject to Whittredge's *Autumn, Hunter Mountain* (plate 51). Both images are dated 1866, and it is likely that Gifford and Whittredge made the sketches together in the summer of 1865. It is possible that McEntee's *Autumnal Landscape* (plate 109) was made at the same time.

Throughout the 1860s and 1870s, Whittredge was fascinated by the effects of broken sunlight in forest interiors. Tuckerman wrote of his work, "There is sometimes not only a feeling *for* but *in* his color, which betokens no common intimacy with the picturesque and poetical side of nature. In a little autumn scene, the deep crimson of a creeper, . . . the true rendering of the trunk and branches of a tree, the clear, dark, calm lake, the many-tinted woods, and the manner in which the pervading light reveals and modifies all these, show that Whittredge unites to the American fidelity to nature in feeling, much of the practical skill derived from foreign study."[6] His first major painting of a forest interior was *The Old*

Plate 126. Worthington Whittredge, *White Birches*, c. 1868.
Courtesy Yale University Art Gallery.

Hunting Ground, exhibited at the National Academy in 1864 and now in the collections of the Reynolda House. During the rest of his career, Whittredge produced many forest interiors, including such major paintings as the previously mentioned *Woods of Ashokan* (1868), *The Trout Pool* (c. 1868-1870; Metropolitan Museum of Art), and *Trout Brook in the Catskills* (c. 1875; The Corcoran Gallery of Art). The National Academy of Design's exhibition records indicate that Whittredge exhibited a forest interior nearly every year from 1864 until the end of his career. *White Birches* (c.1868; plate 126) is no less concerned with light effects than his other interior views. The subject is similar to the Reynolda House's *Old Hunting Grounds;* like that painting, it introduces a deer to represent the permanence of nature as opposed to the transience of man. In *I Come from Haunts of Coot and Hern* (plate 52),[7] Whittredge has dropped this kind of staffage altogether to concentrate even more intensely on the effects of light. The result is a dazzling display of the technique that had impressed Tuckerman. Man has disappeared from view, though he leaves a trail, inevitably to be overgrown, behind.

Whittredge was married in 1867 and served as president of the National Academy from 1874 to 1877. He moved to Summit, New Jersey, in 1880, where he died on 25 February 1910.

MF

1. The key biographical sources are John I. Baur, ed., "The Autobiography of Worthington Whittredge," 1-68; Cheryl Cibulka, *Quiet Places: The American Landscapes of Worthington Whittredge* (Washington, D.C.: Adams-Davidson Galleries, 1982); Munson-Williams-Proctor Institute, *Worthington Whittredge Retrospective* (Utica, NY: Munson-Williams-Proctor Institute, 1969); and Anthony Janson, "The Paintings of Worthington Whittredge" (Ph.D. diss., Harvard University, 1975).

2. "Domestic Art Gossip," *The Crayon* 7 (December 1860): 353.

3. James Suydam to John Kensett, 7 August 1861, Kensett Papers on microfilm at the Archives of American Art (reel #N68-85).

4. Gifford's *Bear Trap* is in his 1861 sketchbook on microfilm at the Archives of American Art (reel #688). Whittredge's *Bear Trap* is in the Mead Art Gallery at Amherst College.

5. The identification of the seated figure as McEntee was aided by the Illinois State Museum's Kent Smith, who consulted the museum's version of *The Arch of Titus* to determine that the figure identified as McEntee in that picture had red hair. Suydam may have neglected to mention McEntee in his letter to Kensett, as McEntee would already have been at his Rondout home since the spring.

6. Tuckerman, *Book of the Artists,* 514-515.

7. The title is from an 1851 Tennyson poem called "The Brook." It is unclear when this title was placed on the painting, but it may not be the original title, as none of Whittredge's exhibited paintings had poetic titles. It has not been established, however, that this painting was ever exhibited under any title.

Plate 127. John Williamson, *Valley of the Hudson,* 1878. Courtesy Lucille and Walter Rubin.

JOHN WILLIAMSON

1826-1885

Valley of the Hudson

Oil on canvas, 1878
20 x 34 in.

Lucille and Walter Rubin
Plate 127

Born at Toll Cross near Glasgow (Scotland), John Williamson immigrated with his family to the United States in 1831. He was raised and lived most of his life in Brooklyn. Williamson began exhibiting at the National Academy of Design in 1850 but was not elected an Associate until 1861. In the same year, he joined with Régis Gignoux and J. A. Oertel to found the Brooklyn Art Association, of which he became secretary. Williamson painted some still lifes, but most of his paintings were landscapes of scenes in New England, New York, or Pennsylvania. Williamson died at Glenwood-on-Hudson on 28 May 1885.

Williamson exhibited Catskill scenes intermittently throughout his career. The earliest was *Autumn, September Afternoon, Catskill Mountains*, which he showed at the National Academy of Design in 1859. The last was *Trout-Fishing, Stoney Clove, Catskill Mountains*, which he showed at the National Academy of Design in 1881. *Valley of the Hudson* is a late and very conservative work. It is doubtful that Williamson ever exhibited it. It is a view of the Catskills from the east bank of the Hudson, although Williamson has adapted the shape of the mountains. The Catskill Mountain House is clearly indicated on the shoulder of South Mountain. The *repoussir* trees and the foreground cattle recall the similar staffage found in *View in the Catskills* (1844; plate 84) and other early landscapes by Asher B. Durand.

ENOCH WOOD

1759-1840

Pine Orchard House, Catskill Mountains

Dark blue transfer-printed earthenware plate
Staffordshire, England, after 1831
10¼ in. in diameter

Albany Institute of History and Art
Plate 21

Sometimes called the "Father of English Pottery," Enoch Wood was born in Burslem, Staffordshire, in 1759. In 1783, he entered into partnership with his cousin Ralph Wood and began to manufacture earthenware. Enoch Wood became sole owner of the firm in 1819, at which time the name was changed to Enoch Wood & Sons. The firm kept this name even after Wood's death in 1840. The reverse of *Pine Orchard House, Catskill Mountain* is marked with an eagle facing right. In his mouth, the eagle holds a scroll attached to a shield. Above him is a banner on which is written "E pluribus Unum." Below him is the title.

The transfer process was invented in the eighteenth century but was not widely used until after 1815. The process was relatively simple. The desired design was drawn onto a lithograph stone. The earthenware was formed and fired. The stone was used to ink thin sheets of paper which were laid over the still unglazed earthenware. The earthenware was then given a second firing in the kiln. Designs were usually based on widely distributed engravings, but the composition of the original source was often simplified or otherwise changed to suit the designer's tastes and needs. Because of the odd shapes of the earthenware, the paper was inked in sections, which were then combined in order to form the desired design. Lines on the finished pieces show the edges where the paper sections met. Early transfer-printed earthenware is dark blue. The deeper the grooves on the stone, the more ink was absorbed onto the paper. And the more ink on the paper, the darker the resulting piece. Consumers preferred the darkest pieces because the dark blue color hid the section breaks and other imperfections in the design. By the 1830s, technological innovation had improved the process, and lighter colors including light blue, mulberry, purple, grey, black, pink, and brown became available.

Transfer-printed earthenware was marketed as a substitute for more expensive Chinese import porcelain and English bone china. Although some wealthy people no doubt bought transfer-printed earthenware in order to use it as "everyday" china, the main market was the emerging English and American middle classes, who thought of it as "good china" and often reserved it for use on special occasions. In the early decades of the nineteenth century, there were fewer wealthy but many more moderately well-to-do families in the United States than in England. It is therefore not surprising that much more transfer-printed earthenware was sold in the United States than was sold in England.

Staffordshire manufacturers knew how dependent they were on their American market and were responsive to the desires of their American consumers. The vast variety and quantity of early nineteenth-century earthenware transfer-printed with scenes from American history or views of American cities or landscapes testifies both to the business acumen of the Staffordshire manufacturers and to the chauvinism characteristic of the early nineteenth-century American public. Enoch Wood & Son produced much more earthenware printed with American scenes than any other Staffordshire manufacturer. As with the light-colored plate produced by William Adams (plate 62), the design on Wood's dark blue *Pine Orchard House, Catskill Mountains* derives from the 1831 engraving after Thomas Cole's *View of the Cattskill Mountain House, N.Y.* (plate 22).[1]

1. Larsen, *American Historical Views on Staffordshire China*, 3d ed., 1-8, 15, 20-21; and Raymond Beecher, "Staffordshire Earthenware with Local Scenes," *Greene County Historical Journal* 9 (1985): 31, 37. For an iconographic history of the view of the Mountain House from the road, see the essay.

NOTES ON CONTRIBUTORS

MARGARET FAVRETTI is a recent graduate of Yale College and is pursuing her doctorate at City University of New York in art history with an emphasis on nineteenth-century American painting.

KENNETH MYERS is a graduate of Cornell University and is a Ph.D. candidate in the American Studies Program at Yale University. He teaches in the American Literature and Civilization Department at Middlebury College.

Artist's entries written by Margaret Favretti are signed "MF." Unsigned entries were written by Kenneth Myers.

Plate 128. J. Loeffler, *Palensville*, c. 1861-1875. Courtesy Greene County Historical Society.

E. & H. T. ANTHONY

Six stereographs: *#4190 The Laurel House* (yellow mount), *#4212 View from the top of the Kauterskill Fall, Looking Down the Glen* (yellow mount), *#398 Kauterskill Falls—from below the Second Fall* (cream mount), *#1279 Kauterskill Falls, from below the Second Fall* (yellow mount), *#402 Cascade in Kauterskill Clove, Near Haines Falls* (yellow mount), *#408 View in the Kauterskill Gorge* (cream mount)
Albumen prints, no dates (c. 1859–1865)
New York Public Library

E. & H. T. ANTHONY

Six stereographs: *#5899 Saloon of the Steamer "Drew," Looking Forward* (yellow mount), *#5553 The Valley of the Catskill, from the Heights North-West of the Village* (yellow mount), *#9045 Rip Van Winkle House in Sleepy Hollow* (orange mount), *#8530 Mountain House, General View* (orange mount), *#8533 The Bluff by Mountain House* (orange mount), *#8535 The Bluff By Mountain House* (orange mount)
Albumen prints, no dates (late nineteenth century)
Courtesy Greene County Historical Society

E. & H. T. ANTHONY

Six stereographs: *#9081 Catskill Mountain House from North Mountain*, *#9079 The Mountain House and Valley of the Lakes from North Mt. High Peak and Round Top in the Distance* (yellow mount), *#9077 The Valley of the Lakes from North Mountain—High Peak and Round Top in the distance—High Peak 3800 ft. from Level of the Hudson River* (yellow mount), *#8549 The Boulder on South Mountain* (orange mount), *#8557 Pallinsville—Hudson River in Distance* (orange mount), *#8544 Looking West from Sunset Rock* (orange mount)
Albumen prints, no dates (late nineteenth century)
Greene County Historical Society

E. & H. T. ANTHONY

Six stereographs: *#9050 The Laurel House and Kauterskill Falls from Prospect Rock* (yellow mount), *#1279 Kauterskill Falls, from below the second Fall* (yellow mount), *#4213 View from the Top of the Kauterskill Fall, Looking down the Glen* (yellow mount), *#4202 Looking down the Kauterskill, from New Laurel House* (yellow mount), *#4194 Glen Mary, at the Laurel House* (yellow mount)
Albumen prints, no dates (c. 1859–1865)
Greene County Historical Society

E. & H. T. ANTHONY
Six stereographs: *#397 Cascade in Kauterskill Clove*
(yellow mount), *#9059 The Fawns Leap—Kauterskill
Clove* (yellow mount), *#9061 The Fawns Leap—Kauters-
kill Clove* (yellow mount), *#9058 Cascade at High Rocks—
Kauterskill Clove* (yellow mount), *#9056 Kauterskill Glen
below the Terrace Cascade* (yellow mount), *#409 Bastion
Fall in the Kauterskill Gorge* (yellow mount)
Albumen prints, no dates (c. 1859–1865)
Greene County Historical Society

J. LOEFFLER
Six stereographs: *#4:293 Burger's Hotel, Palenville*
(orange mount), *#4:305 View near Palensville Bridge*
(orange mount), *#1:226 Palensville* (orange mount),
#1:218 Brocket's (Cauterskill Clove) (orange mount),
#1:292 Fawn's Leap (orange mount), *#1:224 The Falls
below the Bridge (Cauterskill Clove)* (orange mount)
Albumen prints, no dates (c. 1861–1875)
Greene County Historical Society

J. LOEFFLER
Six stereographs: *#1:210 Morning Mist in the Ravine*
(orange mount), *#1:228 View Looking towards the Falls,
from Laurel House Porch* (orange mount), *#1:201 Laurel
House* (orange mount), *#2:244 High Peak and Round Top,
from the Platform at the Head of the Steps* (orange mount),
#1:202 Cauterskill Falls (orange mount), *#2:215 Cauterskill Falls from Prospect Rock* (green mount)
Albumen prints, no dates (c. 1861–1875)
Greene County Historical Society

DETROIT PUBLISHING COMPANY
Catskill Mountain House, Catskill Mountains, N.Y.
Photographic print from glass plate negative, 1901

(From the negative in the Library of Congress)

DETROIT PUBLISHING COMPANY
*The Otis Elevating Railway, Looking Down, Catskill
Mountains, N.Y.*
Photographic print from glass plate negative, 1902

(From an original in the Library of Congress)

DETROIT PUBLISHING COMPANY
*The Otis Elevating Railway and Catskill Mountain House,
Catskill Mountains*
Photographic print from glass plate negative, 1902

(From an original in the Library of Congress)

DETROIT PUBLISHING COMPANY
Kaaterskill Falls and Laurel House
Photographic print from glass plate negative, 1902

(From an original in the Library of Congress)

DR. BERNARD SAMUEL KAHN
c. 1904–1983
Catskill Mountain House #5
Photographic print, June 1958

(From an original in the Haines Falls Free Library)

DR. BERNARD SAMUEL KAHN
c. 1904–1983
Catskill Mountain House #7
Photographic print, June 1958

(From an original in the Haines Falls Free Library)

Plate 129. J. Loeffler, *View near Palensville Bridge* (showing George Henry Hall's studio), c. 1871-1875. Courtesy Greene County Historical Society.

People's Line for Albany. Landing at the Old State Prison Dock... The New and Elegant Steamboat UTICA
Advertising circular, c. 1837
Landauer Collection, The New-York Historical Society

People's Line Steamboats. For New York. From the foot of Hamilton Street... The Steam Boat the North America... Captain Truesdall... June 22, 1841.
Landauer Collection, The New-York Historical Society

Willard's New Map of the Hudson River. Route of the Steamboat Troy.
Advertising broadside, 1844
McKinney Library, Albany Institute of History and Art

Catskill Mountain House Bill
Printed receipt, 19 June 1845
The New-York Historical Society

Catskill Mountain House, Known as the Pine Orchard
Printed advertising circular, c. 1845
New York State Library

Stage Arrangements at Catskill
Advertising broadside, 1847
Vedder Memorial Library, Greene County Historical Society

Stage Coach Ticket Receipt
Printed receipt, no date
New York State Library

Catskill Mountain House Bill
Printed receipt, 28 July 1849
The New-York Historical Society

The Catskill Mountain House
Printed advertising circular, after 1851
Vedder Memorial Library, Greene County Historical Society

From Rochester to New York by Hudson River Railroad... Summer Arrangement
Advertising circular, 1854
McKinney Library, Albany Institute of History and Art

On and after Thursday, Nov. 29, 1860 Trains on the Hudson River Railroad... will run as follows.
Advertising circular, 1860
Landauer Collection, The New-York Historical Society

Catskill Mountain House Register
Printed register, used 18 August 1860—31 August 1865
Vedder Memorial Library, Greene County Historical Society

Climbing the Catskills
Cover engraving by Gray-Parker
The Daily Graphic (31 July 1875)
New York State Museum

Hudson River Line. Steamers Albany and Vibbard
Advertising broadside, 1880
New York State Library

Time Table of Trains from Catskill Mountain Resorts
Advertising circular, c. 1881
22⅜ x 7⅛ in.
Landauer Collection, The New-York Historical Society

Souvenir of the Catskills (The Otis Elevating Railway)
Glass paperweight with photographic print, after 1892
Private Collection

Scenic and Picturesque Catskill Mountains. Aereoplane View of the World-Famed Mountain Region, Showing Motor Highways, Towns and Villages
Advertising broadside, c. 1920–1930
Vedder Memorial Library, Greene County Historical Society

Invitation to Happiness atop the World... Andron's Mountain House
Advertising circular, c. 1930–1941
Vedder Memorial Library, Greene County Historical Society

Long Level and Catskill Mountain House, Catskill Mountains
Postcard, 1912
Haines Falls Free Library

Kaaterskill Falls, Catskill Mountains, NY
Postcard, 1909
Haines Falls Free Library

Greetings from the Catskills, Mr. Kaatskill
Postcard, 1906
Haines Falls Free Library

Hotel Kaaterskill: "At the Top of the American Alps"
Advertising circular, 1922
Private Collection

Souvenir Photo-Tone Views: Catskill Mts., N.Y.
Twenty photographic prints and postcard mailer, c. 1920
Private Collection

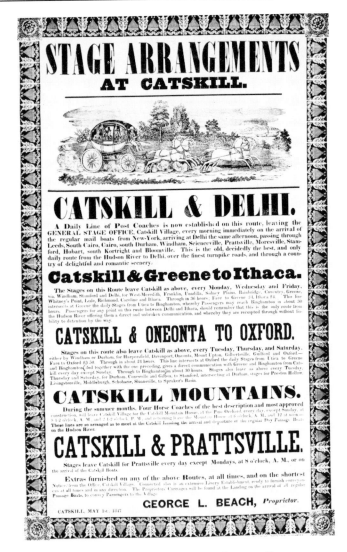

Plate 130. Advertising broadside, 1847. Courtesy Greene
County Historical Society.

Washington Irving
The Sketch Book of Geoffrey Crayon, Gent.
New York: C. S. Van Winkle, 1819
Abernethy Library, Middlebury College

James Fenimore Cooper
The Pioneers
London: John Murray, 1823
Abernethy Library, Middlebury College

William Wade and William Croome
Panorama of the Hudson River from New York to Waterford
New York and Philadelphia: Wade and Croome, 1847
The Hudson River Museum of Westchester; Gift of
Michael Papantonio, 1968

W. Williams
Appleton's Northern and Eastern Traveller's Guide
New York: D. Appleton & Company, 1850
The Hudson River Museum of Westchester

*Hudson River and the Hudson River Rail-Road with a
Complete Map, and Cut Views of the Principal Objects of
Interest Upon This Line*
New York: William C. Locke & Co.; Boston: Bradbury
& Guild, 1851
McKinney Library, Albany Institute of History and Art

Benson John Lossing
The Hudson, from the Wilderness to the Sea
New York: Virtue & Yorsten, 1866
The Hudson River Museum of Westchester; On loan
from the Yonkers Historical Society

William F. Link
The Hudson by Daylight
New York: Day Line Steamers, 1878
McKinney Library, Albany Institute of History and Art

Walton Van Loan
Van Loan's Catskill Mountain Guide
New York: Aldine Publishing Company, 1879
Vedder Memorial Library, Greene County Historical
Society

William Cullen Bryant, ed.
Poems
New York: D. Appleton, 1854
Abernethy Library, Middlebury College

*The Tourist, or Pocket Manual for Travellers on the
Hudson River, the Western Canal, and Stage Road,
to Niagara Falls*
New York: Printed by Ludwig and Tolefree, 1831
McKinney Library, Albany Institute of History and Art

The Scenery of the Catskill
Catskill, NY: Recorder Steam Press, 1876
Vedder Memorial Library, Greene County Historical
Society

Plate 131. E. and H.T. Anthony, *The Fawn's Leap—Kauterskill Clove*, c. 1860-1870. Courtesy Greene County Historical Society.

LENDERS TO THE EXHIBITION

Abernethy Library, Middlebury College,
    Middlebury, VT
Albany Institute of History and Art, Albany, NY
Alexander Gallery, New York, NY
Allen Memorial Art Museum, Oberlin College,
    Oberlin, OH
Arnot Art Museum, Elmira, NY
The Baltimore Museum of Art, Baltimore, MD
Berry-Hill Galleries, New York, NY
The Brooklyn Museum, Brooklyn, NY
Cooper-Hewitt Museum, Smithsonian Institution's
    National Museum of Design, New York, NY
The Corcoran Gallery of Art, Washington, DC
The Dayton Art Institute, Dayton, OH
Mr. and Mrs. R. M. Decker
The Detroit Institute of Arts, Detroit, MI
Judith Filenbaum
George Walter Vincent Smith Art Museum,
    Springfield, MA
Irwin Goldstein, M.D.
Haines Falls Free Library, Haines Falls, NY
Harvard University Art Museums (Fogg Art Museum),
    Cambridge, MA
Hirschl & Adler Galleries, Inc., New York, NY
Historic Hudson Valley, Tarrytown, NY
The Hudson River Museum of Westchester
Indiana University Art Museum, Bloomington, IN
Joslyn Art Museum, Omaha, NB
Kennedy Galleries, Inc., New York, NY
McKinney Library, Albany Institute of History and Art,
    Albany, NY
Mead Art Museum, Amherst College, Amherst, MA
The Metropolitan Museum of Art, New York, NY
Museum of the City of New York, New York, NY
Museum of Fine Arts, Boston, MA
National Museum of American Art, Smithsonian
    Institution, Washington, DC

New Jersey State Museum, Trenton, NJ
The New-York Historical Society, New York, NY
The New York Public Library, New York, NY
New York State Library, Albany, NY
New York State Museum, Albany, NY
New York State Office of Parks, Recreation and Historic
    Preservation, Olana State Historic Site, Hudson, NY
Newington-Cropsey Foundation, Hastings-on-
    Hudson, NY
Orlando Museum of Art, Orlando, FL
The Parrish Art Museum, Southampton, NY
The Art Museum, Princeton University, Princeton, NJ
Mr. & Mrs. Wilbur L. Ross, Jr.
Lucille and Walter Rubin
J. B. Speed Art Museum, Louisville, KY
Sterling Memorial Library, Yale University,
    New Haven, CT
The Margaret Woodbury Strong Museum,
    Rochester, NY
James D. Terra Collection, Terra Museum of American
    Art, Chicago, IL
The George F. McMurray Collection, Trinity College,
    Hartford, CT
Vedder Memorial Library, Greene County Historical
    Society, Coxsackie, NY
Wadsworth Atheneum, Hartford, CT
The Warner Collection of Gulf States Paper Corporation,
    Tuscaloosa, AL
Washington County Museum of Fine Arts,
    Hagerstown, MD
Wellesley College Museum, Wellesley, MA
D. Wigmore Fine Art, Inc., New York
Yale University Art Gallery, New Haven, CT
Private Collections

MAJOR CONTRIBUTORS TO THE HUDSON RIVER MUSEUM

Benefactors

Mr. and Mrs. Herbert L. Abrons
The Hudson River Museum Auxiliary
The Jewish Communal Fund
The Henry Luce Foundations, Inc.
National Endowment for the Arts
National Endowment for the Humanities
New York State Council on the Arts
Mr. and Mrs. Howard M. Pack
The Pope Foundation
Mr. Bernard Rosenshein
Sarah I. Schieffelin Trust
Westchester County
The City of Yonkers

Patrons

Irving Mintz Foundation, Inc.
Mr. and Mrs. Joseph C. Wiener

Major Contributors

Mr. and Mrs. Joseph C. Abeles
Mr. and Mrs. Edward V. Atnally
Mr. Carroll Buchanan
The Cowles Charitable Trust
Mr. Eli Fine
Ms. Evelyn M. Gay and Mr. O. Mahoney
Dr. and Mrs. Donald J. Glotzer
Grand Street Boys Foundation
Mr. and Mrs. Richard Greenwald
Dr. and Mrs. Leonard M. Greene
Mr. and Mrs. Maitland L. Griggs
Mr. and Mrs. Daniel J. Houlihan
Hudson River Contemporary Artists
Mr. and Mrs. Jay Kaufman
Mrs. Arthur Harold Land
Mr. and Mrs. George H. C. Lawrence
Mr. and Mrs. Richard M. Lederer, Jr.
Mr. and Mrs. Ira L. Levinson
Mr. and Mrs. Matthew L. Lifflander
Mr. and Mrs. Leonard H. Mandel
Dr. and Mrs. A. P. Mezey
Mr. and Mrs. A. Charles Miller
Mr. and Mrs. Emanuel Pisetzner
Mr. and Mrs. Paul Pugliese
Mr. and Mrs. Gideon Rabin
Mr. Kenneth Ritchin
Stanley and Elsie Roth Foundation
Mr. and Mrs. Martin Schiffer
Mr. and Mrs. Jerome Siegel
Mr. Howard Stein
Mr. Bronson Trevor
Mr. John Bond Trevor, Jr.
Mr. William H. Wulfing
Mr. Roy Young

Corporate Members

A & J Crane Rental, Inc.
Accent Maintenance Corporation
American Telephone and Telegraph Company
Bank of New York
Blakeslee Prestess, Inc.
The Blum Companies
Campbell Soup Company
Capitol Risk Concepts, Ltd.
Carl Zeiss, Inc.
Chemical Bank
CIBA-GEIGY Corporation
Citibank, NA
Consolidated Edison of New York, Inc.
Corporate Flooring Systems
Cozza & Sons, Inc.
Dalbar Electric Company, Inc.
DeLaurentis Construction Company, Inc.
Diana Gould, Ltd.
Empire Insurance Group
Ensign Bank
Farley, Jutkowitz, Balint & Wiederkehr
Four M Corporation
Friend & Friend Personnel Agency
General Foods Corporation
Gannett Westchester/Rockland Newspapers
Hudson Valley National Bank
ILFORD Photo
JBS Architectural Metals
J.M.R. Concrete of Long Island, Inc.
Levine Brothers Iron Works
Manufacturers Hanover Trust Company
Marine Midland Bank, NA
Mobil Oil Corporation
MONY Financial Services
National Westminster Bank USA
Neiman-Marcus
New England Building Products, Inc.
New York Telephone
Peoples Westchester Savings Bank
Philip Morris, USA
Polychrome Corporation
Precision Valve Corporation
Rosenshein Associates
Safe Flight Instrument Corporation
Soils Engineering Services, Inc.
Stewart Stamping Corporation
Suburban Carting Corporation
Supro Signs
Union Carbide Corporation
United Negro College Fund
Valhalla Garden Center, Inc.
Women's News
Yonkers Industrial Development Corporation